INDIAN FOREIGN POLICY
The Nehru Years

INDIAN FOREIGN POLICY
The Nehru Years

Edited by

B.R. NANDA

Issued under the auspices of
Nehru Memorial Museum and Library

VIKAS PUBLISHING HOUSE PVT LTD
DELHI BOMBAY BANGALORE KANPUR

VIKAS PUBLISHING HOUSE PVT LTD
5 Daryaganj, Ansari Road, Delhi 110006
Savoy Chambers, 5 Wallace Street, Bombay 400001
10 First Main, Gandhi Nagar, Bangalore 560009
80 Canning Road, Kanpur 208004

ISBN 0 7069 0393 5

1V02N1502

Exclusive Distributors in UK, Europe, Middle East, Africa,
Australia, and New Zealand

INTERNATIONAL BOOK DISTRIBUTORS LIMITED
66 Wood Lane End, Hemel Hempstead, Herts, England

PRINTED IN INDIA

At Children's Book Trust Press, Bahadur Shah Zafar Marg, New Delhi 110001,
and published by Mrs Sharda Chawla, Vikas Publishing House Pvt Ltd,
5 Daryaganj, Ansari Road, Delhi 110006

Contributors

B.R. NANDA is Director, Nehru Memorial Museum and Library, New Delhi. He is the author of *Mahatma Gandhi: A Biography; The Nehrus; Gokhale, Gandhi and the Nehrus: Studies in Indian Nationalism* and *Socialism in India* (ed.)

S.R. MEHROTRA was Professor of History, Himachal Pradesh University, and is now Fellow, Indian Institute of Advanced Study, Simla. He is the author of *India and the Commonwealth;* and *The Emergence of the Indian National Congress.*

GIRILAL JAIN is Resident Editor, *The Times of India,* New Delhi. He is the author of *Panchsheela and After;* and *What Mao Really Means.*

M.S. AGWANI is Professor of West-Asian History, Centre of West Asian and African Studies and Dean, School of International Studies, Jawaharlal Nehru University, New Delhi. His published works include *Communism in the Arab East; The United States and the Arab World, 1945-52; The West Asian Crisis 1967* (ed); and *The Lebanese Crisis, 1958: A Documentary Study.*

D.R. SARDESAI is Professor of Southeast Asian History, University of California, Los Angeles, U.S.A. He is the author of *Indian Foreign Policy in Cambodia, Laos and Vietnam, 1947-64;* and *Trade and Empire in Malaya and Singapore, 1869-1874.*

K. SUBRAHMANYAM was until recently Director, Indian Institute of Defence Study and Analyses, New Delhi. He is the author of *Asian Balance of Power in the Seventies; An Indian View; Defence and Development; Our National Security;* and *Perspectives in Defence Planning.*

K.P.S. MENON is a former Foreign Secretary, Government of India and Indian Ambassador to the Soviet Union. He is the author of *Many Worlds: An Autobiography; India and the Cold War; Lenin Through Indian Eyes; Russian Panorama;* and *Lamp and the Lampstand.*

SURJIT MANSINGH is currently teaching history and political science at Washington D.C. She is the co-author (with C.H. Heimsath) of *Diplomatic History of Modern India.*

J. BANDYOPADHYAYA, formerly of the Indian Foreign service, is Professor of International Relations, Jadavpur University, Calcutta. His writings include *Social and Political Thought of Gandhi; Mao Tse-tung and Gandhi: Perspectives on Social Transformation;* and *Making of India's Foreign Policy.*

K.B. LALL, a former member of the Indian Civil Service and Secretary, Ministry of Foreign Trade, Government of India, is now Indian Ambassador in Brussels. He has been closely associated on behalf of India with (GATT) General Agreement on Tariffs and Trade; (EEC) European Economic Community and (UNCTAD) United Nations Commission for Trade and Development.

P.N. KIRPAL was Secretary, Ministry of Education, Government of India for a number of years and later served as Chairman of the Executive Board of the UNESCO. He is the author of *A Decade of Education in India.*

BHABANI SEN GUPTA was until recently Professor of Disarmament, Centre for International Politics and Organization, Jawaharlal Nehru University, New Delhi. He is the author of *Communism in Indian Politics;* and *Fulcrum of Asia: Relations among China, India, Pakistan and the USSR.*

Preface

In 1973-74, the Nehru Memorial Museum & Library organised a series of lectures on Indian foreign policy under Jawaharlal Nehru. The object of these lectures was to attempt an appraisal of India's international relations during this period by experts, who had specialised in this field or actually had a first-hand experience of Indian diplomacy in action.

There is little doubt that as Prime Minister and foreign minister of India for nearly seventeen years, Nehru exercised a dominant influence on the shaping of India's foreign policy. His world-view had been formed by his experience of the national struggle under the leadership of Mahatma Gandhi, as well as by his own perspective of history, which had been sharpened by reading and reflection during his long terms in prison. He had developed an intense hatred of racialism, colonialism and war. The policy of non-alignment with power blocs and peaceful co-existence, which he espoused in the early 'fifties thus really stemmed from ideals which he held with deep conviction.

Some of the papers in this volume pertain to the larger issues of Indian foreign policy, such as non-alignment, the economic content in external relations and the approach to world disarmament, while the others relate to India's relations with particular countries or regions, such as Britain and the Commonwealth, the Arab World, the Soviet Union, the U.S.A., Pakistan, China and Southeast Asia. In my introduction I have, however, attempted a conspectus of Indian foreign policy as a whole. I am aware that these essays will not offer an exhaustive analysis of Indian foreign policy, but hope that they will help to illuminate important aspects of it during the two crucial decades following the emergence of India as an independent State.

I am grateful to the distinguished scholars and diplomatists who agreed to participate in this series of lectures. They had complete freedom to express their views, which, it is hardly necessary to add, do not necessarily represent the views of the editor of this volume or of the Nehru Memorial Museum & Library.

I am deeply indebted to Shri M. Chalapathi Rau, who took the trouble of reading these papers in manuscript and gave me valuable advice in editing this volume. I must also thank Dr. D.N. Panigrahi for the great pains he has taken in seeing the book through the press.

B.R. NANDA

Contents

B. R. NANDA

Introduction

WHEN JAWAHARLAL NEHRU formed the "Interim Government" in
September 1946 and retained the Department of "Commonwealth
Relations" under his own charge, or when a year later—in his first
cabinet he assumed the External Affairs portfolio, no one was
surprised. For nearly twenty years, Nehru had been the mentor of
Gandhi and the Indian National Congress on international affairs.
Through study, travel and correspondence he had kept in touch
with the currents of world politics. At his instance, the Indian
National Congress had denounced Nazism and Fascism in un-
measured terms. His sympathy with the victims of totalitarian
aggression—Republican Spain, Czechoslovakia and China—had
been unequivocally and forcefully expressed. He visited Barcelona
when the fate of the Spanish Republic hung in the balance; he was
in Prague when the shadow of Nazi occupation hovered over it;
in September 1939 he was in Chungking on a goodwill mission
when the Second World War broke out. Nehru made no secret of his
opposition to the policy of "appeasement" of the dictators nor of
his suspicion that Anglo-French policy in those twilight years was
directed less to checkmating Hitler and Mussolini than to erecting
a *cordon sanitaire* round Soviet Russia,[1] a country for which, ever
since his brief visit to Moscow in 1927, Nehru had entertained
much admiration.

As India's first foreign minister, Nehru had to start almost with a
clean slate. Until 1947, the Government of India could scarcely

have a foreign policy of its own; it had simply to keep in step with the policy-makers in Whitehall. Many of the assumptions of imperial foreign policy were in any case largely irrelevant for the government of free India. The British had tried, with a great measure of success, to keep India isolated from other countries. India was not encouraged to make intimate contacts with any country except Britain. Even the United States of America and China were virtually a closed book to the Indian people. Soviet Russia was, of course, beyond the pale. To Jawaharlal Nehru, as he looked out of his South Block window in New Delhi in August 1947, the world must have seemed very different from what it had done to his predecessors under the British regime. He had been deeply influenced by a quarter of century's experience in the struggle for freedom led by Gandhi. He interpreted this struggle as part of the resurgence of Asia. The fact that a predominantly non-violent movement had made it possible to liquidate imperialism in India seemed to prove that physical force was not necessarily the arbiter of the destiny of nations. Thanks to Gandhi and the grass-roots experience of Indian politics, Nehru had also become conscious of the inadequacy of both western capitalism and Soviet communism for India. During his long terms in prison, he had time to read and reflect and to form his own view of the world. He knew enough of the history of mankind to realize that though nationalism could be a liberating force, it was by itself an insufficient answer to the problems of the post-war era. Gandhi's incessant emphasis on the power of the human spirit and on the two-edged nature of violence as an instrument of political and social change had conditioned Nehru against militarism and war. And with his insights into history and science, Nehru was one of the first statesmen of our time to realize the incalculable hazards of the atomic bomb. "The Death Dealer"—this is how he described it in an article in the *National Herald* (July 1, 1946). "Mankind," he wrote, "apparently marches ahead to its doom."[2]

With his passionate hatred of colonialism and war, it is not surprising that the two most important planks in Nehru's foreign policy, immediately after assuming office, should have been the liberation of countries under alien rule, and the promotion of peace among nations. These objectives might sound rather vague and altruistic as state policy, but they stemmed from deeply held convictions of India's first Prime Minister. They also readily appealed to the mood of the euphoric optimism, which a triumphant nationalism

—despite the set-back of the partition—experienced in the years immediately following the transfer of power.

This optimism permeated Nehru's first broadcast on the All India Radio on September 7, 1946 soon after he formed the "Interim Government." In this he spelt out, *inter alia*, his approach to foreign affairs. "We propose as far as possible," he said, "to keep away from the power politics of groups, aligned against one another, which have led in the past to world wars and which may again lead to disaster on an even vaster scale." He looked forward to a cordial and cooperative relationship with Britain and the countries of the Commonwealth, sympathised with Asian countries—such as Indonesia—which were struggling to free themselves from colonial domination. He sent his greetings to the people of the United States of America "to whom destiny has given a major role in international affairs." He made a friendly reference to "that other great nation of the modern world: the Soviet Union....They are our neighbours in Asia and we shall have to undertake many common tasks and have much to do with each other." Of China, he spoke with special warmth: "that mighty country with a mighty past, our neighbour has been our friend through the ages and that friendship will endure and grow."[3]

This broadcast made by Nehru *before* he had any actual experience of administration of the country, foreshadowed with remarkable accuracy, some of the fundamentals of Indian foreign policy for nearly two decades: opposition to racialism and colonialism, willingness to heal the old quarrel with Britain, cooperation with the United States, Soviet Union and China, and countries of Afro-Asia on terms of equality but without any entangling alliances.

II

For an Indian leader, to make such a declaration on foreign policy in September 1946 must have required uncommon prescience and courage. The international scene immediately after the Second World War was confused and even disturbing. The war-time alliance of the Allied Powers had been fractured soon after the defeat of Germany and Japan. The Soviet thrust into Eastern Europe aroused the deep suspicion and wrath of the United States and her West

European Allies. "It was hard," George Kennan writes in his memoirs, "to get the Pentagon to desist from seeing in Stalin another Hitler and fighting the last war all over again."[4] The American policy soon developed into a great crusade to create bastions of anti-communism in Europe and Asia. In this crusade, most Americans expected that independent India under Nehru, with his commitment to democracy and humanism, would join. And if he seemed unwilling to do so, his motives were bound to be impugned. In January 1947, John Foster Dulles, then a member of the United States delegation to the United Nations, was reported to have remarked: "In India, Soviet communism exercises a strong influence through the interim government."[5] Among the epithets bestowed on Nehru in the United States was "the agent of the Soviet Union."[6] In 1949, Dean Acheson, the Secretary of State in the Truman Administration, after long talks with Nehru, described him as "one of the most difficult men with whom I have ever had to deal."[7]

Curiously enough, just when Nehru's independent stance put him out of court with the United States, Soviet Russia under Stalin, refused even to accept that he was the leader of a really independent country. The Russians continued to imagine and assert that India was politically and economically tied to the chariot of western imperialism; they misunderstood her membership of the Commonwealth. Nehru's name hardly ever appeared in the Russian press;[8] no statement made by him was published during these early years of independence; even the fact of the transfer of power from Britain in 1947 went almost unreported in the Soviet Union, and the first Indian Ambassador in Moscow, Mrs. Pandit, did not even receive an audience from Stalin. The initial attitude of Communist China under Mao Tse-tung in 1949 was hardly more cordial towards Nehru and India; in the Chinese political literature, Nehru figured as a stooge of western imperialism.[9]

In the face of a cool and even hostile attitude on the part of the Soviet Union and China during these early years, Nehru's insistence on keeping India out of the western bloc, was an act of faith. Among his colleagues in the Congress party, in the Cabinet as well as in the higher echelons of the civil and military services, there were not a few who believed that India could ensure national security and economic progress through an alliance with the Anglo-Saxon powers. It was obvious that India did not have the military and economic might to play a large part on the world stage. What could she expect to gain by spurning the proferred hand of the western powers? An alliance with Britain and the United States could serve as a protection against dangers from without and subversion from within. The latter did not seem a fantasy to the Indian Government, which had the Telengana revolt on its hands in 1948.

Other practical benefits of a western alliance may have been tempting in 1947-48. The Indian armed forces were dependent on Britain for weapons and even for training in technical arms; indeed the top brass continued to be British for some years. India needed vast quantities of capital, machinery, and knowhow; for all these the obvious sources were western Europe and the United States of America.

If Nehru was able to spurn these immediate advantages and to forge an independent policy for India it was because of his clear-eyed appreciation of the post-war situation in its historical context. He was conscious how the pursuit of short-run national self-interest by nation-states during the inter-war years (1919-39) had ended in a disaster. A much greater disaster in which the victors were unlikely to be much better off than the vanquished, seemed a certainty, if the same policies were pursued in the post-Hiroshima era. Clausewitz's axiom of war being "an instrument of policy, the continuation of politics by other means" had altogether ceased to make sense.

It is not surprising that the anti-communist crusade of the Truman period did not cut much ice with Nehru. He did not have such a horror of communism and communists as American statesmen. He did not agree with all that communism stood for, but he had studied Marx; he was an avowed socialist and admired the achievements of the Soviet Union, especially in the field of education and planned economic development.

Nehru knew that India was not a "great power" but he also knew that she was too big a country to be a satellite of any other country. Indeed India's refusal to align herself with an ideological-cum-military bloc was fundamentally an assertion of her newly-won national independence. Nehru was simply asking for the right of his country to consider each international issue, as it arose, on its merits, instead of tying itself up in advance with "other policies and being conditioned by the wishes and decisions of other countries."[10]

III

For nearly twenty years, Nehru had championed complete independence for India, and rejected out of hand the idea of retaining a connection with the British Commonwealth. However, in 1947, he had—with the rest of the Congress leadership—agreed to Dominion Status, as part of Mountbatten's package plan for the transfer of power. The decision to remain in the Commonwealth had certain practical advantages during the process of transition. It softened the Tory Opposition in the British Parliament; it seemed to offer a useful link with Pakistan even after the transfer of power. It could also help retain the loyalty of the British-dominated civil and defence services and disarm the suspicions of the rulers of princely states and facilitate their integration into the new order.[11]

Two years later, when the task of framing the Indian Constitution was well advanced, and India had decided to become a republic, Nehru began to see the issue of the Commonwealth link in a larger perspective. He saw that the membership of the Commonwealth did not entail any diminution of Indian sovereignty or freedom in conducting relations with the rest of the world. On the contrary, the Commonwealth membership was, (as Peter Fraser, the Prime Minister of New Zealand once put it) "independence with something added and not independence with something taken away."[12] Once Nehru was convinced of this basic fact, the problem was reduced to that of finding a constitutional formula, which could permit India to remain within the Commonwealth even after becoming a Republic. The search for this formula called for much hard work and patience, and among those whose optimism and ingenuity contributed to success were Krishna Menon, then India's High Commissioner in London, B.N. Rau, the Constitutional Adviser to the Indian Government, Gordon Walker, the Secretary of State in the Labour Government and Clement Attlee, the British Prime Minister.

Despite his past denunciations of the British Empire and the Commonwealth, Nehru commended the new formula to his countrymen. He saw it as "a unique and constructive synthesis," and was glad that the old conflict between India and England should have been resolved in a friendly, almost Gandhian way, which was honourable to both countries. "There are," he added, "too many disruptive forces in the world for us to throw our weight in favour of further disruption and any opportunity that offers itself to heal old wounds and further the cause of cooperation should be welcomed."[13] To those who twitted him for betraying the radicalism of his youth, his advice was to "get out of the cage of the past."[14] He never regretted the choice he had made in 1949. Many years, later, as he looked back, he felt that India's membership of the Commonwealth had been a catalytic factor in expediting the freedom of other British colonies and setting "a constructive pattern of transfer from colonialism to freedom."[15]

With India's entry, the Statute of Westminster Commonwealth, which had been "a white man's club,"[16] became a multi-racial as well as a multi-national body. The Indian example was to be followed by most of the other Asian and African countries under British rule. Professor Mansergh, the distinguished historian of the Commonwealth, has called Nehru the real "architect" of the new "Commonwealth, which had grown out of an Empire."[17]

In common with several other Commonwealth statesmen, Nehru discerned in the new Commonwealth the beginnings of a great new experiment in international cooperation, a bridge between races, countries and continents, and even an inspiring example for the rest of the world. He lived long enough to learn that these high hopes of the early 1950s were not only not realised, but were unrealisable. As the Commonwealth became a larger and multi-racial and multi-national body, it also became less coherent in its outlook and interests. Escott Reid, the Canadian High Commissioner in New Delhi reported to his government in 1957 that if the new Commonwealth had any centre it was New Delhi, not London.[18] In fact, London remained the centre of the new Commonwealth, as it had been of the British Empire and the British Commonwealth of Nations. But with the passage of years, the Commonwealth came to take a second place in the strategic and economic calculations of Britain, which began increasingly to look to wider groupings, especially with the United States of America for diplomatic and defence purposes, and to the European market for improving her economic future. The new British orientation was the result, partly, of the cracks in the unity of the Commonwealth which such crises as that over the Suez Canal in 1956, revealed. It was also due to the fact that in the third quarter of the twentieth century, the Commonwealth did not have the economic and military resources to meet fully the needs of Britain or of its other members.[19]

IV

Nehru's quest for a stable equation with Pakistan proved longer, harder and less rewarding than with Britain. He had agreed to the partition of the sub-continent in 1947 as a political solution of an intractable problem and to end the communal acrimony, which had bedevilled Indian politics for several decades. Unfortunately, after 1947, this acrimony was merely transferred to the international plane—between the two successor states. The bifurcation of the country would in any case have been beset with formidable problems. But the unfortunate eruption of mob violence and the flight of minorities across the borders in the summer of 1947 created a gulf between the two successor states. This was further widened by the invasion of Kashmir from across the Pakistan border in October 1947, the accession of that state to India, and the intervention by Indian troops to save the Kashmir valley from being destroyed by fire and sword. The Indian troops chased the raiders back, and the Government of India raised the issue of Pakistani aggression in the United Nations. Even though the balance of military advantage was on the Indian side, Nehru agreed to a ceasefire from the midnight of December 31, 1948. Nehru has been criticised for being in a hurry to end hostilities before completely eliminating the Pakistani military presence from Kashmir, and for referring the issue of Pakistani aggression to the United Nations. The fact is, that he was anxious to avoid a full-scale war between India and Pakistan, almost at any cost. Moreover, he had, until then, little experience of the diplomacy at Lake Success and he failed to anticipate that the Kashmir issue would get bogged down in cold war politics. The real difficulty (apart from a residual hostility to Nehru and India inherited by British officials from the old regime and transmitted by them to the State Department in Washington) was the global strategy of the United States to ring Soviet Russia with military bases. Kashmir held a key position in the Asian heartland, touching India, Pakistan, China and Russia. And unlike non-aligned India, Pakistan was prepared to fall in with the strategic needs of the Pentagon. The plea that Kashmir belonged to Pakistan in accordance with the two-nation theory seemed plausible to those who had only a superficial knowledge of the history of Indian nationalism. Nehru had, of course, never accepted the two-nation theory: so far as he was concerned, the partition was based on a geographical and not on a religious basis. If the latter basis had really been accepted, fifty million Muslims in India and ten million Hindus in Pakistan would have had to emigrate. This is what Nehru meant when he spoke of the "explosive possibilities" of the Kashmir issue, and the dangers inherent in the periodical stoking up of the fires of communal hatred by Pakistan.

In the fifties Pakistan did, what it could, to exploit the cold war so as to steal a march over India. It entered the military pacts sponsored by the United States in South East Asia and the Middle East, and as a reward received vast quantities of arms, ostensibly to strengthen the barriers against the two Communist giants, Soviet Union and China. After 1962 Pakistan formed (in the words of Nehru) an "alliance of animus" with China against India.[20] Incredible as it may seem, when India annexed Goa in 1961, Pakistan was one of the few countries to spring to the defence of Portuguese imperialism.

In retrospect, it seemed to Nehru that the Kashmir issue was more an illustration than the root cause of the tension between the two countries. The leaders of Pakistan continued to follow the tactics which had paid them rich dividends before the transfer of power; they went on behaving as if they were still leaders of a rebellious minority, rather than that of a sovereign state. Just as they had looked to British support for their sectional claims against the Indian National Congress before 1947, they now leaned on the United States of America and its allies to bolster Pakistan's position *vis-a-vis* India.

The continuing rift between the two neighbouring countries, whom history, geography and the well-being of their peoples had obviously destined for a cooperative relationship, was one of the greatest disappointments of Nehru's life. He did his best to remove some of the irritants between the two countries. On such issues as the division of pre-partition assets, the quantum of compensation to refugees and the allocation of the waters of the Indus river basin, he made generous concessions to Pakistan. But these concessions failed to pull Indo-Pakistan relations out of the rut of suspicion and recrimination.

V

The distractions of the Indo-Pakistan disputes did not deflect

Nehru's attention from his wider horizons in international relations. His policy of non-alignment was put to a severe test by the outbreak of the Korean war in June 1950. India voted for the resolution sponsored by the United States in the United Nations Assembly, which declared North Korea as an aggressor. "This is the day," Loy Henderson, the U.S. Ambassador in New Delhi told G.S. Bajpai, Secretary-General of the External Affairs Ministry, "I have been waiting for."[21] Henderson was soon to discover that Nehru had not joined the U.S.-led crusade against communism. While the United States tended to view North Korea's attack on South Korea as a premeditated aggression by the Communist Powers in a "grand design" of world conquest,[22] Nehru saw it in its local and Asian context. From the first, he sought to bring hostilities to an end through a political solution: an agreement among the powers concerned. The Indian stance at the United Nations was determined solely by this consideration, but it only succeeded in, alternately or even simultaneously, irritating the rival blocs led by the United States and the Soviet Union. India's abstention on a U.N. resolution on the establishment of a unified command in Korea, and her efforts to seat Communist China in the United Nations antagonized the United States. Early in October 1950, India relayed a Chinese warning received through K.M. Panikkar, the Indian ambassador in Peking, that if the American forces crossed the 38th parallel, the Chinese would intervene with force. The warning was not heeded, and the result was a tragic extension of the conflict. Nehru persevered in his efforts at a negotiated settlement, but got no thanks for his pains. Public opinion in the United States was so inflamed that there was even an outcry for the use of the atom bomb to save American lives in the Korean battlefields. For his mediatory efforts, Nehru came to be dubbed a communist and "a fellow-traveller." China and North Korea were no less intransigent: indeed not until after Stalin's death in 1953, did they show an inclination to negotiate on the basis of proposals that India had made to the General Assembly.

India's diplomatic efforts to restore peace in Korea were unremitting, strenuous and dismally slow in producing results. Nehru's sole objective was to end the conflict in that part of the world, but the Great Powers deeply suspicious of each other, were primarily concerned with the diplomatic and military gains of each move in relation to their global rivalries. India was, however, able to make a contribution to the closing of the tragic Korean chapter, when on her behalf Krishna Menon evolved a face-saving formula for the exchange of prisoners of war, and an Indian "Custodian Force," under General Thimayya undertook the delicate task of repatriating the prisoners.

The Korean war was a crucial test for Indian foreign policy, but at the end of it, India's position as a non-aligned nation in a bi-polar world and Nehru's stature as a world statesman had been established.

Unfortunately, the end of the Korean war did not bring peace to Asia. The war between France and the Viet Minh in Indo-China, which had continued since 1945, had become involved in the post-war "Great Power" rivalry. Early in 1954 the prospect of massive American support to maintain the French military position was looming large. This was fraught with enormous risks of escalation of the conflict—an escalation which was desired neither by the saner sections of public opinion in France, nor by the government of post-Stalin Russia, which was beginning to grope its way towards the policy of "co-existence." Nehru sensed the change in the political climate and, in the words of Professor Sar Desai, he "caught the straws of peace in the international gale and quickly exploited them for the good of India, Indo-China and the world."[23] In February 1954, he appealed for a ceasefire in Indo-China. Two months later he put forward a six-point proposal suggesting negotiations between "the parties immediately and principally concerned."[24] India was not represented at the Geneva Conference which met in the summer of 1954, but took initiative outside the conference (such as through the Colombo Powers). In the behind-the-scenes negotiations at Geneva, Krishna Menon—through informal contacts—played a pivotal role in hammering out a formula acceptable to the parties.

The Geneva agreement offered a great opportunity for reversing the process of cold-war antagonisms, but it was not seized.[25] The United States was not a party to the agreement, and although it promised not to use force to alter the provisions of the settlement, it used diplomatic pressures to prevent its implementation. Nehru's efforts to end the isolation of the Peking regime by bringing it into the United Nations did not endear him to the United States, which organized the eight-nation pact—the SEATO (the South East Asia Treaty Organization) to contain China. The International Control Commission for Indo-China, of which India was unanimously nominated Chairman, became the target of constant American criticism and ridicule. The Commission failed to win the steady or sincere cooperation of the countries in the region, or of the Great Powers which went on pumping war materials into this area. India thus presided over an uneasy equilibrium, which was continually threatened by shifting diplomatic alignments and escalating hostilities. The gains of the Geneva agreement were quickly dissipated, not only because of the lack of enthusiasm for it on the part of the United States, but because of the strains which Indo-Chinese relation were to undergo from 1958 onwards. Nehru's hopes of a *detente* in Asia were to be deferred, if not dashed, on the rock of Chinese no less than of American intransigence.

VI

India and the United States had (as Surjit Mansingh points out)[26] no real clash of interests; their differences on international issues during the last quarter of a century have stemmed from divergent attitudes towards other countries: to China, Pakistan, Korea, Indo-China. The initial differences over Pakistan were due to the fact that the American State Department tended to take its cue from the British, who were believed to be experts on the problems of the sub-continent. The Indo-Pakistan dispute over Kashmir came to be over-simplified in Britain and the United States as between "Hindu India" and "Muslim Pakistan." The pro-Pakistan "tilt" of the United States was accentuated by considerations of global strategy. The American quest for bases in Asia, designed to "contain" Soviet Russia, happened to coincide with Pakistan's quest for military hardware to attain parity with, if not superiority over India. Pakistan entered the anti-Communist military alliances organized by the United States: the SEATO and the CENTO (Central Treaty Organization). The induction of vast quantities of American arms into Pakistan strengthened its military machine. but as Girilal Jain points out, it also undermined its democratic structure, encouraged anti-Indian postures and policies and poisoned Indo-American relations. The United States "mortgaged the good relations with India for its secret bases in Pakistan."[27]

India's relations with the United States, did not, however, follow a fixed pattern. Writing to President Kennedy in 1961, Galbraith, then American Ambassador in New Delhi, contrasted the relaxation

in the atmosphere with the palpable tension between the two countries he had sensed during his visit to India five years before.[28]
Indo-American cordiality reached its peak in 1962 soon after the
Chinese invasion. President Kennedy's response to the Indian
call for help was prompt and sympathetic, and it seemed as if India
and the United States were going to be aligned at least against
China. However, as the immediate threat on the northern borders
receded after the ceasefire, Nehru swiftly and skilfully steered his
country back into an independent posture. This process was facilitated by the ill-conceived and abortive effort of the Anglo-Saxon
Powers to twist Nehru's arm over Kashmir, and by their reluctance
out of deference to Pakistan—to supply arms to India to make up
the deficiencies in her defences against China.

The question has been asked if Nehru was anti-American.
Chester Bowles, who had two long spells as the American Ambassador
in New Delhi and had opportunities of observing Nehru at close
quarters, dismisses the charge as baseless. However, he hazards
the view that Nehru, who had been reared in the nurseries of British
aristocracy at Harrow and Cambridge at the turn of the century,
"carried some of the upper class British prejudices against the
boisterous and self-assured approach to life of many Americans."[29]
Nehru was often dismayed by the inability of most Americans to
understand the mind of Asia. The high prestige, which the United
States had enjoyed in Asia until the Second World War, had been
due to its detachment from European imperialism; when it began
to form a ring of"client states" in Asia, this prestige was quickly
dissipated. The division of the world into two armed camps struck
Nehru as clumsy as it was dangerous, and he was amazed by the
logic, which included South Africa, Portugal and Taiwan in the
"free world," but excluded Egypt from it.

Nehru's visits to the United States were not as fruitful as they
could have been. His first visit was in 1949 when that country was
in the grip of the anti-communist fever and Nehru's talk of conciliation, bridge-building and peace among nations could hardly
strike many answering chords. The second visit in 1956 unfortunately
coincided with the period when the diplomacy of John Foster Dulles
and military aid to Pakistan had created a yawning gulf between
the two countries. This gulf was largely bridged by the time Nehru
paid his third and last visit to Washington in 1961. President Kennedy
had great admiration for the Indian leader, but Nehru was not in

his best form and this meeting from which much had been expected, proved a damp squib.

Indo-American relations suffered to some extent from the diplomatic style of those entrusted with the execution of foreign policy. The self-righteous statements of John Foster Dulles, contemptuous of Nehru's non-alignment, hurt India. Similarly, V.K. Krishna Menon's rapier thrusts at the United Nations contributed much to the alienation of American opinion.

Nehru was conscious of the democratic and humanistic values which India and America shared. He kept on his desk a bronze, cast of Abraham Lincoln's hand, the touch of which pleased and inspired him. In the United States, there was always at least a core of informed and influential opinion which did not let the interests of India go completely by default. The differences on the "cold war" notwithstanding, the two countries were able to extend cooperation in economic and cultural matters. The United States Government did not initiate an imaginative plan like the Marshall Plan for Asia, but in 1957, it established a development fund for procurement of capital goods in the United States, In the following year, largely with American support, the World Bank formed the Aid-India Consortium. In 1960, the United States made a large contribution to the Indus Valley Development Fund. Three years later, a thirty-years agreeent for cooperative development of atomic power plants was signed.

VII

With the other Super Power, Soviet Russia, India's relations, after a rather tardy start, underwent a process of spectacular development to which Nehru's own contribution was most significant. He had been almost alone in the top leadership of the nationalist movement in his belief that Soviet Russia would have a large part to play in the post-war era, and that there would be scope for a close and cooperative relationship between independent India and the Soviet Union. He refused to be put off by the icy reserve which he initially encountered from the Soviet leadership. His optimism was well rewarded from 1951 onwards there were signs of a thaw. In 1952, a Soviet delegate at the United Nations broke his country's prolonged silence on the Kashmir issue by endorsing the Indian stand. Three months later, S. Radhakrishnan, the Indian Ambassador in Moscow, was received by Stalin for the first time.

The turning point in Indo-Soviet relations, however, came in the post-Stalin period. In June 1955, Nehru visited the Soviet Union and the Soviet leaders, Khrushchev and Bulganin, paid return visits to India later that year. Indo-Russian cordiality was facilitated by the Kremlin's rejection—in the light of the stark realities of the atomic age—of two basic Leninist doctrines: the inevitability of war between capitalism and socialism and of violent revolution as the "midwife of socialism." From this followed policies of co-existence with the West, and, of acceptance of the constructive role of "national bourgeois" leadership in economically under-developed and diplomatically uncommitted nations. The new Soviet line broadly fitted in with the view of the world which Nehru had been propagating for nearly eight years. His concept of non-alignment suited the strategic interests of the Soviet Union; it offered to the newly independent countries of Asia and Africa, an alternative to the military alliances which the United States was sponsoring to "contain" Russia.

From 1955 onwards, there was a progressive improvement in Indo-Russian relations. The Soviet Union extended diplomatic support to India at the United Nations on issues—Kashmir and Goa for example—which intimately concerned her. Trade and economic cooperation between the two countries grew rapidly; Russian help for India's heavy industry was particularly welcome.

It is noteworthy that during the very years India was developing closer relations with the Soviet Union, her relations with the United States were also improving. Indeed it seemed during the years 1956-60 as if India was going to be "a workshop of peace" in which Russians, Britons, Americans, Rumanians and others would compete with each other in building oil refineries, steel plants and tool-making factories. By 1962 Nehru's prestige on the international stage as an elder statesman stood higher than ever. He had lived down the early suspicions by the rival power-blocs. He commanded the respect of statesmen of both the East and the West: Kennedy and Macmillan, De Gaulle and Nasser, Khrushchev and Tito, all held him in high esteem. Nasser saw in Nehru the "expression of the human conscience itself."[30] The British philosopher, Bertrand Russell, haunted by the nuclear nightmare, declared that Nehru stood "for sanity and peace in a critical moment of human history.

Perhaps it will be he who will lead us out of the dark night of fear into a happy day."[31] Ironically enough, just when Nehru seemed to have reached the pinnacle of his fame and influence, a cloud from across the Himalayas seemed to threaten his life's work.

VIII

Nehru had long cherished the vision of "a thousand million strong cooperative of the Chinese and Indian peoples, the base of a larger Asian-African cooperative and ulimately a new cooperative world order."[32] In the 1930s and 1940s this vision did not seem as romantic as it might do today. Both India and China had ancient civilisations; both had suffered from the ravages of western imperialism; both had to make up the leeway of centuries; and both required decades of peace and hard work to raise the living standards of their peoples. Nehru had cosistently lent his moral support to the Chinese cause; at the Brussels Congress of Oppressed Nationalities in 1927, he had denounced the use of Indian troops in China by the British; in 1937, when Japan invaded China, Nehru condemned it as an act of wanton aggression. In 1949 India was one of the first countries to recognise the new regime in Peking. In 1950, when China asserted its authority in Tibet and the centuries long autonomy of the Tibetan people was being destroyed, Nehru showed extraordinary restraint; despite provocations from China and the clamour of the press and the politicians in India he avoided a confrontation with China on this issue. His approach to China was deliberately designed to disarm its suspicions and fears. The problem, as he saw it, was one of giving to China "the assurance of normal peaceful growth and removing the bitter complexes and frustrations of a giant that had been suppressed and oppressed for centuries." He was prepared to make every possible concession to Chinese misgivings in order "to bring them round to an uninhibited, peaceful and good neighbourly attitude."[33] In 1954, the two countries signed an agreement on Tibet which proclaimed the "Panchsheel" doctrine, which enunciated the five principles of peaceful co-existence: mutual respect for each other's integrity and sovereignty, non-aggression, non-interference in each other's national affairs, equality and mutual benefit and peaceful co-existence.

Nehru was later blamed for his naivete in trusting the security of

India's northern borders to a mere scrap of paper, the "Panchsheel" agreement.

The fact is that Nehru never took a simplistic view of Indo-Chinese relations. There is evidence to indicate that very early after the emergence of the Maoist regime in Peking he had discerned a long-term threat posed to India by a powerful and centralized Chinese State.[34] He hoped to reduce this potential threat by exposing China to the winds of international politics and blunting the edge of her isolation and militancy. He was eager to convince China that India had no territorial or ideological ambitions against her, and that the two countries had everything to gain from a cooperative relationship. At the back of Nehru's mind, however, was the possibility that the Chinese Revolution may go astray. He, therefore, gave instructions for strengthening the defences in the border areas and he tried to build up India economically. As he was to put it later, the Five Year Plans of the country were also the defence plans of the country.

The Chinese attitude to India was, however, less sentimental. Its leadership was obsessed with the doctrine of confrontation between capitalism and communism, and tended to see the world in sharply contrasted colours. In retrospect it seems that even during the years 1954-59, when Indo-Chinese relations seemed ostensibly smooth, there was little of the meeting of minds. This became clear when the controversy on the Indo-Chinese border burst into the open in 1959. The Chinese claims to large chunks of Indian territory, hurt, angered and baffled Nehru. He saw that they involved "a fundamental change in the whole geography of India," and to concede them was tantamount to handing over the Himalayas as a "gift" to the Chinese.[35]

At first Nehru kept back information about the Chinese claim and incursions from the Indian Parliament and the press in the hope that the differences between the two countries would be ironed out through the channels of confidential diplomacy. He had long cherished the sense of an Asian identity and he hated the idea of a controversy and conflict with China, but he also hated being bullied. He was not averse to minor rectifications here and there of the international *de facto* boundary line between India and China, but what he saw of the Chinese style of diplomacy could hardly have encouraged him to reopen the whole question of the 3000-mile-long northern border. It is significant that later Soviet Russia adopted a similar approach to the claims for border revision by China.

Nehru's response to the Chinese claims and provocations from 1959 onwards was neither hasty nor impulsive. The problem had indeed been weighing on his mind at least since 1958 and in later years it almost crowded out other anxieties. China had eight million men under arms; the Indian army had not even half a million men. General Thimayya's opinion that India could not take on China alone[36] was basically not unsound. But an all-out Chinese attack across India's northern border did not seem to be on the cards. China had on her hands a long, bitter and an apparently interminable confrontation with the United States in South East Asia and the Far East; her relations with Soviet Russia, the other super power— as Nehru knew too well—had visibly begun to deteriorate. It seemed likely therefore that the Chinese would not go beyond probing tactics, and attempting minor encroachments in the frontier areas. If the Indian government could register its effective presence at suitable points in the sparsely populated mountainous areas along the border, the Chinese would be less tempted to nibble on territory on the Indian side of the traditional border. Unfortunately even this limited objective was not achieved fast enough because of administrative failures on the part of the Government of India: the construction of the road net-work in the mountainous terrain of the border areas had been badly delayed. Indeed, on the whole vital issue of the Indo-China boundary problem, there was a curious lack of urgency in the 1950s, and a lamentable "communication gap" between the political leadership, the civil service and the generals, leading to lacunae in the state of Indian preparedness which were tragically revealed when the Chinese invasion came in the autumn of 1962.

We now know a great deal about the hopes and fears, the calculations and miscalculations in that fateful year on the part of Nehru and his government, but we know very little about the motives and aims of the Chinese. It is possible that the ideologues in Peking became the victims of their own theoretical formulation, that the "national bourgeois government" headed by Nehru was swerving to the right and deliberately manufacturing a border dispute with China to divert the attention of the Indian people from a political and economic crisis in India.[37] It is possible that the Soviet economic and (until 1962) very limited military aid, to India and the agreement on production of MiGs. were taken amiss in Peking. It is possible that the hawks in the Chinese leadership, especially the military leaders, got the upper hand for a while in 1962, and the attack on India was a by-product of the intra-party tussle in Peking. It has also been argued that Indian efforts to occupy the areas on the Indian side of the border (the socalled forward policy) provoked the Chinese into a pre-emptive strike. On this view the Chinese were only forestalling what they fancied was a potential Indian attack. To take such an interpretation seriously is to under-rate China's intelligence services and its hardheaded leadership. After all, the Chinese leaders had refused to be "provoked" over disputes with America over Formosa and Vietnam and with Russia over the Chinese-Russian border. It is not improbable that in 1962, the hawks in China were "provoked" by the state of Indian un-preparedness on the Himalayan border. Nehru's judgment in ruling out a full scale Chinese operation from across the Himalayas according to the alignment of world forces was not irrational; neither the United States nor the Soviet Union could afford to see India overrun by the Chinese military machine. Nehru, however, failed to take out the double insurance which his daughter did, nine years later, when India entered into a Treaty of Friendship with one of the "super powers," and thus warned off other countries against fishing in the troubled waters of the Bangladesh conflict. In 1962 China also cunningly timed its invasion so as to coincide with the fateful Cuban crisis, the effect of which was temporarily to immobi-lise both the "super powers."

One can only guess at the motives of the Chinese in attacking India. They may have hoped to kill several birds with one stone: with a quick overwhelming blow, they could humble India, the chief protagonist of non-alignment, compel her to divert her re-sources from economic development to defence, to weaken the appeal of the Indian democracy and mode of development (which were often cited as an alterative to the Chinese way to the new nations of Asia and Africa) and finally to score a point against the Soviet Union in the bitter doctrinal debate on co-existence and non-alignment which was raging within the Communist camp.

The Indo-Chinese conflict darkened the last days of Nehru's life. It was a blow to his prestige both at home and abroad. Nevertheless, during the eighteen months which were still left to him, he took measures in the spheres of diplomacy and defence, which were to stand India in good stead. Not only was India able to preserve and pursue an independent foreign policy, but also to plug holes in her defensive armour, and thus was she better equipped to meet the challenges from the military dictatorship of Pakistan which were to come in 1965 and 1971.

IX

Nehru's diplomatic style was peculiarly his own; it owed a great deal to his experience for nearly three decades as the leader of Indian nationalism, when he was continually (and publicly) analysing problems and presenting solutions in intellectual-moral terms. He was accused of sermonizing and reading homilies to other nations. The fact is that he was one of the most articulate of men, who felt a compulsive need to carry conviction. His habit of thinking aloud, formed in the days of political agitation, served well the needs of India's parliamentary democracy, but it exposed him to much misunderstanding. His instant and candid comments on world events, especially in the early fifties, evoked resentment in the West. It was alleged that his criticisms of the actions (such as in Hungary)[38] of the Soviet Union tended to be more cautious and modulated than his criticisms of the actions (such as over Suez) of the Western Powers. In the case of the latter, Nehru could directly appeal to public opinion, but in the case of the former, he had to deal only with the governments. In any case, his object was (as he once put it) to "bring about results rather than put peoples' backs up." On such issues as those of Berlin[39] and the independence of Austria,[40] Nehru's influence—through personal appeals to Khrushchev in favour of moderation cast behind the scenes, was much greater than has been assumed. At the Bandung and Belgrade Conferences, his was a steadying influence over the Afro-Asian countries. And, it must be stated to Nehru's credit that he exercised a sobering influence on nationalist passion inside India; as an Australian diplomat noted, Nehru "insisted on a level of restraint and patience in dealing with small neighbours often acting unjustly to India such as Burma, Ceylon and Nepal, which is rare in foreign relations."[41]

In the External Affairs Ministry, Nehru was not content to merely give guidelines. He "liked to do much of his civil servants' work for them."[42] This mode of functioning was certainly a tribute to his prodigious energy and intellect; but it retarded the growth of the habits of rational and systematic policy formulation within the External Affairs Ministry. Another result was the relative neglect of certain aspects of foreign relations for which Nehru either did not have the aptitude or the time. With its three or four secretaries of equivalent status at the top, the External Affairs Ministry was not organized for quick, vigorous and coordinated functioning. Despite Nehru's own awareness of the importance of the economic factor in foreign policy,[43] India's international relations did not adequately develop an economic edge through commercial exchanges, industrial collaboration, financial coopera- tion and mutual technical assistance. While he directed his attention to "crisis-management" in the quest for world peace, not enough homework was done in his foreign office on development of bi-lateral relations, especially with countries in South East Asia, Africa and Latin America.

X

Ten years after Nehru's death, it is possible to see his foreign policy in better perspective. Its essential significance lies in the historical context of the crucial decade following the end of the Second World War, when in the words of a distinguished American diplomatist and historian, the world was confronted with "the seemingly almost insoluble conflicts of outlook and aspiration that divided the United States, and the Soviet Union."[44]

In this troubled decade Nehru brought to international relations the vision, fervour and methods of an idealist and a gifted amateur in diplomacy. He braved the opposition of both the power-blocs. In 1947-49 when India unfurled the banner of non-alignment it seemed neither the best way of ensuring her national security nor of obtaining economic aid. Not until many years later did "non- alignment" become respectable, and aid to developing countries could pass for sound economics as well as good diplomacy. If non- alignment finally turned out to be the strategy by which Nehru derived out of the world balance of forces the maximum cover for Indian security,[45] it was neither Nehru's initial aim, nor was it a result predictable in 1947. It is a tribute to his sagacity that he was able to find points of convergence between the interests of India and interests of world peace. And whenever peace seemed in jeopardy, whether in Korea, the Suez, the Middle East or the Congo, Nehru volunteered India's good offices for conciliation and even for the thankless tasks of international policing. He became a link, a bridge between warring ideologies, races and nations. He had fought against colonialism in Asia and Africa, but in later years, as this imperialism was being liquidated, he tried to exercise a sobering influence on the leaders of Afro-Asia, urging them not merely to flog the dead horse of imperialism, but to switch their minds from the past to future, to tasks of reconstruction.

A recent critic of Nehru's foreign policy has reminded us how at the time of his death his "foreign policies lay in ruins."[46] Whatever the validity of this verdict in 1964, it would need to be substantially modified ten years later. Non-alignment which initially earned so much odium in the West has so far ceased to be a dirty word in 1974 that an American Secretary of State can publicly pay a tribute to Nehru for perceiving "the impermanence of the post-war world into which India was born—of frozen hostility between the super powers and their insistent efforts to enlist other nations on one side or the other."[47] Nehru's view that Communism was not a monolithic political force and in any case could not be fought with military means, was angrily rejected by the West in the 1950s, but this view has now become an orthodoxy of international relations. Nehru foresaw the changes in the Soviet Union, the potential for Indo-Soviet friendship and cooperation, and the possibilities of the Sino-Soviet rift long before they became realities. His advocacy of the admission of Communist China in the United Nations brought him many brickbats, but was to be vindicated more than twenty years later. His warnings against great power involvement in Indo-China proved prophetic. He had predicted, and passionately pleaded for a detente between the super powers. His irrevocable adherence to secularism helped India to retain Kashmir and to make possible the new alignments in the subcontinent after 1972. It is true that he tragically misjudged Chinese intentions and policies towards India, but his hope that the Chinese Revolution, like the Russian Revolution, would also be mellowed by experience and the facts of international life might yet come true.

One could differ with Nehru's handling of particular problems or crises, but there is no doubt that, by and large the policies he framed—almost intuitively—for India's relations with the outside world have stood the test of time. In framing these policies, he could take a longer view, because his vision was a happy amalgam of western liberalism, Marxism and Gandhism. In a period of deep cynicism and doubt he was an incorrigible idealist, but his idealism was, as he once put it, "the realism of tomorrow." It is a measure of Nehru's understanding of the era, which emerged from the ruins of the Second World War, that Indian foreign policy in the nineteen seventies has been spared the drastic changes and the about-turns which the Great Powers—the United States, the Soviet Union and China—have been compelled to execute to keep abreast of the facts of international life.

S. R. MEHROTRA

Nehru and the Commonwealth

INDEPENDENT INDIA'S DECISION in 1949 to remain a member of
the British Commonwealth—even after the Indian Constituent
Assembly had on January 22, 1947 declared its "firm and solemn
resolve to proclaim India as an Independent Sovereign Republic"[1]—
came as a surprise to many people in India and abroad, more so
because this decision was taken by a government headed by
Jawaharlal Nehru, who, since the late 1920s, had been a bitter
opponent of the idea of Dominion status and an ardent advocate
of complete independence for his country. In this paper I shall try
to answer two inter-related questions: first, why did Nehru decide
in 1949 to keep India in the Commonwealth? and, second, what
did the Commonwealth mean to Nehru?

In the 1920s and 1930s Nehru considered the very idea of a vast
and ancient country like India remaining a Dominion of England
to be ridiculous and humiliating. He did not believe in reforming
imperialism by entering into a partnership with it. He was firmly
of the view that the British Commonwealth, in spite of its high
sounding name, did not stand for true international cooperation.
It was an exclusive system whose membership would deprive India
of the freedom to develop contacts with the world at large, especially
with the other countries of Asia. He did not stand for a narrow,
isolated nationalism, but he felt that a true commonwealth of
nations could not grow out of the British Empire.[2]

Nehru was a severe critic of British foreign policy in the 1920s and 1930s, particularly as witnessed in Britain's dealings with the countries of the Middle East, with China, and with Fascist Italy and Nazi Germany. He denounced Britain as the greatest enemy of national freedom, of disarmament and peace throughout the world. One of his great objections to Dominion status for India was that it would mean India's involvement in the reactionary foreign policy followed by Great Britain. He regarded Britain as "the arch-priest of imperialism," India being the pivot of her imperial policy. In order to retain her hold on India, Britain had subjugated the other parts of Africa and Asia. Indian soldiers had been used to do "the dirty work of British imperialism." The independence of India would, Nehru argued, be a death-blow to British imperialism and the signal for the liberation of other oppressed nations.[3]

It was the Lahore session of the Indian National Congress, presided over by Jawaharlal Nehru, which on December 31, 1929 defined the word "Swaraj" in the Congress constitution to mean "Complete Independence."[4] Nehru was the chief draftsman of the "Independence Day Pledge" which Congressmen repeated year after year from January 26, 1930 onwards and which, among other things, said: "The British Government in India has not only deprived the Indian people of their freedom but has based itself on the exploitation of the masses, and has ruined India economically, politically, culturally, and spiritually. We believe, therefore, that India must sever the British connection and attain Purna Swaraj or complete independence."[5]

Like most leading Indian nationalists Nehru was a keen observer of developments in other parts of the British Empire. In 1933 he surveyed the developments within the British Empire since the Anglo-Irish Treaty of 1921 in a letter to his daughter, Indira:

The formation of the Irish Free State led to some far-reaching consequences in Britain's imperial policies. The Irish treaty had given Ireland a greater measure of independence than was possessed at the time, in law, by the other Dominions. As soon as Ireland got this, the other Dominions automatically took it also, and the idea of Dominion status underwent a change. Further changes in the direction of greater independence of the Dominions followed some Imperial Conferences which were held between England and the Dominions. Ireland, with her strong republican movement, was always pulling towards complete independence.

So also was South Africa with her Boer majority. In this way
the position of the Dominions went on changing and improving
till they came to be considered as sister-nations with England
in the British Commonwealth of Nations. This sounds fine, and
no doubt it does represent a progressive growth towards an equal
political status. But the equality is more in theory than in fact.
Economically the Dominions are tied to Britain and British capital,
and there are many ways of bringing economic pressure to bear
on them. At the same time as the Dominions grow, their economic
interests tend to conflict with those of England. Thus the Empire
gets weaker. It was because of this imminent danger of the cracking
of the Empire that England agreed to the loosening of the bonds
and admitting political equality with the Dominions. By wisely
going thus far in time, she saved much. But not for long. The
forces that separate the Dominions from England continue to
work; they are in the main economic forces. It was because of
this, as well as the undoubted decline of England, that I wrote
to you of the fading away of the British Empire. If it is difficult
for the Dominions to remain tied to England for long, with all
their common traditions and culture and racial unity, how much
more difficult must it be for India to remain tied to her. For
India's economic interests come into direct conflict with British
interests, and one of them must bow to the other. Thus a free
India is most unlikely to accept this connection, with its corollary of subordinating her economic policy to that of Britain.[6]

Writing in *Vendredi* of Paris in 1936, Nehru remarked:

Some people imagine that India may develop into a free dominion
of the British group of nations like Canada or Australia. This
seems to be a fantastic idea. Even the existing dominions, in spite
of their numerous links with Great Britain, are gradually drifting
apart as their economic interests conflict. The drift is greatest
in the case of Ireland, partly for historical reasons, and South
Africa. There are few natural links between India and England,
and there is a historical and ever-growing hostility between them.
In many parts of the Empire there is racial ill-treatment and a
policy of exclusion of Indians. But more important still, there
is a conflict of economic interests. So long as India is controlled
by the British Government this conflict is resolved in favour
of Britain, but the moment India becomes a real dominion the

two will pull in different ways and a break would become inevitable, if the present capitalist order survives till then. There is another interesting aspect of this question. India, by virtue of her size, population, and potential wealth, is far the most important member of the British Empire. So long as the rest of the Empire exploits her, she remains on the imperial fringe. But a free India in the British group of nations would inevitably tend to become the centre of gravity of that group; Delhi might challenge London as the nerve centre of the Empire. That position would become intolerable for England as well as the white dominions. They would prefer to have India outside their group, an independent but friendly country, rather than be boss of their own household.[7]

But even while inveighing against the British Empire and the idea of Dominion status for India, Nehru never forgot to emphasize that the Indian nationalist movement was not directed against Britain or the British people. "Our quarrel is not with the people of England but with the imperialism of England," he said. "The day England sheds her imperialism," he affirmed, "we shall gladly cooperate with her." India could have no truck with British imperialism. Nor could she have "a real measure of freedom within the limits of the British Empire." "Before a new bridge is built", he insisted, "on the basis of friendship and cooperation, the present chains which tie us to England must be severed. Only then can real cooperation take place."[8]

Presiding over the Lahore session of the Indian National Congress in 1929 Nehru had remarked: "Independence for us means complete freedom from British domination and British imperialism. Having attained our freedom, I have no doubt that India will welcome all attempts at world cooperation and federation, and will even agree to give up part of her own independence to a larger group of which she is an equal member." He had reiterated his opposition to Dominion status, but left the door open to friendship with Britain: "India could never be an equal member of the Commonwealth unless imperialism and all it implies is discarded."[9]

Jawaharlal Nehru was the most internationally-minded man in India. Not only was he free from narrow nationalism, he had no bitterness against the British people as such. As he wrote in his *Autobiography* in the mid-1930s:

It is not a question of an implacable and irreconcilable antagonism to England and the English people, or the desire to break from them at all costs. It would be natural enough if there was bad blood between India and England after what has happened. 'The clumsiness of power spoils the key and uses the pick-axe,' says Tagore, and the key to our hearts was destroyed long ago, and the abundant use of the pick-axe on us has not made us partial to the British. But if we claim to serve the larger cause of India and humanity we cannot afford to be carried away by our momentary passions. And even if we were so inclined the hard training which Gandhiji has given us for the last fifteen years would prevent us. I write this sitting in a British prison and for months past my mind has been full of anxiety, and I have perhaps suffered more during this solitary imprisonment than I have done in gaol before. Anger and resentment have often filled my mind at various happenings, and yet as I sit here, and look deep into my mind and heart, I do not find any anger against England or the British people. I dislike British imperialism and I resent its imposition on India; I dislike the capitalist system; I dislike exceedingly and resent the way India is exploited by the ruling classes of Britain. But I do not hold England or the English people as a whole responsible for this, and even if I did, I do not think it would make much difference, for it is a little foolish to lose one's temper at or condemn a whole people. They are as much the victims of circumstances as we are.

Personally, I owe too much to England in my mental make-up ever to feel wholly alien to her. And, do what I will, I cannot get rid of the habits of mind, and the standards and ways of judging other countries as well as life generally, which I acquired at school and college in England. All my predilections (apart from the political plane) are in favour of England and the English people, and if I have become what is called an uncompromising opponent of British rule in India, it is almost in spite of myself.

It is that rule, that domination, to which we object, and with which we cannot compromise willingly—not the English people. Let us by all means have the closest contacts with the English and other foreign peoples. We want fresh air in India, fresh and vital ideas, healthy cooperation; we have grown too musty with age. But if the English come in the role of a tiger they can expect no friendship or cooperation....

Indian freedom and British imperialism are two incompatibles, and neither martial law nor all the sugar-coating in the world can make them compatible or bring them together. Only with the elimination of imperialism from India will conditions be created which permit of real Indo-British cooperation.[10]

Nehru's avowed partiality for England and the English appears to have received a temporary set-back in the late 1930s and the early 1940s. He disliked intensely the British policy of appeasing Fascism and Nazism. He was shocked and hurt by the brutal manner in which the British government suppressed the Quit India movement in 1942. While imprisoned in the Ahmednagar Fort—incidentally, Nehru's longest ever imprisonment—he wrote in *The Discovery of India* in 1944:

I had always looked forward in the past to a visit to England, because I have many friends there and old memories draw me. But now I found that there was no such desire and the idea was distasteful. I wanted to keep as far away from England as possible, and I had no wish even to discuss India's problems with Englishmen. And then I remembered some friends and softened a little, and I told myself how wrong it was to judge a whole people in this way. I thought also of the terrible experiences that the English people had gone through in this war, of the continuous strain in which they had lived, of the loss of so many of their loved ones. All this helped to tone down my feelings, but that basic reaction remained. Probably time and future will lessen it and give another perspective.[11]

Time did lessen Nehru's adverse reaction and gave him another perspective. Post-war Britain obviously aroused Nehru's sympathy and admiration. She had fought and suffered in the cause of democracy and freedom. Immediately after victory had been achieved on the western front she had rejected Winston Churchill and the Tories and voted a Labour government to power with Clement Attlee as Prime Minister. And Attlee and his colleagues lost no time in applying themselves to the task of translating into reality the policy, which they had long advocated, of giving independence to India.

As one examines Nehru's utterances in the year immediately

preceding the transfer of power on August 15, 1947 one notices a gradual but discernible trend in his thinking towards the maintenance of friendly relations with Britain and the Commonwealth. Speaking as head of the newly-formed Interim Government, Nehru remarked on September 27, 1946: "In spite of our past history of conflict, we hope that an independent India will have friendly and cooperative relations with England and the countries of the British Commonwealth."[12] Again, on December 13, 1946, while moving the *Objectives Resolution* in the Indian Constituent Assembly, he said: "We want to make friends, in spite of the long history of conflict in the past, with England also." He referred to his recent and disappointing visit to England in connection with the deadlock over the Cabinet Mission proposals, but added: "... we seek the cooperation of England, even at this stage, when we are full of suspicion of each other. We feel that if that cooperation is denied, it will be injurious to India, certainly to some extent, probably more so to England, and, to some extent, to the world at large."[13] Once again, on January 22, 1947, while replying to the debate on the *Objectives Resolution* in the Indian Constituent Assembly, Nehru observed:

Now, what relation will...[the future Indian] Republic bear to the other countries of the world, to England and to the British Commonwealth and the rest? For a long time past we have taken a pledge on Independence Day that India must sever her connection with Great Britain, because that connection had become an emblem of British domination. At no time have we ever thought in terms of isolating ourselves in this part of the world from other countries or of being hostile to countries which have dominated over us. On the eve of this great occasion, when we stand on the threshold of freedom, we do not wish to carry a trail of hostility with us against any other country. We want to be friendly to all. We want to be friendly with the British people and the British Commonwealth of Nations.... If we seek to be [a] free, independent, democratic Republic, it is not to dissociate ourselves from other countries, but rather as a free nation to cooperate in the fullest measure with other countries for peace and freedom, to cooperate with Britain, with the British Commonwealth of Nations, with the United States of America, with the Soviet Union, and with all other countries big and small. But real cooperation would only come between us and these other nations when we know that we are free to cooperate and are not imposed upon and forced to cooperate. As long as there is the slightest trace of compulsion, there can be no cooperation.[14]

Thus it is clear that even before the transfer of power in August 1947—in fact, even before the Attlee declaration of February 20, 1947 regarding " the transference of power into responsible Indian hands by a date not later than June 1948,"[15] or the arrival of Lord Mountbatten as Viceroy in India in March 1947—Nehru was inclined to keep India in the Commonwealth. The manner in which the British transferred power in August 1947 undoubtedly created a favourable impression on the minds of Nehru and his associates and reinforced their desire to let India remain in the Commonwealth. Nehru's friendship with the Mountbattens certainly strengthened his resolve and eased the process by which a republican India stayed in the Comonwealth. But the fact cannot be over-emphasised that already in late 1946 and early 1947 Nehru's thoughts were tending in the direction of maintaining friendly relations with Britain and the Commonwealth.

There were many Indians and Britons who thought that the resolution of the Indian Constituent Assembly of January 22, 1947, which had declared that India would become "an Independent Sovereign Republic," had already prejudged the issue of Commonwealth membership, for a republican India could not remain in the Commonwealth. This was not Nehru's view. He repeatedly stated that "this business of our being a republic" had "little or nothing to do with what relations we should have with other countries, notably with the United Kingdom or the Commonwealth," and that India's membership of the Commonwealth was "something apart from and in a sense independent of the Constitution" that she adopted.[16] Nehru was encouraged in this belief by the fact that Eire, though a republic in all but name since 1937, had continued as a member of the Commonwealth. [17]

The fact that Nehru and other Indian leaders accepted the transfer of power in August 1947 on the Dominion-status basis, albeit, as a temporary arrangement in order to facilitate a speedy change-over, was not without some significance. It indicated that he and his associates recognized that the concept of Dominion status had changed and that it now meant virtually complete independence.

It also indicated that they were not averse to the idea of India remaining in the British Commonwealth. More significantly, it left independent India in the British Commonwealth.

Discussing the probable reasons which prompted India to remain in the Commonwealth, Professor Nicholas Mansergh writes: "There was, however, one immediate factor which may well have been decisive. Pakistan was committed to Commonwealth membership. If India seceded, did not that, in view especially of pre-partition disputes on division of assets, evacuee property, river water and above all Kashmir, mean the likelihood of an anti-Indian Commonwealth?"[18] It is true that Indian leaders were anxious that Muslim League (later Pakistani) politicians should not be allowed to make political capital out of their loudly proclaimed intention to stay in the Commonwealth. Many Indian leaders were even apprehensive that if India went out of and Pakistan remained in the Commonwealth, Pakistan might become a base of British imperialism. They were also advised by their British friends that the best way of neutralizing anti-Indian elements in Britain and the Commonwealth—and these were not insubstantial—was that India should remain in the Commonwealth.[19] But until we have access to the papers of Nehru—both private and official—which are still closed to the public, we shall not be able to judge precisely how much the thought of using the Commonwealth membership "as a counterpoise to Pakistan"[20] weighed with Nehru in his calculation of India's self-interest while deciding to keep India in the Commonwealth.

It was as Prime Minister of the Dominion of India that Nehru first attended the meeting of Commonwealth Prime Ministers in London in October 1948. Personal experience further convinced him of the value of the Commonwealth connection. In a broadcast from London on October 26, 1948 he spoke of the old colonial empire of Britain gradually changing into a combination of free Dominions and non-self-governing countries and expressed the hope that "this change-over will be complete soon, so that the Commonwealth of Nations will become a real commonwealth of free nations." He referred to the mutual understanding that resulted from the meeting and added: "We may not agree about everything, but it was surprising what a large measure of unanimity there was, not only in the objectives to be aimed at, but also in the methods to be pursued.....
This meeting has shown me that there is great scope for the Commonwealth to function in this way, and not only to help itself but to help

others also." [21]

On his return from London, Nehru, speaking in the Indian Constituent Assembly on November 8, 1948, alluded to the private and unofficial discussions he had had with other Commonwealth Prime Ministers regarding India's continued membership of the Commonwealth and remarked that he had made it clear to them that India "desired to be associated in friendly relationship with other countries, with the United Kingdom and the Commonwealth" even after becoming a republic, but how this could be done was a matter for careful consideration by all concerned.[22]

The Congress party endorsed Nehru's stand. Meeting in its annual session at Jaipur, it passed a resolution on December 18, 1948, which, among other things, said:

> In view of the attainment of complete independence and the establishment of the Republic of India which will symbolize that independence and give to India the status among the nations of the world that is her rightful due, her present association with the United Kingdom and the Commonwealth of Nations will necessarily have to change. India, however, desires to maintain all such links with other countries as do not come in the way of her freedom of action and independence, and the Congress would welcome her free association with the independent nations of the Commonwealth for their common weal and the promotion of world peace.[23]

After months of consultation and deliberation a formula was evolved which permitted India, if and when she became a republic, to remain a member of the Commonwealth, without damaging the monarchical basis of the other members, or destroying the common bond of the Crown on which the Commonwealth was built. The future Indian Republic would owe no allegiance to the Crown, nor would the Monarch have any place in her government. She would, however, remain a full member of the Commonwealth and would acknowledge the King as a symbol of the free association of its independent member nations; and, as such, the Head of the Commonwealth.[24] The formula was accepted by the Commonwealth Prime Ministers at their meeting in London in late April 1949.[25] It was approved both by the Indian Constituent Assembly[26] and by the Congress party[27] in May 1949.

The settlement of April 1949 was, as Professor Mansergh has rightly pointed out, specific, not general, in application.[28] There was no decision that a republic as such could be a full member of the Commonwealth. But the exception soon became a category and later the majority of the Asian and African Commonwealth states opted to follow the same course.

In any discussion of the reasons which prompted Nehru to decide in 1949 that India should continue to stay in the Commonwealth we must also keep in mind the following important facts. When India became independent in 1947, she had been a member of the Commonwealth for thirty years, having been admitted to the Imperial Conference in 1917[29]. The decision that India had therefore to make on achieving independence was not whether to join the Commonwealth or not, but whether to remain in the Commonwealth or leave it. Though the Indian Constituent Assembly had already, on January 22, 1947, declared its "firm and solemn resolve to proclaim India as an Independent Sovereign Republic," the government of independent India wisely suspended its judgement on the question of Commonwealth membership until 1949—unlike Burma which decided to stay out of the Commonwealth immediately after gaining independence. This suspension of judgement for two years by India was made possible by the fact that India was already in the Commonwealth. It was very fortunate, for it gave India and the other members of the Commonwealth time to think over the problem and to prepare for the necessary adjustments. It also enabled Nehru to attend the Commonwealth Prime Ministers' Conference in London in October 1948, where he had the opportunity of seeing things from inside and of becoming convinced that the Commonwealth was a free association of equal nations, in no way subordinate one to another, and that "membership in the Commonwealth meant independence plus, not independence minus."[30] Had India not already attained her special status in the Commonwealth in 1917, it is doubtful whether she would have chosen to remain a member in 1949, and also whether the other members of the Commonwealth would so readily have accepted her, especially as a republic.

India's continued association with the Commonwealth was also made possible by the manner in which the Indian nationalist movement was conducted and the way the British responded to it. The inevitable bitterness created by the nationalist movement and its periodical repression did not fail to colour Indian patriotism with a strong antipathy to their rulers; it was intensified by a distrust of British intentions, and in the minds of many Indians the sense of subjection bit so deep that they wanted, as it were, to cut themselves away from their past by severing all relations with Britain. They demanded that the Indian National Congress— the party which led the Indian freedom movement—should commit itself to secession from the British Commonwealth. But some of the leaders of the Congress—chief among whom was Mahatma Gandhi—consistently opposed this demand. Gandhi argued that if Britain offered India an equal and honourable partnership, it would be "petulant", "vindictive" and "religiously unlawful" on India's part to refuse it. He told the Congress in 1924:

The better mind of the world desires today, not absolutely independent states warring against one another, but a federation of friendly inter-dependent states. The consummation of that event may be far off. I want to make no grand claim for our country. But I see nothing grand or impossible about our expressing our readiness for universal inter-dependence. It should rest with Britian to say that she will have no real alliance with India. I desire the ability to be totally independent without asserting the independence. Any scheme that I would frame, while Britain declares her goal about India to be complete equality within the Empire, would be that of alliance and not of independence without alliance.[31]

When in 1929 the Congress rejected—much to Gandhi's distaste— the ideal of Dominion Status for India in favour of "Complete Independence," Gandhi saw to it that the Congress was not committed to secession from the British Commonwealth.[32] At the Round Table Conference in London in 1931 he remarked: "The Congress contemplates a connection with the British people—but that connection to be such as can exist between two absolute equals—I have aspired—I still aspire—to be a citizen, not in the Empire, but in a Commonwealth; in a partnership if possible—if God wills it an indissoluble partnership—but not a partnership superimposed upon one nation by another. Hence you find that the Congress claims that either party should have the right to sever the connection, to dissolve the partnership".[33] Gandhi did not allow

Indian nationalism to become narrow, violent, racial and isolationist. He saved the Congress from getting into the straight-jacket
of secession. He never sought outside help to free India. He kept
the quarrel between India and England what it was in essentials,
a family quarrel. "I know the English and they know me; ours
is a deadly but friendly struggle," he was fond of telling foreign
visitors. It is rare for a nationalist leader to avow openly and
incessantly—as Gandhi did—that he had been and remained a
sincere friend of the country against which he was waging a non-
violent war. Nor was it insignificant that his war was non-violent.
Had the Indian nationalist movement turned violent, it would
in its turn have invited violent repression, and ended by leaving
a legacy of bloodshed, which would have been (as the examples of
Ireland and South Africa prove) extremely hard to overcome. If
the transfer of power in India in 1947 could be what Lord Samuel
called it, "a treaty of peace without a war,"[34] credit is due as much
to Gandhi's leadership as to enlightened British policy.

It can well be argued that Britain was often too slow and
grudging in making political concessions to Indians. But she never
adopted an attitude of uncompromising hostility to Indian political
aspirations. Concessions were periodically made to Indians, if only
just in time, and what is more important, they were actually made
to moderate-minded Indians. This kept alive the faith of many
Indians in British good intentions, strengthened the hands of the
moderates against the extremists in India, and prevented the drift
of the Indian nationalist movement towards violence. British
policy in India thus differed essentially from that in Ireland, where
concessions had to be made to extremism and violence long after
they had been denied to moderation and reason.

Probably nothing became the British in India so much like their
leaving it. The timing and manner of the transfer of power in India
made a profound impression on the Indian mind. "The British
had set an example of voluntary withdrawal with grace. They had
been magnanimous. Shall India be mean and petty, and continue
nursing old wrongs? No, she must also rise to the occasion and
set an example of magnanimity by clasping the extended hand
of the erstwhile adversary." This is how Nehru and many other
Indian leaders argued. Describing the feelings which were uppermost
in his mind when he decided to continue India's membership of the
Commonwealth in 1949, Nehru remarked: "I wanted the world

to see that...India was prepared to cooperate even with those with whom she had been fighting in the past...." [35]

Another reason—and this was perhaps the most important—which persuaded Nehru to keep India in the Commonwealth in 1949 was that there was a Labour government in Britain at that time. The Labour party contained many old friends of India. It had supported the cause of Indian self-government over the years. It had given India independence and redeemed its pledge. It wanted India to remain in the Commonwealth, but gave her freedom to remain or quit. All these things were important. There was—and remains—in India a deep and long-standing dislike of the Conservatives. Had there been a Conservative government in Britain in 1947 or 1949, it is very doubtful whether India would have remained in the Commonwealth. The Labour government gave Indians what they had been demanding ever since 1920—the right to secede from the Commonwealth. It was the denial of this right in the past which prejudiced opinion in Ireland against the Commonwealth connection. It was the denial of this right which was the cause of so many attacks upon Commonwealth membership in India during the 1920s and the 1930s. It is significant that soon after 1942—when the right to secede from the Comonwealth was first explicitly conceded in the famous Cripps proposals of that year[36]—prejudice against the Commonwealth connection lessened in India. On the question of the Crown, Nehru and other Indian leaders were prepared for a give-and-take. If the Commonwealth was willing to retain a republican India, they did not mind recognizing "the King as the symbol of the free association of its independent member nations and as such the Head of the Commonwealth."

Nehru knew that the Commonwealth had changed and was changing and that it was no longer a Western or Anglo-Saxon club. He rightly judged that the Commonwealth would grow and that in the course of time there would be many more Asian and African countries in it, and that India's membership of the Commonwealth would facilitate this development.[37]

Nehru was a liberal-internationalist, not an isolationist. He did not want India to live the life of "a frog in the well." He was conscious of India's important position in the world. He was inspired by the conviction that India, having come into her own, had a distinct contribution to make towards solving international problems. He was eager to develop new relationships with the outside world and he felt that it would look ridiculous for India to sever old, established ties with Britain and the Commonwealth while trying to establish new ones. The Commonwealth, he rightly reasoned, not only offered India an established network of international relationship which it would be foolish on her part to throw away, but could also help her in developing new contacts..[38]

Immediately after independence India was faced with tremendous problems. There were the ill effects of partition. There was the problem of the Indian princely states, especially those of Hyderabad and Kashmir.[39] Her defences were weak. She was new to the international community. She had few friends in Asia. Her experience of the Asian Relations Conference held at Delhi in March 1947 had not been very encouraging. Her relations with Pakistan and the Soviet Union were far from being cordial. In a note written in 1949, Sir B.N. Rau, then Constitutional Adviser to the Indian government, argued that "this is no time for leaving the Commonwealth and venturing into the unknown, for she [India] may thereby create for herself a new set of problems even more baffling."[40] Nehru emphasized the same point in 1949. He said: "If we dissociate ourselves completely from the Commonwealth, then for the moment we are completely isolated. We cannot remain completely isolated, and so inevitably by stress of circumstances we have to incline in some direction or other. But that inclination in some direction or other will necessarily be on a basis of give-and-take. It may be in the nature of alliances: you give something yourself and get something in return. In other words, it may involve commitments far more than at present. There are no commitments today."[41] Membership of the Commonwealth gave India friends and a sense of security and stability in the difficult early years of her freedom.

Justifying his government's decision to continue India's membership of the Commonwealth, Nehru remarked in the Indian Constituent Assembly on May 16, 1949 that it was "beneficial to us and to certain causes in the world that we wish to advance."[42] Of the benefits to India there could be little doubt. There were the advantages of cooperation in the economic and political fields, in education and diplomacy, and even in defence. The bulk of India's trade was then with the Commonwealth; her foreign exchange reserves were tied up in the sterling area; there were substantial communities of Indian settlers in various parts of the British

Empire;[43] her armed forces depended on British-made weapons; she had a common concern with the Commonwealth in the defence of the Indian Ocean area and in the maintenance of a balance of power in the whole Eurasian continent.

What of the larger causes in the world that Nehru wished to advance? Let us first see what were these causes which he had at heart. They were peace, freedom for colonial peoples, the fight against racialism, international cooperation, especially cooperation with Asian and African nations, and raising the living standards of under-developed countries. All these causes, Nehru thought, India could serve better by remaining in the Commonwealth, and he has been proved right.

As Professor Nicholas Mansergh rightly observes, "Nehru reinterpreted the idea of the Commonwealth to fit his own philosophy of international relations."[44] He viewed the Commonwealth as an association of governments and peoples brought together by history and maintained for the promotion of certain common interests and ideals. It was a bridge between the East and the West, between various continents, races and cultures, a grouping of friendly nations making widely differing responses to the cold war, and thus cutting across the frozen configuration of international politics. It was an instrument of peace. It had brought "a touch of healing"[45] to an embittered world. It was an example to the world of the Gandhian principles applied to relations between nations.[46]

Nehru did not consider the Commonwealth to be a super-state or even the embryo of such a state. He believed that the Commonwealth was a free association of sovereign states and that it could only survive as such. He was opposed to all proposals for giving the Commonwealth supra-national authority as being misconceived and potentially dangerous. He would not allow the Commonwealth to interfere in the domestic affairs of any member nation. He objected to the setting up of a Commonwealth tribunal or to the Commonwealth assuming mediatory responsibilities in intra-Commonwealth disputes. Replying to the criticism in India that he had failed to raise the issue of racial discrimination by the South African Government at the Commonwealth Prime Ministers' Conference, Nehru remarked in May 1949:

It was a dangerous thing for us to bring that matter within the purview of the Commonwealth. Because then the very thing to which you and I object might have taken place. That is, the Commonwealth might have been considered as some kind of a superior body which sometimes, acts as a tribunal, or judges, or in a sense supervises, the activities of its member nations. That certainly would have meant a diminution in our independence and sovereignty, if we had once accepted that principle. Therefore, we were not prepared and we are not prepared to treat the Commonwealth as such or even to bring disputes between member nations of the Commonwealth before the Commonwealth body. We may, of course, in a friendly way discuss the matters; that is a different matter.[47]

Consistent with this view, Nehru resolutely opposed the raising of the Indo-Pakistani dispute over Kashmir at the Commonwealth Prime Ministers' Conference in London in 1951, but agreed to talk about it informally with interested Prime Ministers outside the forum of the Conference.[48]

Nehru did not regard the Commonwealth as a political bloc. In fact he decided to keep India in the Commonwealth because it was not a political bloc and because he did not wish her to join any one of the existing political blocs. Though he was anxious to promote greater understanding, cooperation and agreement among members of the Commonwealth, he did not think that the Commonwealth could have a common foreign policy. He believed that any attempt to have uniform policies among Commonwealth countries— so differently conditioned, both geographically and historically— was doomed to failure, and that a friendly approach and the desire to consult and cooperate with each other was more important than an artificial unity in policy.

Nehru valued the Commonwealth as a friendly association that neither circumscribed India's political and constitutional independence nor came in the way of her pursuing her own independent policies in international affairs. As he said in 1950:

Presumably some people imagine that our association with the Commonwealth imposes some kind of restricting or limiting factor upon our activities, be they political, economic, foreign, domestic or anything else. In the case of the United Nations or the International Monetary Fund, some limiting factors certainly come in, as they must, if we join an international organization of that type; but in our association with the Commonwealth, there is not the least vestige of such a limiting factor....We may carry out any policy we like regardless of whether we are in the Commonwealth or not.[49]

The Commonwealth represented a form of international cooperation which, according to Nehru, suited India best, being intimate and informal, beneficial and yet not binding. In 1956 Nehru remarked: "Of all the types of associations we have between nations, probably this rather invisible type of association is stronger than alliances or treaties." He would like to see, he added, a world develop in which all the nations were associated in some such friendly way with each other.[50] But while membership of the Commonwealth did not bind or commit India in any way, it certainly exposed her to other influences. This, however, in Nehru's view was neither a disadvantage nor a one-way traffic. "When people think of the Commonwealth influencing us in our policies," he remarked in 1950, "may I suggest to them the possibility that we may also greatly influence others in the right direction?"[51]

Nehru prized the Commonwealth machinery for the exchange of information and opinion. He valued the Commonwealth for its technical assistance, educational facilities and trading privileges. But great as these advantages were, they were not in Nehru's opinion decisive. Membership of the Commonwealth according to Nehru, had been most useful to India in that it had allowed her to pursue policies which were dear to her heart, and to exercise a greater influence in the world than she would have otherwise done. It had enabled her to help towards the transformation of the Commonwealth in a direction which she favoured. It had helped her to develop closer contacts with countries in Asia and Africa. It had saved her from the distasteful necessity in the modern world of leaning too heavily on one super-power or the other. It had helped her to remain independent and non-aligned, and to reach out and influence opinion in all parts of the world.[52]

GIRILAL JAIN

India, Pakistan and Kashmir

PARTITION AND ITS aftermath in the shape of awesome communal
riots and exchange of over twelve million refugees in 1947, did not
settle the key issues of primacy, the viability of Pakistan and
the pull of the ideology of Islamic nationalism in the subcontinent.
They had not been settled even seventeen years later at the time
of Jawaharlal Nehru's death on May 27, 1964. The events of 1971
culminating in India's decisive military victory in the war with
Pakistan and the rise of the state of Bangladesh have however,
done that with such finality as there can be in human affairs. Indeed,
the Simla agreement whereby Pakistan agreed to replace the old
cease-fire line in Jammu and Kashmir with the line of control, and
to settle in principle all disputes between the two countries through
bilateral negotiations is an indication that the ruling elite in Islamabad
is no longer totally averse to accommodation with this country
on a realistic basis.

There should be little doubt now that India has emerged as the
first power in South Asia, that its lead over its neighbours is too
big to be made up by them, and that Pakistan has disintegrated not
so much under pressure from this country as under the weight of its
internal contradictions. The ideology of Islamic nationalism has lost
much of its appeal and pull. The acceptance by the predominantly
Muslim Bangladesh of the concept of secularism, with its accent on
the equality of all citizens irrespective of religious considerations,
as the basis of its constitution is proof enough of the reduced pull

of Islamic nationalism. But as it happens, even Pakistan is under compulsion to play down the talk of Islamic nationalism and to try to meet the legitimate aspirations of its linguistic and cultural minorities on a practical basis.

It would be a case of wisdom by hindsight to say that these developments are a logical culmination of events leading to, and following, the partition of the sub-continent in 1947. For, the Pakistan Government could have prevented the drift towards its disintegration at various points of time if its leaders had the foresight and the courage to do so. There was, for instance, nothing fatally inevitable about President Ayub Khan's gamble in Jammu and Kashmir in 1965, or Zulfiqar Ali Bhutto's decision to oppose the Tashkent accord in 1966, or Islamabad's refusal to normalise relations with New Delhi after the 1965 war, or President Yahya Khan's inept handling of Sheikh Mujibur Rahman and his Awami League before and after the general elections in December 1970. In other words, it was possible for Pakistan to avoid aggravating tensions with India and to win over the East Bengal leaders through a policy of conciliation and there by ease the crisis in 1971.

However, this is another way of saying that Pakistan could have avoided the disaster of 1971 if it had reconciled itself to India's primacy, if it had not challenged the *status quo* in Jammu and Kashmir as it emerged from the cease-fire on January 1, 1949, and if it had acceded to East Bengal's demand for autonomy. Perhaps it would have moved in that direction under the force of circumstances if the United States had not intervened in the affairs of the sub-continent through its treaty of mutual security with Pakistan (1954) and consequently upset the natural power balance in the sub-continent, on the one hand, and the internal arrangement in Pakistan, on the other. Ironical though it may appear, the treaty sowed the seeds of Pakistan's disintegration. For it not only aggravated tensions between India and Pakistan but also paved the way for the rise of the military dictatorship which denied East Bengal its legitimate share in political power and thus alienated it.

This is not to suggest that everything would have gone well for Pakistan in the absence of American intervention. On the contrary, three points can be made to show that the situation resulting from partition in 1947 or even the cease-fire in Jammu and Kashmir on January 1, 1949, could not have been frozen.

First, it is a common-place that Pakistan, as it emerged in 1947,

was a physical monstrosity, divided as it was by a thousand miles
of Indian territory, and that the cultural and linguistic differences
between its eastern and western wings were so marked that tension
between them was unavoidable. The dominant West Pakistani ruling
elite exploited East Bengal and denied it its legitimate share in
power and developmental resources and thereby accelerated the rise
of Bangla nationalism. But even wiser and more far-sighted men at
the helm of affairs in Pakistan could at best have delayed the crystalli-
sation of the feeling of language-and-culture based identity in
East Bengal and made its fulfilment less painful. They could not
have prevented the rise of Bangla sub-nationalism for the simple
reason that by destroying the geographical, administrative and
political unity of the sub-continent, Mohammed Ali Jinnah wrecked
the very basis on which the unity of the Indian Muslim community
could rest and paved the way for the rise of linguistic nationalism
in East Bengal and possibly in Sind, the NWFP, Baluchistan
and finally even in Punjab as well. (Developments in Pakistan since
this was written bear out the accuracy of this assessment).

It is also well known that Pakistani leaders decided to transfer the
pre-partition conflict with the Indian National Congress, which
had helped the Muslim League bring large segments of the Muslim
community, specially the middle class intelligentsia, under its
influence, to the state level after partition on the calculation that
hostility towards India could keep the two wings of Pakistan united.
But in choosing Kashmir as the symbol of the struggle against this
country, they made sure, *albeit* unwittingly, that the East Bengalis
could not share their view of Pakistan's security requirements.

This divergence of interests became apparent at the time of the
Indo-Pakistan war in 1965 when East Bengal lay open to an Indian
attack and Z.A. Bhutto as Foreign Minister made the astounding
statement that its security was guaranteed by China. The Pakistan
government further weakened its position by refusing to resume
trade with India after the war. This hurt East Bengal which, for
instance, had to import coal at four times the price at which it
could have secured its requirements from India. This provided the
East Bengali elite another proof that Rawalpindi did not care for
its economic well-being. It was in this setting that Sheikh Mujibur
Rahman formulated his six-point programme asking for a measure
of autonomy which bordered on independence.

Secondly, whatever one's appreciation of the factors that led to the establishment of Pakistan in 1947, it could not be said to have settled that basic conflict in the sub-continent. It was, therefore, unavoidable that there would be a trial of strength between it and India. Contrary to what Pakistanis have said and believed, most Indians were not unhappy either with the fact and the results of partition or with the outcome of the war over Kashmir, and were therefore willing to freeze the *status quo*. Indeed, Nehru's entire policy towards Pakistan can best be understood in those terms. But Pakistan functioned under different compulsions and was determined to upset the *status quo*.

Finally, India's decision to adhere to the policy of secularism in spite of unprecedented communal riots on both sides of the new border and the influx of millions of refugees, made the trial of strength with Pakistan more and not less likely. In the very act of being true to its professions India constituted an affront to Pakistan because the ideology of secular nationalism posed a challenge to the rival concept of religion-based nationalism. However strange it may appear on a surface view, Pakistan would have welcomed a government in New Delhi which claimed to speak in the name of Hindu nationalism because that would have vindicated the two-nation theory which constituted its sole *raison d'etre*. There is no conflict between these two viewpoints. In fact they reinforce each other. For, if the *status quo*, as it emerged between India and Pakistan, on the one hand, and within Pakistan, on the other, as a result of partition and the war over Kashmir (in 1947 and 1948), was unstable, America's generous military assistance to the Pakistan Government obviated for it the need to seek accommodation either with India or with the aspirations of the people of East Bengal.

It was argued, almost endlessly in the west till the 1971 war, that having agreed to partition on the basis of religion, India should have allowed Pakistan to annex Kashmir, or at least abided by its promise of a plebiscite. This is a long story which has been told again and again and need not be repeated. All that needs to be said here is that the issue has been one of principles, indeed, of ideology because, at stake in Kashmir, have been India's concept of secular nationalism and Pakistan's concept of religion-based nationalism. And surely India could not have compromised on this issue without compromising to some extent the right of almost sixty million Muslims to equal citizenship under the law. This is the crux of the matter and the Indo-Pakistan conflict either during Nehru's tenure of office or subsequently cannot be understood without a proper understanding of this central fact.

II

The main source of conflict between India and Pakistan has been so thoroughly confused that it is necessary to go to the basic point whether such a thing as Indian nationalism has existed before and after independence. This is specially so, because even well-intentioned commentators not only abroad but in India have taken the simplistic view that the concept of Hindu nationalism would have triumphed in India if Nehru had not been at the helm of affairs. But while his role in ensuring the acceptance of the secular path by India cannot be denied, it needs to be remembered that Nehru was not an aberration. He was the product of the twin movements of social reform and political independence which have shaped the Hindu elite in the 19th and 20th centuries. In other words, he was operating in a political milieu which was not at all hostile to his philosophy of life and aspirations. How else could he have become the unchallenged leader of the Congress party and led it to victory in three successive general elections in 1952, 1957 and 1962?

The absurdity of it all is that some commentators have gone to the extent of describing Gandhi, (who named Nehru as his heir), as a revivalist, if not a communalist. Much of this denigration of the Mahatma is deliberate and motivated. But there are some who have genuinely failed to understand that the social reform and nationalist movements in the Hindu society were subject to the laws of dialectics, that revivalism as such did not acquire a hold over the Hindus and that the distinction between the so-called moderate and rationalist national figures like Gopal Krishna Gokhale and the so-called Hindu radicals like Lokamanya Tilak is rather arbitrary. The two groups and viewpoints complemented one another, though on a superficial view they seemed to contradict and oppose each other. The Mahatma embodied both these trends in his person and therefore could work with conservatives and radicals alike. As Professor C.H. Heimsath points out, while the inspiration and the human compassion of Hindu *bhaktas* on occasions enriched 19th century social reform movements, these were not in any way the products of the *bhakti* spirit and they did not function primarily in the spirit of religious devotion. They began with individual revolts against existing customs, took shape under the influence of western methods of organisation and propagation, and recruited their supporters from men who were English-educated or who had imbibed western ideas indirectly. Thus while some of the social doctrines underlying the social reform movements were not unlike the ideals to be found in Hindu thought, they derived their sustenance from "the western ideas of individualism, natural rights, the ethical duties of individual to society at large, the possibility of human progress, 'social efficiency' and the religious doctrine of acquiring merit through good works. Although a few reformers accepted some of those ideas on faith, most of them used reason as their standard of judgment, a Western approach to ethical principles."

It was inevitable that there should have been a reaction against such an open and unashamed acceptance of western ideals and forms in an ancient society like India's whose pride in its past had been aroused by western scholars. This reaction took several forms—revivalist movements, radical nationalism within the Indian National Congress, the Hindu Mahasabha and subsequently the Rashtriya Swayamsewak Sangh. But two points need to be noted. First, it is well known that no programme of social change can win broad acceptance unless it can be presented as the product of authentic native traditions, social, religious and intellectual. Secondly, virtually all of the outstanding nationalist leaders, who identified themselves with the revival of genuine Indian values, were themselves endowed with western training and the bulk of their aspirations for Indian society was derived from it. "The vociferousness of the pleaders on behalf of traditional India could not conceal a great selectivity when they described the Indian society of traditional eras."

The social reform as well as the nationalist movement among the Hindus were by and large based on western ideas of humanism, rationalism, liberalism, utilitarianism and so on and the so-called revivalists only legitimised the changes that the reformers were suggesting.

It has been argued, not always by partisan commentators, that the social and political reform movements produced Hindu nationalism and not Indian nationalism. This view is based on the fact that mostly the Hindus manned and led the freedom struggle, and by and large the Muslims kept out of it. But a nationalism based on an acceptance of the western concepts of individualism and secularism, which recognises the autonomy of the political and economic realm and makes religion a matter of conscience for the individual, cannot exclude members of minority communities irrespective of whether they join the mainstream or not.

This is not to claim that India has reached a stage where it can claim to be fully secular in its polity. But it is not a small achievement that she adopted a liberal and secular constitution, which makes no concession to the religion of the majority, and that communal parties have not proved attractive to most Hindus. Witness the result of the general elections in the past two decades.

It is, indeed, remarkable that in spite of the enormous strains to which the Hindu society has been exposed in the process of modernisation and industrialisation, it has not thrown up any significant revivalist movement, which harks back to some mythical golden age. The Ram Rajya Parishad of Swami Karpatriji, which made a brief appearance in the 'fifties, can be said to be the only exception. But such success as it won in Rajasthan depended on the support of the princely order rather than on its own appeal to the people. The Jana Sangh falls in a different category. It is not a revivalist party in that it does not believe that modern Indian society can be organised on the basis of old scriptures. Similarly, while it equates the Hindu ethos with the Indian ethos, it does not exclude the non-Hindus, including the Muslims, from its ranks.

Unfortunately a similar reform movement did not strike roots among the Muslim community in India in the 19th century, though men like Sir Syed Ahmed Khan made an attempt to re-interpret the holy *Koran* in terms of the western principles of rationalism. On the contrary, revivalism became the dominant theme among the Muslims because it offered them solace in the period of their political and economic decline. As such their elite defined the community's identity in religious and not in territorial terms. The problem was further complicated by the Muslim elite's memories of rule over the Hindus, its inability to compete with them in modern professions, trade and industry, and its dependence, psychologically and otherwise, on British power.

These factors account partly for the rise of the demand for partition in 1940, though even today we do not know enough about the role of the British government. But be that as it may, if the demand for a separate homeland was a logical culmination of the claim that Muslims constituted a separate nation, it also constituted a repudiation of this claim because over one-third of the Muslims were bound to be left in India whatever the boundaries of the proposed state of Pakistan. It would have been more logical for Jinnah and the Muslim League to ask for a bi-national state. And if they did not deem that possible, they should have gone to the logical extreme and asked for an exchange of population. Instead, they demanded a Pakistan in which the Muslims would have enjoyed a safe but not an overwhelming majority. This was an absurd proposition, and the absurdity of it was fully exposed when in the wake of partition Jinnah called upon all citizens of Pakistan to forget religious distinctions.

Why then did Jinnah raise the demand for partition? There are two possible explanations. First, it is possible that he reckoned that once he had vanquished his opponents and rivals in the Muslim community and mobilised it fully on the basis of the demand for partition, he would be able to make a deal with the Congress on his own terms. If Maulana Azad's account in his book, *India Wins Freedom,* is to be accepted at its face value—Jinnah nearly succeeded in 1946 when the Congress accepted the Cabinet mission proposals. That the arrangement could not have worked is an altogether different proposition.

Secondly, it is plausible that Jinnah calculated that he would be able to galvanise Pakistan into an effective instrument for the restoration of Muslim hegemony in the sub-continent. In any event, such a sentiment was pretty strong among his supporters, specially in Hindu-majority provinces, that is, among the people who rallied behind the demand for partition largely out of the fear that they would be submerged by the numerically stronger Hindu majority.

But whatever Jinnah's original calculations, once he had destroyed whatever unity Indian Islam possessed by virtue of the geographical, political and administrative unity of the sub-continent, he was bound to be drawn to try to restore it by disrupting India and bringing it under Pakistan's hegemony. All this might appear to be too far-fetched. But Jinnah's actions speak for themselves.

He tried to persuade the Hindu Maharaja of Jodhpur to accede to Pakistan; he accepted the accession of the Nawab of Junagadh in utter disregard of the fact that the state was located three hundred miles from the nearest point in Pakistan; he encouraged the Nizam to try to carve out an independent kingdom in the heart of India; and having failed to browbeat the Maharaja of Jammu and Kashmir he ordered the invasion of the state by well-armed tribals led by regular officers of the Pakistan army.

Jinnah failed in all these attempts. Jodhpur acceded to India. The Nawab of Junagadh had to flee when his people rose in revolt against him. The Kashmir valley was saved because of the timely arrival of Indian troops and the resistance organised by the local Muslim community under the leadership of Sheikh Abdullah. Finally, Hyderabad, too, was brought into the Indian Union after a brief action by the army.

It was an accident of history that the Indian army should have been scheduled to move into Hyderabad within hours of the announcement of Jinnah's death on September 12, 1948. But the two events summed up the situation in the sub-continent. The Indian State was overcoming the last major obstacle in the path of its consolidation as Pakistan was losing the only leader with sufficient moral authority to place it on a firm footing. By then Pakistan's attempt to seize Kashmir had also failed.

III

India, of course, did not choose Kashmir as the testing ground. It only responded to the challenge flung by Jinnah. But the point cannot be over-emphasised that nothing less than the credibility of the Indian state was at stake in the tribal invasion of Jammu and Kashmir. If Jinnah had been allowed to succeed in Jammu and Kashmir, the very basis of the relationship between the two countries could have been transformed to India's great disadvantage. It was not just a question of the concrete demands Jinnah might have made in respect of Assam, and a corridor linking West Pakistan with East Bengal, but of the triumph of one ideology and the defeat of the other. By acquiescing in Kashmir's conquest, India would have for all practical purposes conceded Pakistan's claim to the loyalty of all Muslims in the sub-continent.

Notwithstanding the claim of the Indian National Congress that the sub-continent was not divided in 1947 on the basis of religion or the two-nation theory, Pakistan could not in reality have been reduced to the status of a breakaway state if India had not accepted and met Jinnah's challenge in Kashmir. If he had got away with the gamble there, Pakistan would have been well placed to claim to be the spiritual, if not the actual, homeland of all Muslims in the sub-continent. As things turned out, in the process of being forced out of the Kashmir valley, Pakistan was condemned to impotent rage. With the defeat in Kashmir it lost some of its elan which it has not been able to recapture.

The Pakistani ruling elite has consistently represented its actions as being defensive. It has argued that, not to speak of "Hindu chauvinists", even a man like Nehru was not reconciled to partition and worked for Pakistan's dismemberment. The charge is patently fatuous. Nehru did not make any move which can by any stretch of imagination be said to have been aimed at the dismemberment of Pakistan. On the contrary, Maulana Bhashani disclosed in New Delhi in 1971 that when he approached Nehru for his support for organising a secessionist movement in East Bengal, he advised him (Maulana Bhashani) to work for a democratic set-up in Pakistan as a whole.

But by the very fact of working ceaselessly for a genuinely secular regime in India, which would accord fair treatment to all minorities, by continuing to repudiate the two-nation theory and by refusing to be browbeaten into surrender on Kashmir, Nehru created a serious psychological problem for Pakistan's ruling elite, for self-consciously ideological regimes like Pakistan's ideological challenge is as grave a threat as a physical one.

Jinnah's death was followed by Liaquat Ali Khan's assassination (October 16, 1951) and the dismissal of Khwaja Nazimuddin as Prime Minister (April 17, 1953). By 1953 the predominantly Punjabi military bureaucratic elite was in control in Pakistan. Since it was not the product of the Muslim League's struggle against the Congress it could have quietly laid aside the two-nation theory, reached a practical solution of the Kashmir dispute more or less on the basis of the cease-fire line, and settled down to peaceful co-existence with India. The then Governor-General, Ghulam Mohammed, clearly the ablest man in the coterie in power in Karachi, wanted to make a deal with India and to bury the hatchet. But apparently the pull of the past, the influence of the hawks in the establishment and the fear of the refugees, who had virtually taken over the capital city and had become a major factor in the country's life, proved too much for him. Instead, he went in for a treaty with the United States.

It is not necessary here to go into the details of either the United Nations mediatory efforts or the direct talks between the leaders of the two countries, principally between Nehru and Mohammed Ali Bogra, partly because these have been discussed in detail in various publications on Indo-Pakistan relations, and partly because these were fore-doomed to failure because of the very nature of the conflict. For India, Kashmir was the test of its secular nationalism and for Pakistan of its concept of Islamic nationalism. There could have been no compromise except on the basis of the *status quo*, which the Pakistani rulers found unacceptable.

In parenthesis, however, it may be noted that in the early 'fifties Pakistan could have embarrassed India, if during the discussions, both direct and under United Nations auspices, it had agreed to vacate its aggression, or if it had not insisted on Admiral Nimitz as the plebiscite administrator. But apparently it did not feel secure enough to withdraw its troops, or to accept a leading figure from a neutral country like Burma, Indonesia or Ceylon as the plebiscite administrator. Its intransigence negated the commitment that India had made to hold a plebiscite within the terms of the United Nations resolution of August 13, 1948. Meanwhile, the situation within Jammu and Kashmir and in the Indian sub-continent evolved in a manner that made the original Indian offer of a plebiscite wholly out of date.

Throughout the 'fifties, two leading western powers, the United States and the United Kingdom, were partial towards Pakistan and generally unsympathetic towards India on the Kashmir issue. This was the result of a variety of factors. The British ruling class had, it seems, by and large not forgiven the Congress for having led the struggle for independence and in the process having undermined the entire fabric of the empire. It had also entertained a prejudice against the "wily" Hindus because their religion, way of life and thinking processes were much too complicated and subtle for most of its members. In terms of *real-politik*, it looked upon Pakistan as a bastion against the so-called Soviet expansionist drive, on the one hand, and the restless Arabs, who were beginning to stir, on the other.

The article Sir Olaf Caroe wrote anonymously in *Round Table*, London, in its March 1949 issue, has often been quoted. As perhaps

the most lucid exposition of the Anglo-American strategic appreciation at that stage, one paragraph in it deserves notice even today.
It said:

> The Mesopotamia campaign of the first war and the strategic
> movements of the allies in the second war were made possible
> from the Indian base....At present the establishment of indepen-
> dent States on the Indian peninsula entails a new approach to old
> problems. In this quarter, as on the north-west frontier, Pakistan
> has succeeded to much of India's responsibility, for the Gulf opens
> directly on Karachi, in a real sense its terminus....The importance
> of the Gulf grows greater, not less, as the need for fuel expands,
> the world contracts, and the shadow lengthens from the north. Its
> stability can be assured only by the closest accord between the
> states which surround this Muslim lake, an accord which is under-
> written by the great powers whose interests are engaged.

Sir Olaf Caroe was still not prepared to write off India. For, he
added that "any concept of defence in this region must take account
...of India as the geographical centre of Southern Asia."

It is possible that Sir Olaf was hopeful that despite his policy
of neutrality, Nehru would be willing to cooperate with the western
world because both Stalin and Mao Tse-tung were highly critical
of his govenment and of him personally. But by 1951 when he
published his famous book, *The Wells of Power*, things had greatly
changed.

It had become clear beyond doubt, specially after the outbreak
of the Korean war, that Nehru was serious about his policy and that
anti-imperialism and cooperation among Asian countries were as
important features of it as neutrality in the cold war. The United
States administration to which Sir Olaf was primarily addressing
himself had also become much more allergic to Nehru because of
his refusal to side with it in its policy of containing China by establishing a *cordon sanitaire* around it. Sir Olaf therefore wrote that
if India's help is to be acceptable in a region "where Pakistan stands
in the first line, it will be for India...to adjust her differences with
the sister state in such a way as to strengthen and not weaken their
mutual defences. Failing a new approach in this matter the pattern
will assume a different shape and the Indo-Pakistan frontier will
become a permanent limit between two systems."

But even then he added: "Because a political vacuum will not endure, let us divide the Indian Ocean into three—a small circle including Pakistan with south-western Asia and extending up to the arc of danger, another gate gathering Tibet, Nepal, Burma and south-east Asia in with India, and the third an oceanic theatre based on the Australian continent and including Ceylon." This means that even then India figured in Sir Olaf's scheme of things in the context of China.

Sir Olaf's formulations are believed to have played a major role in persuading the United States to go in for a mutual security pact with Pakistan in the face of protests of well-informed Americans such as George Kennan and Chester Bowles. Ironically enough, the British acted more discreetly than the American leaders, whose thinking was completely dominated by the cold war so much so that Nixon, for instance, urged an alliance with Pakistan not for its defence value but as a "counter-force to confirmed neutralism of Jawaharlal Nehru's India."

This having been said, two points need to be made. First, it is not particularly surprising that even honest and unprejudiced foreigners found it difficult to appreciate the Indian stand on Kashmir and interpreted the issue either in terms of the long-standing Hindu-Muslim conflict or of the Indian promise of holding a plebiscite. For, as noted earlier, only a few outsiders have had the time and the patience to study and understand the complex developments that have led to the rise and growth of Indian nationalism.

Secondly, it is only fair to note that, however strong its annoyance with Nehru, no United States administration in the 'fifties or the 'sixties ignored India or tried to tilt the military balance too heavily in favour of Pakistan. It just could not afford to do so as long as China was its principal preoccupation. India did not line up behind the United States in its confrontation with Peking. On the contrary, it espoused China's case for recognition and admission to the United Nations. But Washington could not see it weakened lest that should automatically strengthen China's position in the region. That is why fairly generous United States' aid to "neutralist" India and President Kennedy's ready response to Nehru's appeal for military aid in 1962.

As it happened, India was very well placed in 1954 when President Eisenhower concluded the pact with Pakistan. Nehru's personal stock in the world was high in view of his defiance of the still dominant western alliance and his role in Korea and Indo-China. Peking had long since abandoned its carping criticism of the Indian Prime Minister and so had Moscow, specially since Stalin's death in March 1953. In 1954 India and China concluded an agreement over Tibet. Even if it turned out to be rather unsatisfactory from the Indian point of view in subsequent years, at that time it was widely regarded as a symbol of understanding and friendship between the two countries. Chou En-lai visited India and Nehru visited China in that year. Though Nehru's trip to Moscow and Khrushchev's and Bulganin's tour of India took place in subsequent years, there were by early 1954 indications that Moscow was preparing itself to respond to New Delhi's overtures. These factors, in addition to its own policy of containing China, obliged the United States to try to convince India with words as well as deeds that its treaty with Pakistan was not directed against it.

Pakistan itself was on the defensive. As noted earlier, Jinnah's efforts to keep India off-balance by encouraging some of the members of Indian states not to accede to it, and by trying to grab Kashmir had failed. His death and Liaquat Ali Khan's assassination added to the prevailing sense of uncertainty among the people which the bureaucratic-military elite could not overcome. Thus while India made a success of democracy, adopted a constitution in 1950, held the first general election under it in 1952 and launched on a programme of economic development under its first five-year plan in 1951, Pakistan was floundering as a result of bitter quarrels between the two wings, shifting alliances among politicians who owed no loyalty to any cause higher than self-aggrandisement, and intrigues by the men actually in control of the State machinery. The sense of purpose and direction in India contrasted sharply with wide-spread frustration and cynicism in Pakistan.

It is, in fact, possible to argue that domestic factors were primarily responsible for persuading the Pakistani "hierarchs" to seeking an alliance with the United States. They needed external assistance to maintain their military establishment at the existing level. Ghulam Mohammad had dismissed Khwaja Nazimuddin as Prime Minister in 1953 partly because the latter had decided to reduce the defence budget to cope with a serious economic crisis. The "hierarchs" were not averse to the idea of getting a new foreign protector in place of the British. These men had loyally served the British and had no qualms in accepting another overlord if he was prepared to underwrite their rule and cough out enough money. The United States was only too willing to do both.

Nothing can illustrate the mentality of the men who were ruling Pakistan in the mid-fifties better than the then Prime Minister, Suhrawardy's statement on November 28, 1956, in connection with the unprovoked Anglo-French-Israeli aggression against Egypt. He criticised Egypt for having blocked the Suez. He said: "...there are many countries who, with us, wonder what requirements of military strategy or tactics necessitated the sinking of so many ships in the canal, thereby adversely affecting the lifeline of so many countries who depend upon it for their trade and their essential supplies." Inevitably this stance added to Pakistan's isolation from what may be called, the mainstream of Asian nationalism and reduced its leverage in dealing with its allies as well as its opponents.

The point has often been made that, unlike other communist countries, China did not in the 'fifties endorse India's claim to Jammu and Kashmir and that in fact soon after the Bandung conference, it sent an emissary to Karachi to assure it that there was no clash of national interests between the two countries and that Peking accepted its explanation for its adherence to SEATO. But the more pertinent fact is that Pakistan's foreign policy thinking and diplomacy were so immobilised by its alliances with the west that it did not make any significant overture to China between 1959, when the Sino-Indian border conflict had erupted into the open, and 1962. On the contrary, in April 1959 President Ayub Khan offered a joint defence arrangement to India against the common danger from the north. When Nehru turned down the proposal, President Ayub Khan tried to explain it away. But as is evident from his version in his autobiography, *Friends Not Masters*, this was an unconvincing attempt. Indeed the title itself speaks for the Pakistani elite's self-image in the fifties and the early sixties.

The Pakistani rulers were naturally pleased with the military and economic assistance they received from the United States during the Dulles era. They also found a psychological satisfaction in his statement denouncing neutrality in the cold war as immoral. His death in 1958 and the consequent change in the style of American policy towards non-aligned countries in general, and India in particular, leading to President Eisenhower's visit to this country in November 1959, therefore came as a great shock to them. They slowly began to wake up to the fact that the United States remained sensitive to India's susceptibilities and interests despite the latter's adherence to the policy of non-alignment. But it was only in 1961 that they took the first meaningful step to bring their country's foreign policy in accord with the realities of the international situation. This took the form of an agreement with the Soviet Union regarding oil exploration. So complete had been Pakistan's subordination to the United States till then that this relatively minor deal was regarded as an act of daring and Z.A. Bhutto, who signed it on Pakistan's behalf, earned a great deal of credit in his country on this account.

Kennedy's election as America's President in 1960 alarmed the Pakistani rulers in view of his observations about India before and after the election. His warm references to Nehru and his decision to extend substantial economic assistance to India caused virtual panic in Rawalpindi and sent President Ayub Khan rushing to Washington in search of an assurance that the United States was not about to abandon "its good friends for people who may not prove good friends." He returned home to claim that his visit had been a great success, but in fact he began reorienting Pakistan's foreign policy leading to the border deal with China in 1962 and better relations with the Soviet Union.

But if President Ayub Khan hoped that his deal with China and overtures to the Soviet Union would enable him to blackmail India into surrender over Kashmir, he had once again miscalculated as he had done in April 1959 when he held out the carrot of joint defence to India. After India's debacle in NEFA in November 1962, his old allies could have helped him if he was realistic. Indeed, under pressure from the United States and Britain, India agreed to make substantial territorial concessions to Pakistan over Kashmir, partly because New Delhi wanted to concentrate its attention and resources on meeting the Chinese threat, and partly because it did not wish to alienate President Kennedy and Prime Minister MacMillan, who had come to her assistance at the time of the armed conflict with China. But the Pakistani rulers asked for virtually the entire state of Jammu and Kashmir. The talks failed, and with it disappeared the last chance for Islamabad to secure a chunk of the coveted valley.

Towards the end of his life, Nehru not only released Sheikh Abdullah but also allowed him to go to Pakistan to explore the possibility of a settlement of the Kashmir issue in the wider framework of a confederation. But he could not have expected results. As an idealist he wanted to bring India and Pakistan closer together before his death, which he knew was approaching. But as a realist and a keen student of history he would have known that feuds of this nature are not easy to settle. Nehru was at once a man of peace, almost a pacifist—and a nationalist. He hated war and violence but he hated surrender on issues of principle and national interests even more. The final result of the Sheikh's visit to Pakistan could not therefore have been different if Nehru had not died in the meantime.

The Pakistani leadership had convinced itself that India would begin to disintegrate after Nehru disappeared from the scene. In 1965 it also felt that since it was on friendly terms with the United States, the Soviet Union and China—President Ayub Khan visited the three capitals in that year—it could give India a push and realise its ambitions. It also grossly underestimated Lal Bahadur Shastri, then India's Prime Minister, and India's determination to meet any challenge. It, therefore, sent over five thousand armed guerillas into Jammu and Kashmir. The attempt failed and with it began the decline of President Ayub Khan and the end of the most stable period in Pakistan's chequered history. This set in train events which culminated in the break-up of the country. Both in 1965 and 1971 the Pakistani rulers expected China to come to their rescue because they failed to understand that country's complicated approach towards India.

In a broad survey of this nature it is not possible to discuss, much less to do justice, to the disputes over evacuee property and the division of the river waters which loomed so large in the 'fifties. These have therefore been left out. But it should be noted in passing that the river waters dispute could not have been settled in 1960 under the auspices of the World Bank if India had not agreed to contribute generously to the construction of the new canal system in Pakistan. Similarly, Nehru was large-hearted in virtually giving up the Indian claim to compensation for the properties which the Hindu refugees had left in Pakistan.

Nehru adopted a balanced approach towards Pakistan fairly early and did not deviate from it throughout his long tenure of office as India's Prime Minister under pressure either from the hawkish elements at home or the Great Powers. While he was generous to a fault on financial and other issues, he did not compro-

mise on the Kashmir question because that would have weakened
the very basis of the Indian state and hurt the interests of the Muslim
minority. The same consideration led him to acquiesce in Sheikh
Abdullah's overthrow and arrest in August 1953. It is also a great
tribute to Nehru that he did not allow his difficulties with Pakistan
to dominate his thinking on larger problems of foreign policy and
to prevent him from articulating the aspiration of the newly independent countries and colonial peoples still struggling to be free.
For a whole decade he was widely regarded as the most important
spokesman of the third world. A smaller man may have either
succumbed to western pressures or leaned heavily towards the
Soviet bloc. He did neither, not even in the wake of the Chinese
attack.

Nothing would have pleased him more than to have settled the
Kashmir problem before his death. But that was not to be. Pakistan's
rulers had not given up the hope that they could clinch the issue some
day in their favour by military means.

M.S. AGWANI

India and the Arab World

ACROSS THE ARABIAN Sea from the western coast of the Indian subcontinent lies the Arabian Peninsula. The Arabian Sea washes the shores of both the landmasses. The Arabian peninsula was the original home of the Arabs, who, in the middle of the seventh century A.D., embarked on an unprecedented career of empire-building. In less than a century they established a vast empire stretching from the Indus river in the east to the Atlantic coast of North Africa and the Pyrenees mountains in south-west Europe. This empire, like the empires that preceded it, did not last very long. Nevertheless, unlike many empires of the past, it left a lasting ethno-cultural impact on a vast stretch of territory spreading from the Persian Gulf to the Atlantic shores of Morocco. Its people were arabized. In other words, they adopted the Arabic language, and the literature, folklore, mores, and customs that went with it. The Arab world was not a racial entity even though the Arab stock penetrated, in varying degrees, the distant nooks and corners of the Arab Empire. It was not a religious entity although Islam was the religion of a vast majority of its inhabitants. Nor was it a political entity, except for a relatively short period. Indeed, the one factor that has sustained the concept of the Arab world through the centuries is the element of common culture and a common way of life. The Arab world occupies some five million square miles or one-tenth of the earth's land surface and is inhabited by about a hundred million people.

II

In considering Independent India's inter-action with the Arab world it is important to underscore the distinct geo-political features of the area as well as its recent political evolution. The landmass of the eastern Arab world forms a link between the continents of Asia, Africa, and Europe. Geostrategists have described it variously as "the gateway of Asia and Africa" and the "backdoor of Europe." As such it has been a hotbed of international rivalry throughout recorded history. With the opening of the Suez Canal (1869), which established a link between the Mediterranean and the Red Sea, the Arab world became the nerve-centre of international communications, both over land and sea. Indeed, to the nineteenth-century Europeans the Arab world served as a half-way house to the East which offered vast opportunities for lucrative trade and military adventures. In both the world wars the area served as one of the principal battlefields where rival powers fought some decisive battles. During the second World War, the Allied powers used North Africa as a vital base for mounting offensives against Hitler's Europe. Moreover, in the course of the last fifty years or so the Arab world has emerged as a major producer of a much-coveted commodity, namely oil. According to current estimates, the Arab World accounts for nearly 56 per cent of the world's proven reserves of petroleum and over one-fourth of the world's total production. That the Arab world is one of the two biggest suppliers to the world oil market (the other being Venezuela), in addition to being a source of immense profit to the foreign-owned oil companies, explains why this area has been the scene of many an international friction and crisis in recent years.

The commercial and political penetration of the Arab world and India by European powers started about the same time. However, it was only after the first World War that the entire Arab world came under European domination. On the eve of the war, much of Arab Asia was actually or nominally under the Ottoman Turkish rule. This was largely a result of the British policy of preserving the Ottoman Empire with a view to preventing intrusion by rival European powers into an area which commanded the imperial communication lines to India. It was also for reasons of imperial interests that Britain seized Aden (1839) and Egypt (1882) and established a chain of protectorates in the Persian Gulf area in the course of the nineteenth century. Towards the end of the century, Britain recognized France's special position in Algeria, Morocco, and Tunisia. Italy, a late-comer in the scramble for colonies, conquered Libya in 1911. The collapse of the Ottoman Empire following the First World War enabled Britain and France to divide the Fertile Crescent comprising Palestine, the Lebanon, Syria, and Iraq between themselves under the so-called Mandates System.

The inter-war period witnessed the rise of Arab movements for national freedom resulting in sustained conflict between the nationalists on the one hand and the Britain and French authorities on the other. In Palestine, Arab nationalism came into conflict with the mandatory authority and also with the Zionist immigrants who had begun to colonize Palestine under the auspices of the British. After the Second World War, while the Zionists succeeded in establishing the State of Israel comprising more than half the Palestinian territory, the Arabs in other areas began to march steadily towards national independence. The French forces withdrew from Syria and the Lebanon in 1946. During the same year, Transjordan became a kingdom; and after the annexation of the west bank of river Jordan in 1949 the country's name was changed to Jordan. Libya became independent in 1952. Egyptian independence was consummated with the withdrawal of British forces from the Suez Canal zone under the 1954 Agreement. Morocco, Tunisia, and the Sudan achieved independence in 1956. The Iraqi revolution of July 1958 put an end to British privileges in that country. Kuwait attained freedom in 1961. Algeria fought a war of national liberation for seven years until it achieved full independence in 1962.[1]

III

The objectives of India's Arab policy during the Nehru era were defined by the country's historical background and by its political and economic needs and interests. In the early years after independence memories of the recent past largely conditioned the Indian approach to the Arab world. It was only in later years that practical considerations began to play a decisive role.

India's political, economic, and cultural contacts with the Arab world, which lies next door to it, go back to very ancient times. The intrusion of European powers into the Arab world and India during the nineteenth and twentieth centuries practically cut off these direct contacts. The nationalist resurgence in the two areas during the inter-war years, however, served to forge new bonds of fellowship. While the nationalist movement in India sympathized with the national aspirations of the Arabs the latter realized that their own emancipation was tied up with the outcome of the Indian struggle. Reminiscent of this emotional affinity is a letter written by an eminent Iraqi statesman, Kamil El-Chadirchi, to Jawaharlal Nehru in December 1938:

> Your country has been truly great from time immemorial, nature having given it inexhaustible resources. Though, from the dawn of civilization, India has not been as great as it is today when its intellectual seeds burst into bloom of such men as the country is in need of, more especially since a personality as unique as your own appeared on the horizon of the Orient, filling my imagination and that of my brethren....We wholeheartedly appreciate your struggle, and wish we had the opportunity to share in it though in a small measure, for we both are in the same boat. True endeavour in the campaign against imperialism and exploitation must not be considered in separate units, but rather that neither geographical frontiers nor political obstacles can suppress it.[2]

Independent India, therefore, felt emotionally and morally committed to the national aspirations of the Arab peoples to gain their rightful place in the comity of nations.

Underneath this emotional euphoria lay questions of India's political, economic, and, above all, security interests. And these began to shape the broad outline of India's policy towards the region.

One of the basic considerations governing India's policy towards the Arab world was the question of security. At the beginning of this century an English writer defined the "Middle East" as comprising "those regions of Asia which extend to the borders of India, and which are consequently bound up with the problems of Indian political as well as military defences."[3] Indeed, throughout the nineteenth and early twentieth centuries the Arab world had remained a bone of contention among the Great Powers desirous of securing a foothold in India. Whether it was the British anxiety over the security of the imperial communication lines, Napoleon's expedition to Egypt, Tsarist Russia's drive towards the Persian Gulf or the German *drang nach osten*, the ultimate object had invariably been India. British withdrawal from India and the emergence of independent states in the Arab world, coupled with the rise of the United States and the Soviet Union as new global Powers, no doubt changed the form, though not the substance, of international rivalries in the region. Hence history, no less than the facts of contemporary international life, served to bring into sharp focus the relevance of the Arab world to India's security problems. This point was underscored by Prime Minister Jawaharlal Nehru in a statement before the Constituent Assembly in March 1949:

> If you have to consider any question affecting the Middle East, India inevitably comes into the picture. If you have to consider any question concerning South-East Asia, you cannot do so without India. So also with the Far East. While the Middle East may not be directly connected with South-East Asia, both are connected with India.[4]

Closely connected with India's security interests was the question of the international communication lines which lie across the Arab world. In ancient and mediaeval times Indian goods were carried to Europe by sea and land routes passing through Arab territories. Unsettled political conditions in the area during the fifteenth century A.D. induced the Portuguese explorer, Vasco da Gama, to discover the Cape of Good Hope route to India. In 1869, when the Suez Canal was completed and opened to international traffic, the West Asian route was resumed. The Suez Canal indeed cut down the maritime distance between Bombay and London by 4,500 miles and in course of time became the veritable life-line of world trade. About three-fourths of India's import and export trade passed through the Suez Canal. The importance of this waterway for India's foreign trade was pointedly driven home in the fall of 1956 when the Anglo-French-Israeli attack on Egypt resulted in the temporary closure of the Suez Canal. It again became clear after the Arab-Israeli war of 1967. Besides, while the Suez Canal offers the shortest sea-route to Europe, Cairo and Beirut are important halting stations for India's west-bound air services.

The third important reason for India's interest in the Arab world was the steadily growing trade between the two areas. In ancient times Indian textiles and spices found a flourishing market in the Arab world. To these were added tea and jute manufactures in modern times. With the expansion of Indian industry after Independence, India also started exporting some non-conventional items to the Arab countries. These included electrical gadgets, machine tools, diesel engines, chemicals, iron and steel products, and sugar and textile mill machinery. The expansion of Indo-Arab trade was, of course, a two-way affair and was immensely beneficial to the developing economies on both sides. Indian imports largely consisted of raw materials such as the long-staple cotton from Egypt and Sudan and crude oil from the Gulf. Towards the end of the period under review the two-way trade between India and the Arab world exceeded 1,000 million rupees per annum and held out prospects of further expansion.[5] Trade also paved the way for wider economic and technical cooperation between India and the Arab world in later years.

Finally, India was naturally interested in promoting the welfare of the sizeable Indian community of traders settled in the Arab world. For centuries Indian trading communities have flourished in this region, particularly in the Persian Gulf and Aden. Ibn Batuta, a fourteenth century Arab traveller, indeed refers to Aden as "the port of Merchants of India" to which came "great vessels" from Cambay, Quilon, Mangalore, and Goa.[6] In recent years, this trading community in the Gulf region has been reinforced by Indian technicians and workers mostly employed in the oil industry.

IV

The choice of instruments for the conduct of foreign policy is determined as much by the objectives that a country seeks to achieve as by the resources it can afford to allocate for the pursuit of these objectives. At the dawn of freedom India was faced with vast problems of economic development and nation-building which called for a sustained mobilization of its resources on a long-term basis. This inevitably circumscribed India's capacity to project itself in world affairs. But this deficiency was not peculiar to India and was indeed common to most of the newly independent countries of Asia and Africa. It was, however, in part compensated by the moral stature which India's protracted struggle for freedom and active cooperation with similar movements in the Arab world had imparted to it. This gave Indian diplomacy a measure of influence which cannot be explained in terms of India's actual power and resources.

Hence, in the early years of independence, India could not but rely mainly on political and diplomatic means for the pursuit of its broad objectives. At a later stage these were reinforced by selected measures in other fields such as joint industrial enterprises, commercial credits, and technical assistance. All these served to generate a climate of goodwill, understanding, and cooperation between India and the various Arab countries.

In the early phase of its relations with the region India encountered a two-fold challenge to its interests in the region: the British drive to bring about a military grouping of the West Asian countries which would safeguard its oil and imperial interests in the region; and Pakistan's design to forge a Pan-Islamic alliance of Arab and other West Asian states. While the former threatened to bring the cold war between the East and the West to India's doorstep, the latter sought to isolate India from a region so vital to its security and economic well-being. By 1955 the two forces converged, and the Baghdad Pact was born.

India endeavoured to counteract this ominous development by projecting the concept of non-alignment into the region. Non-alignment as conceived by Nehru was rooted in the commonsense assumption that national independence cannot be sustained without independence in foreign affairs. It must, however, be added that in the early years India's preference for non-involvement in the power blocs did not make much of an impact on the Arab states. Even so, Nehru clearly saw the relevance of non-alignment not only for India but for other newly independent states as well. Speaking before the Constituent Assembly in December 1947 he observed:

> I have no doubt that fairly soon, in the course of two or three years, the world will find this attitude justified and that India will not only be respected by the major protagonists in the struggle for power, but a large number of the smaller nations which today are rather helpless will probably look to India more than to other countries for a lead in such matters.[7]

In the course of the next decade the principle of non-alignment made considerable headway in the Arab world even though it was not universally endorsed. Resurgent Arab nationalism strongly resisted the western overtures for the creation of a Middle East Defence Organization which, it believed, was intended to perpetuate western supremacy in the region. An early indication of the alternative course open to the Arabs was made in an official Egyptian announcement soon after Nehru's visit to Cairo in 1953. It said:

> We must remember that there is in the world today a great force which aims at goodness and which will not permit itself to be an instrument of evil....This great force, representing one-third to the world, which has been used in the past was as an instrument of death in the hands of the imperialist powers, will no longer allow itself to be used as cannon fodder in the service of imperialism in any future war.[8]

After the conclusion of the Baghdad Pact, which deeply embittered Arab nationalist opinion, the concept of non-alignment found vigorous and widespread support in the Arab world. It also helped to create conditions for active cooperation between India and the Arab states in political, economic, and commercial spheres.

On a wider plane India also strove to promote cooperation and understanding with the Arab states through treaties of friendship as well as trade and cultural agreements. These were reinforced by frequent consultations on issues of common interest in the United Nations and at formal gatherings of like-minded nations such as the two non-aligned summit conferences.

With the gradual abatement of the cold war in the last years of the Nehru era, the West Asian military pacts tended to lose their original meaning and significance. While affinity of outlook on world affairs continued to bind India closely to the non-aligned Arab states, there was a marked shift of emphasis from political to economic issues in India's approach to this region. This new initiative prepared the ground for the launching of several joint ventures, including shipping and industrial undertakings, in later years.

V

At this point, a word about the principal actors and influences that shaped India's approach to the Arab world would be relevant. The political ethos generated by India's freedom struggle, particularly after the early twenties, exercised marked influence on free India's official policies and popular attitudes towards the Arab problems. As Mahatma Gandhi transformed the Indian National Congress from an elite debating society into a mass organization dedicated to political emancipation and social regeneration, it began to take increasing note of nationalist movements in the neighbouring regions and to relate them to India's own struggle. An awakened India naturally regarded the Mandates System as imperialism in disguise and evinced deep solicitude for Sa'ad Zaghlul's struggle in Egypt and Abd al-Karim's revolt in Morocco. At the Congress of Oppressed Nationalities in Brussels (February 1927) Nehru made personal contacts with some of the national leaders of Syria, Palestine and Egypt. In 1928 letters were sent to the nationalist organizations of Tunisia, Egypt and Palestine inviting fraternal delegates to the annual Congress Session. These contacts were considerably strengthened in the following decades.

On a personal plane, Gandhi, Nehru and Azad played a significant role in shaping the Indian approach to the Arab world both before and after Independence. Mahatma Gandhi established personal contact with leaders of the Egyptian *Wafd* Party and showed keen interest in the struggle of the Palestinian Arabs. He frankly disapproved of the Jews' dependence "on American money or British arms for forcing themselves on an unwelcome land," and pleaded that "Palestine belongs to the Arabs in the same sense that England belongs to the English, or France to the French."[9]

Jawaharlal Nehru's abiding interest in Asian resurgence and world affairs led to his close association with the national leaders of Asia and Africa. Among them were Egypt's Mustafa Nahas, Syria's Faris al-Khuri and Iraq's Kamil al-Chadirchi. After Independence he established close rapport with Gamal Abd-al-Nasser, which sometimes invited the undeserved criticism that his Arab policy placed excessive reliance upon Egypt. In fact, Nasser's thinking on foreign policy and economic planning were admittecly influenced by Nehru.[10] Finally, Abul Kalam Azad, an eminent Congress leader and a distinguished scholar of Islam, acted as Nehru's principal adviser on Arab affairs: in the pre-Independence period he favoured close cooperation with Arab nationalist movements; after Independence he played a conspicuous part in moulding India's

Arab policy.

Alongside these major influences, which largely fashioned India's policy, some opposition parties and interested groups evinced active interest in developments in the Arab world and in India's official response to them. A major issue which attracted criticism of several opposition parties was the Arab-Zionist dispute over Palestine. The Socialist Party of India and its offshoots, the Praja Socialist Party (PSP) and the Samyukta Socialist Party (SSP) established fraternal ties with the Israeli labour movement and tended to look upon the Jewish state as a beacon of democratic socialism in West Asia. The Jana Sangh, ever suspicious of the Muslim Arab states, saw in their adversary, Israel, a potential ally of India. The Rightist Swatantra Party, too, was persistently critical of India's policy of not giving enough weight to the claims of the pro-western Israel against the Left-leaning Arab nationalism. All these opposition parties ceaselessly stressed the need for cultivating close political and economic ties with Israel. It must, however, be added that the Indian Socialists at first opposed the partition of Palestine; and after partition the SSP consistently advocated an Arab-Israeli federation. The Jana Sangh joined them in strongly condemning the Israeli attack on Egypt in the fall of 1956.

The Indian communists originally favoured the creation of Israel; but their larger interest in the Arab liberation struggle as also the radical orientation of some Arab countries induced them to support the Arab national causes. They fervently endorsed Nehru's opposition to the Baghdad Pact, but complained that India's support for Arab National liberation—whether in Algeria or in Palestine—was inadequate and half-hearted.

Industrialists and business houses having economic and commercial interests in the Arab world were naturally sensitive to developments in the region. But the national Press—of which a sizeable part is owned or controlled by some leading industrialists and businessmen—not infrequently offered trenchant criticism of India's Arab policy even though this indictment could scarcely be justified on grounds of national self-interest.

VI

The formulation and working of India's Arab policy must be

seen in the context of major problems of the region, namely, the colonial question, the Baghdad Pact, the Suez crisis, the Arab-Israeli conflict, and the Pan-Islamic issue.

The Colonial Question. "We in Asia," said Jawaharlal Nehru in a speech before the United Nations General Assembly in November 1948, "who have ourselves suffered all these evils of colonialism and imperial domination, have committed ourselves inevitably to the freedom of every other colonial country . . . . Countries like India who have passed out of that colonial stage do not conceive it possible that other countries should remain under the yoke of colonial rule."[11] Thirteen years later Nehru told the leaders of the non-aligned nations—most of them ex-colonial countries—meeting in Belgrade that the era of classical colonialism was dead and gone, and stressed the primacy of peace in a world menaced by grave dangers of nuclear conflagration.[12] This was no *volte-face*. The shift in India's attitude *vis-a-vis* the colonial question indeed reflected the great transformation in Asia and Africa from colonial rule to freedom in the intervening period.

In the case of the Arab countries India favoured elimination of all vestiges of direct or indirect rule by foreign powers. On the eve of Independence, India gave firm support to Syria and the Lebanon on the question of French withdrawal from those countries. India, however, viewed the Anglo-Egyptian dispute over the future of the 1936 Treaty on a different plane. While opposing foreign interference with Egypt's sovereignty and independence, India recognized the fact that Egypt was in treaty relations with Britain and that the differences over British presence in the Suez Canal zone should be settled by the two countries in "a friendly way and on a firm and workable basis."[13] Moreover, India offered its good offices to help settle the Anglo-Egyptian dispute. As regards the problem of Sudan, India gave moderate support to Egyptian interests in the unity of the Nile Valley, but clearly recognized the Sudanese people's right to self-determination. Following the Anglo-Egyptian accord on Sudan in February 1953, the Government of Sudan invited an Indian to head the Sudan Electoral Commission; both the Sudanese government and people widely acclaimed the services he rendered them.

The colonial problem in North Africa, however, proved to be rather intractable partly because of the presence of sizeable numbers of French settlers in Algeria, Morocco, and Tunisia, but mostly because of lack of political realism on the part of successive French Governments. Besides, India herself was engaged in delicate negotiations with Paris over Pondicherry. India, nevertheless, recognized the right of the North African peoples to freedom and joined the Asian-African States in the United Nations in the quest for a negotiated settlement of that intricate problem.

The colonial issue in the Persian Gulf did not come to the fore until the 'fifties. Here, too, India favoured the need for decolonization. When the question of Aden came to a head in the early 'sixties, India backed Aden's demand for national self-determination.

In sum, Nehru's approach to the colonial question in the Arab world was based on two principles: support for freedom movements; and adherence to a peaceful approach. India sought to advance the cause of freedom in the region but without impairing political stability or aggravating international tensions.

The Baghdad Pact: In October 1951, the British, French, Turkish, and the United States governments jointly presented a proposal to the Egyptian government for a Middle East Defence Organisation. An accompanying note from the Government of Great Britain made the British evacuation of the Canal zone conditional on Egypt's acceptance of the proposal. The Egyptian government, which had only recently revoked the Anglo-Egyptian treaty of 1936, flatly rejected the proposal. With that the prospects of a western-sponsored military pact for the region were shattered for the time being.

About this time Pakistan realized that a pan-Islamic alliance with the West Asian nations was not feasible, and began to look farther west for friends and allies. Early in 1954 Pakistan signed a pact with Turkey, a member of the North Atlantic alliance. This paved the way for the conclusion of the Baghdad Pact between Turkey, Iraq, Iran, Pakistan, and Britain in 1953. The United States joined the Economic and Counter-Subversive committees of the Pact in 1956.

India strongly opposed the creation of this military alliance on several grounds. First, it aggravated political tensions in the Arab world. Secondly, it unwittingly encouraged and helped the very forces that it intended to restrain or suppress. In other words, it provoked the Soviet Union to enter the region in a big way with offers of massive arms and economic aid to the Arab states which were opposed to the pact. But most important of all, Pakistan's membership of the pact posed a serious threat to India's security. Nehru declared that the Baghdad Pact tended to "encircle" India. and added:

> Surely, nobody here imagines that the Pakistan Government entered into this Pact because it expected some imminent or distant invasion or aggression from the Sovet Union. The Pakistan newspapers and the statements of responsible people in Pakistan make it perfectly clear that they have joined this Pact because of India. Either they are apprehensive of India, or they want to develop strength and, as the phrase now goes, speak from strength. Whatever it is, they have joined the Baghdad Pact and SEATO essentially because of their hostility to India.[13]

New Delhi was aware that other members of the pact bore no hostility towards India. But, as Nehru put it, when countries "get inter-locked with one another, each pulls in a different direction and in a crisis they are pulled away in a direction they never thought of going."[14] Hence India's instinctive reaction was to draw closer to the non-aligned pan-Arabist forces, particularly Egypt. India may not have shared Saudi Arabia's contention that the pact was "a stab in the heart of Arab and Muslim states," or Nasser's belief that it was "a conspiracy against Arab nationalism," but it did believe that Arab nationalism possessed the means as well as the urge to resist big power pressures in the area which prejudiced India's security.

It must also be noted that India's full-throated support for Arab nationalism produced some unavoidable complications; for to support pan-Arabism was after all tantamount to supporting Nasser, whom Nehru once described as "the most prominent symbol of Arab nationalism."[15]   And this was taken amiss by many an Arab state which otherwise swore by Arab unity and neutralism. The irritants thus caused were partly mollified by India's conscious effort to eschew involvement in intra-Arab disputes. This was significantly borne out by India's recognition of the secessionist Syrian regime (1961) and its non-partisan stance in Saudi-Egyptian conflict over the Yemen.

Suez Crisis: That Egypt's decision to nationalize the Suez Canal Company came closely in the wake of Nehru's meetings with Nasser at Brioni and Cairo caused visible embarrassment to India. Nehru took the earliest opportunity to inform the Indian parliament that his discussions with the Egyptian leader "did not relate to the Suez Canal or any aspect of Anglo-Egyptian relations."[16] But immediately after the Egyptian announcement New Delhi got in close touch with Cairo and London to counsel moderation on both sides and to help resolve the dispute in a manner satisfactory to Egypt as well as the users of the Canal.

India's deep concern about the Suez dispute was the result of practical considerations no less than its anxiety to promote stability and peace in the area. As Nehru put it, in the course of his first detailed policy statement on the Suez issue, India "is not a disinterested party. She is a principal user of this waterway, and her economic life and development is not unaffected by the dispute, not to speak of worse developments, in regard to it."[17] At the same time it could scarcely ignore the wider aspects of the dispute. For one thing, Egypt's impulsive resolve to take over the administration of the Suez Canal was precipitated by a series of moves initiated by Washington and London to deflect Egypt from its declared preference for non-alignment. The last of these moves was the Anglo-American decision to withdraw the promised financial support for building the Aswan High Dam. Besides, India believed that the blatant British and French threats to use force against Egypt gravely prejudiced the prospects of a negotiated settlement. Finally, the Indian approach took full account of the fact that under the Constantinople Convention (1888) the Suez Canal formed an integral part of Egypt and that a settlement of the Suez dispute must be sought within the framework of this acknowledged principle.

In short, India's policy was to seek a peaceful solution which would safeguard the legitimate interests of the users of the Canal without detracting from the sovereign rights of Egypt. Accordingly, the Indian delegate to the London Conference (August 1956) proposed the creation of a "consultative body" of Canal users "on the basis of geographical representation and interests" and charged with "advisory, consultative and liaison functions." Other important ingredients of what was termed "the Indian plan" were: recognition of the Suez Canal as an integral part of Egypt; freedom of navigation in accordance with the Constantinople Convention; the tolls and charges to be just and equitable and the Canal facilities to be accorded to all nations without discrimination; and maintenance of the Canal in accordance with latest technical requirements relating to navigation.[18]

The Indian plan, endorsed by nations as diverse as Ceylon, Indonesia and the Soviet Union and hailed by Cairo as a practical basis for negotiations,[19] was, however, rejected by the western powers in favour of the American plan envisaging an "international Suez Canal Board" which would wield effective sanctions. India, in turn, took strong exception to the British Prime Minister's suggestion (12 September 1956) to set up a Suez Canal Users' Association in order to "assert" the users' rights unilaterally. Simultaneously, Indian diplomacy got actively engaged in dissuading London and Washington from any precipitate action; and Krishna Menon, the chief Indian spokesman at the Suez talks, evolved fresh proposals similar to those subsequently endorsed by the Security Council.

India's further efforts for the peaceful settlement of the Suez problem were cut short by the Israeli invasion of Egypt and the landing of British and French troops in the Canal Zone. This evoked a sharp reaction in New Delhi. Nehru bluntly described it as "a naked aggression", and a "reversion to the past colonial methods" and pleaded for speedy action by the United Nations to halt it.[20] Subsequently, India played an active role in the United Nations in securing the withdrawal of foreign forces from Egyptian soil and in vindicating Egypt's sovereign rights.

Arab-Israeli Conflict: India's approach to the Arab-Zionist conflict over Palestine was influenced by a mixture of moral and practical considerations. In the pre-Independence period, as we have already noted, Gandhi, Nehru, and the Indian National Congress had opposed the imposition of a "Jewish National Home" on the reluctant Palestinian Arabs. While Gandhi strongly condemned the inhuman treatment meted out to the Jews in Hitler's Germany, the Zionist plan to penalize the Arabs for the wrongs done by the Nazis was revolting to his conception of justice and fair-play. Nehru, on the other hand, saw in the Palestine problem a manifestation of the wider problem of colonialism: the British trying to put up Jewish religious nationalism against Arab nationalism in order to protect their own imperial interests. These factors broadly defined India's approach during 1947-48, when the Palestine question was being actively considered by the United Nations.

As a member of United Nations Special Committee on Palestine

(UNSCOP) India did not subscribe to the majority plan recommending partition of Palestine. Instead, it put forward, along with Iran and Yugoslavia, the proposal to create an independent federal State of Palestine comprising autonomous Arab and Jewish units. In a separate note, Sir Abdul Rahman, the Indian member of the Committee, pleaded that partition would not lead to a lasting solution and argued that the two states sought to be created would not be politically viable.[21] As it happened, the General Assembly endorsed the majority plan, and Palestine was partitioned.

The State of Israel was created on May 14, 1948. This event was attended by the outbreak of Arab-Israeli hostilities in the course of which the Israelis seized 77 per cent of the Palestinian territory (as against 55 per cent allocated by the UN resolution) and expelled about 800,000 Palestinians from their ancestral homes. These developments added new difficulties to an already complex situation. The armistice agreements concluded by the belligerent states in 1949 offered little more than a precarious armed truce.

India was one of the seven non-Arab countries which voted against the partition plan. But its attitude towards Israel was in the main determined by the complexities that arose from the 1948 war. When the issue of Israel's admission to the United Nations was raised in May 1949, India voted against its admission. M.C. Setalvad, India's chief delegate, pleaded that his government "could not recognize an Israel which had been achieved through the use of force and not through negotiations."[22] Another factor which entered Indian calculations at this stage was the desire not to ruffle Arab susceptibilities at a time when Pakistan was fervently canvassing for an anti-Indian pan-Islamic alliance with the West Asian countries.

After much hesitation New Delhi eventually recognized Israel on September 17, 1950. An official statement, however, hastened to add that India's recognition of Israel did not mean that it endorsed the Israeli position regarding its boundaries.[23] In the meantime, India continued to support legitimate Arab demands concerning the rights of the Arab refugees. At Bandung, Nehru urged the Arabs not to rule out negotiations as a means of settling the Palestine issue and joined other Asian-African states in calling for implementation of the United Nations resolutions on Palestine. In later years, India also backed the Arab case for an equitable distribution of the Jordan river waters. These measures, combined with New Delhi's reluctance to establish diplomatic relations with Israel, indicated India's

solicitude for the Arabs.   On balance, however, India supported
only the legitimate demands of the Arabs and at no time did it
subscribe to the wider claims advanced by some Arab circles.

Pan-Islamism: Finally, the issue of pan-Islamism. The strains of
Indo-Pakistani relations, together with Pakistan's sustained efforts
since 1947 to arouse the sentiment of Islamic solidarity in its inter-
actions with the Arab world, alerted New Delhi to the possible
consequences of pan-Islamism.

Curiously, there was a tendency both in Pakistan and in India
to rate the political efficacy of pan-Islamism higher than was
warranted by empirical realities. In the nineteenth century Pan-
Islamism had signified the response of the Muslim peoples to the
colonial thrust of Europe in Asia and Africa. Jamal-ad-Din Afghani,
its chief exponent, had many supporters in Egypt and other Arab
countries; but his efforts fell far short of the challenge posed by
European imperialism. After Afghani's death the pan-Islamic
sentiment progressively yielded to Islamic reform, nationalism, and
political modernization, but was not altogether extinguished. In
the meantime, rivalries between European Powers for political
influence and economic privileges in the Muslim world gave a new
twist to pan-Islamism.

At the beginning of the present century Germany began to make
studied appeals to the pan-Islamic sentiment in an attempt to outwit
its European rivals. After the Second World War, the British too
seemed inclined to take refuge in pan-Islamism in a desperate
effort to stem the tide of Arab nationalism. The British proposals
for a regional military alliance of West Asian nations were accordingly prefaced with appeals to Islamic solidarity. And when the
British debacle at Suez prompted the United States to take an
active hand in Arab politics pan-Islamism was once again trotted
out as a political gimmick.

Thus, over a period of time, pan-Islamism lost its anti-colonial
charge and became a handy expedient of foreign powers anxious
to acquire a foothold in the Arab world. Internally, it became a
battle-cry of conservative elements anxious to neutralize pressures
for social and political change. All in all, the politics of pan-Islamism
barely masked the interplay of factors wholly unrelated to Islam.
Similarly, the so-called Islamic conferences degenerated into a game
which every participant played with an eye on the political advantages to be gained for his own nation.[24]

In this connection Prime Minister Nehru's directive of 1955 outlining New Delhi's approach to various Muslim conferences of pan-Islamic character may be mentioned. Nehru stressed the need to oppose any Islamic grouping, but added that non-official delegations might participate in Islamic conferences. Dilution of the latter part of the directive in the post-Nehru era resulted in official delegations being sponsored for the various Islamic conferences. That this was both unnecessary and unwise was subsequently revealed by the distasteful Rabat episode.

In conclusion it might be said that India's policy towards the Arab world passed through distinct stages of evolution. In the early period the hangover of the colonial past evoked an emotional interest in the developments of the region. Opposition to colonial rule and support for political and economic rights of the Arab nations characterized the Indian approach during this period. By the mid-fifties, awareness of India's security requirements and of the need for political support in a world sharply divided between two power blocs gave a practical orientation to India's policy. This shift in emphasis yielded tangible results. The Arab world survived the formidable pressures exerted by the rival power blocs. Also, Arab nationalism became sufficiently strong to withstand the pan-Islamic campaign. Besides, India considerably strengthened its economic, commercial and cultural relations with the Arab countries. An appreciable lessening of Cold War tensions in the early sixties marked the beginning of a new phase in which greater attention could be given to questions of trade and economic co-operation.

Above all, India's Arab policy bore the imprint of the personality of Jawaharlal Nehru. His unflagging commitment to enlargement of freedom, to de-colonization, and to ever-increasing cooperation among nations influenced the entire spectrum of Independent India's relations with the Arab world. It also earned for India a measure of respect which outweighed transitory disagreements.

D. R. SARDESAI

India and Southeast Asia

THE MAGNITUDE OF the subject compels a selective treatment
inhibiting both a discussion of India's bilateral relationship with
each country of Southeast Asia and a comprehensive review of all
aspects—economic, political and cultural.[1] What will be attempted
here is an analysis of Indian attitudes to two issues which were
closest to the statesman in whose memory this series of lectures
has been instituted: the questions of freedom and peace. Preoccupation with world events, particularly affecting these two factors had
always been a matter of passion for Jawaharlal Nehru. Events in
Southeast Asia obviously claimed considerable attention from him
not only because of the fight for freedom which is still continuing
but also because this region has developed, in the last two decades,
into one of the two most explosive areas of the world threatening
global peace. While it would be true to say that India's bilateral
relations with the countries of the region did not consequently get
proportionate attention, the concern with larger issues was not
entirely a matter of Nehru's personal fancy, as is proved by the fact
that statesmen and intellectuals all over the world have seen their
efforts frustrated in solving the problems of Southeast Asia over
the last decade. In that sense, a survey of India's relations with
Southeast Asia during the Nehru era has an abiding relevance to
the present times.

On the eve of India's independence in August 1947, Indian
contacts and knowledge about Southeast Asia were vague, illusory

and uncertain. Except for a handful of area specialists and those closely related to the Indian immigrants in the area, very few Indians knew as much about their neighbours in Southeast Asia as they knew of Europe or America. A proud memory of Hindu colonies established in some dim historical past, a vague impression of Indian immigrants' trading activities, and a recent reminder of a region in which Subhas Chandra Bose had organized a movement and an army for India's liberation—these summed up an average educated Indian's awareness of this region. The colonial interlude referred to by Sardar K.M. Panikkar, as the Vasco-da-Gama epoch in Asian history,[2] had effectively separated India from a region long styled "Greater India." The divergent political, and economic ambitions of the colonial powers, with attendant tariff and travel barriers and varying administrative and educational patterns, made the colonial peoples more closely oriented towards their respective metropolitan powers than towards one another. Indo-China, Indonesia and the Philippines were even less in touch with India than were the British-ruled Burma and Malaya. If the historical ties with the region were to be restored in the new era of emergent nationalism and decolonization, imaginative bridges of vital common interests in various fields would be necessary.

Even so, the Indian interest in the neighbouring countries of Southeast Asia has not been very intense. Thus, during the Nehru era, Southeast Asia figured relatively prominently in the Indian thinking on international affairs for only three brief periods: 1947-49, 1954-55 and 1959-61. Of these, only the first shows a direct regional interest as such, while on the other hand latter two were dominated by Indian concern with crises in Southeast Asia in so far as they affected the global issues like communism and anti-communism, co-existence and confrontation, peace and war.

II

In the post-World War II period, the binding force between India and other Asian countries was nationalism. Indian nationalists welcomed the establishment of republics by their Vietnamese and Indonesian counterparts, who had taken advantage of the time-gap between Japanese surrender and arrival of western troops to proclaim their freedom. Therefore, the news of the use of Indian troops

by Mountbatten's South-East Asia Command (charged under the
Potsdam Agreement with the task of disarming the Japanese) to
suppress Vietnamese and Indonesian nationalists angered the
Indian National Congress.[3] Nehru, wanting to go to Indonesia
in response to Sukarno's appeal and denied travel facilities by the
British Government, voiced indignant India's reactions:

> We have watched British intervention there with growing anger,
> shame and helplessness that Indian troops should thus be used
> for doing Britain's dirty work against our friends who are fighting
> the same fight as we [are] . . . .[4]

That was on the last day of 1945. Events moved rapidly thereafter
in India leading to the establishment of an Interim Government
on September 2, 1946, headed by Nehru himself. The responsibilities
of high office introduced in him a certain amount of restraint in
foreign policy pronouncements and execution. This was best reflected
in the Indian government's differing attitudes towards the movements in Indo-China and Indonesia.

In the beginning of 1947, soon after the Franco-Vietnamese
hostilities broke out, Ho Chi Minh's unofficial representative in
India, Mai The Chau, appealed to the Indian government and
people for help in his countrymen's "fight to death."[5] He approached
Sarat Chandra Bose, a member of Nehru's Cabinet, who had, on
his own already succeeded in recruiting a volunteer force drawn
from India and neighbouring countries.[6] Bose wrote to Nehru and
his Cabinet colleagues requesting transport and passport facilities
for the journey to Indo-China and back for his volunteer force.
Nehru refused the requisite travel facilities, stressing the legal
aspects of intervention in Indo-China, pointing out that "so long as
the Government of India is not at war with another country it
cannot take action against it."[7]

The Vietnamese issue figured prominently at the Asian Relations
Conference in the following month, from March 23 to April 12, in
New Delhi. Indo-China was represented by two delegations, representing Ho Chi Minh's DRV (Democratic Republic of Vietnam)
and the French-backed regimes of Cambodia, Laos and Cochin-
China. The DRV delegation wanted the Indian government to help
the Indo-Chinese movement in at least three positive ways: by
recognizing the government of the DRV, using influence at the

United Nations to take up the Indo-China issue, and taking practical steps to stop French reinforcements.[8]

Neither Bose's nor the DRV's appeals would convince Nehru of the propriety of intervention in Indo-China by outside countries, even on grounds of a common struggle against colonialism and for Asian freedom. Nehru said he did not see how the Indian government, or for that matter, other Asian countries, could be expected to declare war on France. His government had already taken steps to limit the number of French aircraft which might fly across India.[9] He promised, however, to bring sufficient pressure to bear on France, which could not "obviously be done by governments in public meetings."[10]

Nehru's attitude towards the Indonesian nationalist movement was markedly different from that towards Indo-China. Thus, a few months later, when the Dutch attacked the Indonesian Republic on July 20, 1947, Nehru warned: "No European country, whatever it may be, has any right to set its army in Asia against the people of Asia. The spirit of new Asia will not tolerate such things."[11] He tried to get the British government to mediate with the Dutch government. Failing in his efforts, he persuaded Australia to join India in sponsoring a cease-fire resolution in the Security Council, which offered its good offices for settlement of the dispute by arbitration and peaceful means.[12] When the Dutch renewed their attacks in December 1948, an enraged Nehru, in a spectacular move, called a Conference on Indonesia to meet in New Delhi in the following month. India denied facilities to all Dutch aircraft and shipping and successfully persuaded Pakistan, Ceylon, Burma, Saudi Arabia and Iraq to apply similar sanctions. She sent a Red Cross medical unit to Indonesia and granted asylum to Sjahir.[13] The Indian Government extended *de facto* recognition to the Indonesian Republic, which enabled her to characterize the Dutch action as an act of war against the Indonesian Republic. The Conference on Indonesia, attended by eighteen countries from Asia and Africa heard Nehru launch a bitter and outspoken attack against Western colonialism:

We meet today because the freedom of a sister country of ours has been imperilled and dying colonialism of the past has raised its head again and challenged all the forces that are struggling to build up a new structure of the world. That challenge has a deeper significance than might appear on the surface, for it is a challenge to a newly awakened Asia which has so long suffered under various forms of colonialism.[14]

Two weeks earlier, he had promulgated the Asian Monroe Doctrine as he addressed the Jaipur session of the Indian National Congress.

Our foreign policy is that no foreign power should rule over any Asiatic country. The reaction of the Dutch action will be heard soon over all the Asiatic countries and we will have to consider what we will have to do under the circumstances.[15]

Nehru sent the Conference speeches, resolutions and recommendations to the United Nations where the Security Council adopted a resolution five days later urging cease-fire, release of political prisoners and re-establishment of the Republican government in Jogjakarta.[16] These recommendations were substantially identical with the demands made by the Delhi Conference.[17] The negotiations that followed between the Netherlands government and Indonesian leaders led to the ultimate transfer of sovereignty to Indonesian hands on December 27, 1949. Not for the last time could India take legitimate pride in helping the birth of a nation.

India did not take any comparable measures in regard to Indo-Chinese movement before or after 1949. Among the reasons that restrained Nehru's enthusiasm were the character of the nationalist leadership in Vietnam and the coincidence of continued French hold over five small possessions in India itself. After 1949, a more decisive factor was the emergence of a communist regime in China with a common border with a communist-led movement in Vietnam. The resulting attitude was less one of indifference or neglect than of calculated circumspection.

The communist leadership of the Vietnamese nationalist movement must have made for some difference in the Indian attitude at that time. Yet, the Indian antipathy to communism did not conform to the western dichotomy between the "free" and communist worlds. As Nehru himself was to say later to the Institute of Pacific Relations in Lucknow in October 1950:

No argument in any country of Asia is going to have weight if it goes counter to the nationalist support of the country, communism or no communism. That has to be understood.[18]

The natural preference in India was indeed in favour of the establishment of democratic institutions in the newly emerging states as in India itself. If a nationalist movement were dominated by communism and if the only choice lay between perpetuation of colonial rule and the rise of national communism, India deemed it a duty to support the latter, although in practice her enthusiasm under such circumstances would be quite restrained.

III

Nehru's attitude towards communist nationalism and nationalism impeded by communist elements deserves analysis. He resented communist hampering of nationalist efforts in Indonesia, Malaya and Burma almost as much as within India itself. India did not object to the Indonesian Republican government arresting communist leaders like Mohammed Jusuf in February 1946 or Tan Malaka the following March, or fighting communist rebellion led by Musso, Suripno and Sjarifuddin in 1948. In Burma, within three months of independence, communists attempted to overthrow the government through armed rebellion. The Indian government supplied the U Nu government with arms, ammunition and monetary assistance.[19] And later, in March 1950, India's mediation resulted in the decision of five Commonwealth countries to lend Burma six million pounds as assistance to meet the communist threat to that country. India contributed one-sixth of the sum.[20] The Indian Government openly condemned the communist rebellion in Malaya. On his return from a Southeast Asian tour, B.V. Keskar, Deputy Minister of External Affairs, said that the Malayan movement could not be described as a nationalist struggle, and that the insurgents there were nothing but bandits who did not care what or whom they opposed.[21] In 1948, the Home ministry of the Indian government found conclusive evidence that the communist rebellions that took place in that year in Malaya, Burma, Indonesia and Telangana had been hatched at the apparently innocent Calcutta Conference of the Southeast Asian Youth in February 1948.[22] The communist uprising in Telangana was effectively crushed and communists were arrested and detained on a large scale in India. Nehru openly denounced Indian communists in February 1949, for their programme of "murders, arson, and looting, as well as acts of sabotage." and for their determination to "create a chaotic state in the country."[23] The Communist Party itself was banned in a number of states like West Bengal, Mysore, Madras, Hyderabad and Travancore-Cochin.[24] The Indian leadership demonstrated its strong resolve not to permit the hard-won fruits of Indian nationalism to be destroyed by violent communism.

While Nehru directly or indirectly helped in the suppression of communists in Burma, Malaya, Indonesia and India, he recognized that the situation in Vietnam was different. The communists in Vietnam were genuine nationalists and there was no other compara-ble nationalist rival rallying point for people's aspirations in that country. Even if Nehru did not like the communist leadership of that movement, he could not bring himself to condemn it as long as it was anti-colonial.

Franco-Indian relations were an important factor in determining Indian attitudes towards the French Indo-China question. India experienced unexpected inflexibility on the French part concerning the granting of independence to the five small pockets of French territory on Indian soil. In August 1947, when India became inde-pendent, the French government had agreed to study in common with the Indian government "ways and means of friendly regulation of the problem," taking into consideration "the interests and aspira-tions of the population of these territories, . . .the historical and cul-tural links of these people with France and. . .the evolution of India."[25] However, it was not until October 21, 1954, seven years later and three months after the Indo-China settlement had been reached, that the French government signed an agreement to transfer *de facto* sovereignty over the territories to the Indian Republic.[26] The interregnum was covered by deliberate delays in negotiations and recriminations on either side.[27] To the French, their Indian possessions were important for strategic and military considerations. They provided refuelling and other facilities for the pursuit of the Indo-China war. If it was politic for France to adopt dilatory tactics on the issue of transfer of their Indian territories, it was equally politic for India in the national interest to adopt a restrained and less belligerent attitude on the Indo-China question.

India's attitude toward the Ho Chi Minh-led movement became even more circumspect after the establishment of the People's Republic of China in October 1949. Geographically, culturally as well as ideologically, the Chinese were closer than India to the

Vietnamese, who now openly disclosed a strong communist affiliation. In November 1949, some of the Vietnamese communists attended the famous Peking meeting of the World Federation of Trade Unions of Asia and Australia, at which Liu Shao-chi exhorted the colonial countries to adopt the Chinese path in their struggle for national independence and people's democracy.[28]

The proximity of the communist-led movement of Vietnam to Communist China held possibilities for extension of the communist movement southward. The geopolitics did not fail to impress Nehru, who always emphasized the geographical factor in Indian foreign policy formulation.[29] He was aware of Chinese expansionist tendencies through history,[30] dramatically confirmed by the forcible occupation of Tibet in 1950. Besides, the leaders of new China expressed themselves clearly concerning their intentions to help communist movements in South and Southeast Asia. Liu Shao-chi described countries like India, Burma, the Philippines and Indonesia as "semi-colonies", which must be freed from the stranglehold of western imperialism.[31] Another party theoretician described the western support for nationalists like Nehru, U Nu, Soekarno and Hatta as "dykes against the surging force" of revolutionary communism.[32] Mao Tse-tung himself, in a message to the Communist Party of India, expressed the hope that under its leadership, India would certainly not remain long "under the yoke of imperialism and its collaborators."[33] There were innumerable references in Chinese political literature to Nehru as an "imperialist running dog," "stooge of Anglo-American bloc," "member of the political garbage group in Asia," and the highest Chinese decoration of dishonour—"the Chiang Kai-shek of India."

India continued her policy of circumspection and non-interference in Indo-China until early 1954. Despite economic and military aid to the rival sides from communist China on the one hand and United States on the other, the Indo-Chinese conflict had essentially remained a bi-partisan conflict between France and the Vietminh. But towards the end of 1953 and early 1954, while the French Government appeared weary of the war, the French military authorities in Vietnam manifested a stiffening, belligerent attitude. These elements, interested in the continuation of the conflict at any cost, succeeded in persuading the Republican administration in the United States to augment its economic and military aid to the war effort in Indo-China. They interpreted the Vietminh thrust in Laos and Cambodia in the spring of 1953 as indicative of a well-planned strategy of aggressive communism to engulf all of Indo-China and Southeast Asia. The United States Secretary of State, John Foster Dulles, held the Soviet Union and communist China directly responsible for the increased Vietminh activity, warning them on September 17, 1953, that if they persisted in promoting war in Indo-China, their conduct would be taken "as proof that they adhere to the design to extend their rule by methods of violence."[34] Within a fortnight, on September 30, the State Department announced a Franco-American agreement whereby additional financial resources up to 385 million dollars would be made available to the French government before December 31, 1954, "in support of the plans of the French government for the intensified prosecution of the war against the Vietminh."[35] What appeared to be representative of American determination was the statement of the then Vice-President, Richard Nixon, in November 1953 in Paris that under no circumstances could negotiations take place that would "place people who want independence under bondage" adding: "it is impossible to lay down arms until victory is completely won."[36] Dulles predicted such a military victory in 1954.

On the other hand, the remaining Big Powers appeared potentially receptive to the idea of peace when the foreign ministers of the Big Powers met in Berlin in February 1954. While France was weary of the war, Great Britain was wary of an escalation in the conflict which might result on account of Dulles' brinkmanship. As for the communists, conditions had changed considerably since Stalin's death. The new Russian line of peaceful co-existence, followed by Malenkov and later by Khrushchev recognized neutrality as a valid approach in international affairs, marking a *volte face* in Maoist China, which had so far categorically rejected the existence of a "third" path other than the communist or capitalist.[37]

IV

Nehru perceived the altered situation, deftly caught the straws of peace in the international gale and quickly exploited them for the good of India, Indo-China and the world. In February 1954, he contributed to the breaking of the political stalemate by calling for an immediate cease-fire in Indo-China. He attempted to secure for

India representation at the Geneva Conference on Indo-China, on the plea that this was an Asian question which should not be decided by non-Asians in Europe. He used the forum of the Colombo Conference of five Asian Powers on April 10 to discuss his six-point proposal for a settlement and sent his emissary, V.K. Krishna Menon, to Geneva to explain the Asian point of view to the powers assembled there. The Indian peripheral participation at Geneva was so considerable as to lead the French premier, Pierre Mendes-France to speak of the Conference as "this ten-power conference—nine at the table—and India."[38]

Indian diplomatic intervention in 1954 was on a large scale, comprehensive and to a certain extent conclusive. It was befitting a country that aspired, despite Nehru's repeated protestations, to a role of leadership in Asia and Africa. It was not an entirely altruistic action as chauvinistic enthusiasts of Indian foreign policy would make it appear. As Nehru himself admitted India's interest in peace was not only in principle, but also because of her interest in India's own progress. As he wrote to the Presidents of the state (provincial) Congress Committees in July 1954, the progress of India and other Asian countries depended upon peace, which may not be guaranteed indefinitely but was certainly worth striving for even if it lasted for a few years.[39] "Peace to us is not just a fervent hope," he told the Indian Parliament earlier in April 1954, "it is an emergent necessity."[40] It was desirable to have world peace, but it was even more essential to have peaceful conditions nearer home in Asia. The difference in Nehru's protests about SEATO, MEDO and American military aid to Pakistan can be contrasted with his attitude towards the more distant NATO in this context.[41] If the Korean problem interested him more than the German, it was because of the former's proximity to India and the prospect of Chinese and American intervention bringing war to Asian soil; similar possibilities in Indo-China caused him greater concern, because of greater proximity to India. To quote again from his speech in the Parliament:

Indo-China is an Asian country and a proximate area....The crisis in respect of Indo-China therefore moves us deeply and calls from us our best thoughts and efforts to avert the trends of this conflict towards its extension and intensification and to promote the trends that might lead to a settlement.[42]

Throughout the period of the Indo-China talks, New Delhi proved to be one of the few world capitals in which the future of Indo-China was being decided. Of all the visits of diplomats and statesmen in that connection to New Delhi, Chou En-lai's visit was certainly the most important. *Le Monde* described it as "an extension of the Asian Conference of Geneva, where China was a reluctant invitee and India an official outcast."[43]

The Chou-Nehru meeting was a crucial turning point in Asian politics and indeed in Indian diplomatic history, inaugurating a new phase and injecting the single most important factor into Indian foreign policy until almost the close of the decade. The joint communique issued at the end of Chou's visit contained the five principles or Panchsheel of which the most important was "peaceful co-existence." This was the culmination of a long-term effort on Nehru's part to arrive at a sound basis of relationship with China.

The Nehru-Chou communique also hoped that the five principles would be applied "to the solution of the problem in Indo-China." Panchsheel was presented as a panacea for political ills of a power-dominated world, bipolarized between communist and non-communist blocs of nations. If these two could not co-exist, the Sino-Indian agreement implied that the communist and the non-aligned nations could. The Indian and Chinese Premiers further hoped that the five principles would be "applied in their relations with other countries of Asia as well as in other parts of the world."[44] India felt sure that the extension of similar agreements to Southeast Asia could safeguard the integrity and sovereignty of the states in that region. Therefore, Indian diplomacy geared itself in 1954 to preventing further internationalization of the Indo-Chinese conflict by forestalling Chinese military intervention on behalf of the Vietminh and preventing the Americans from upgrading their assistance to the French military effort to the point of using nuclear weapons. China had to be assured of safe southern frontiers free from massive American military presence; at the same time, the states of Indo-China were to be protected from being brought under Chinese influence. In the behind-the-scenes parleys at Geneva, India, therefore, secured from Great Britain and France promises to China not to let the Americans have bases in Laos and Cambodia. On the other hand, Nehru secured Chinese assurances to guarantee the neutralization of Laos and Cambodia. Such exchanges of assurances between the East and the West obtained through Indian mediation, were in the Indian estimate, vital footnotes to the Geneva Agreements. Further at China's suggestion, India was appointed Chairman of the International Control Commission, whose tasks included supervision of imports of foreign armaments (including those of Chinese origin) into Laos, Cambodia and Vietnam. It was further indicative of the new Chinese confidence in Indian friendship for it virtually entrusted India with policing China's southern frontier in Laos and Vietnam.

To reinforce such unwritten clauses of the Geneva settlement, India pursued efforts on the diplomatic plane to oblige the DRV and China publicly to pledge adherence to the Panchsheel. Thus, at the Afro-Asian Conference at Bandung, Nehru arranged meetings of Cambodian, Laotian, North Vietnamese and Chinese premiers[45] at which Chou En-lai and Pham Van Dong gave promises of non-intereference in Laos and Cambodia. The DRV specifically agreed that the question of the political settlement in Laos was an internal one, in which North Vietnam would not interfere.[46] The Geneva Agreements, read in the context of the Panchsheel pledges, constituted in Indian eyes, a non-military defence system for Southeast Asia.

India's hopes and expectations that the Geneva settlement would bring lasting peace in Asia were not realized. Both India's unofficial role in the negotiations and her philosophical basis of the settlement were exaggerated. Enthusiasm and optimism got the better of political realities, since the Indian External Affairs ministry hoped to integrate the Indo-Chinese peace with the Sino-Indian peace. The twin instrumentalities for achieving these goals were the Panchsheel and the ICC. The former was dependent not on a military deterrent, like the .one maintained by the peace-loving Emperor Asoka, but on a misplaced faith in India's northern neighbours. As for the ICC, it was not an agency with powers to enforce peace, but only a commission charged with the supervision of a truce. There were too many ifs for its successful functioning: the continued presence of the French military command to ensure logistic facilities; the withdrawal of the Vietminh from Laos and Cambodia and of the Pathet Lao into the two Laotian provinces before disbandment. Even more important was the cooperation of the local governments. It was clear that the South Vietnamese government, with tacit support from the United States, would oppose the implementation of certain articles of the Geneva Agreements. Within the ICC itself, the cooperation of Canada and Poland would be forthcoming only as long as the east-west entente persisted. The Indian foreign office tended, in the first two years of the Geneva settlement, to underestimate some of its defective and difficult aspects.

India's approach conflicted with American policy in Indo-China. The Secretary of State, John F. Dulles, who held China responsible for the worsening situation in Indo-China, believed that only a collective security organization could deter China from advancing further in Southeast Asia. Apprehensive of communist designs, the United States had refused to subscribe to the Geneva settlement, and although she promised not to use force to alter the provisions of the Agreements, she employed diplomatic pressure to stall their implementation. After the Geneva Conference, Dulles took the initiative in organizing the eight-nation SEATO. With only three Asian members, two of them from Southeast Asia, SEATO became the target of Indian attacks, while the ICC under Indian chairmanship became the target of bitter American criticism.

India was more intensely interested and became far more successful in her relations with Laos and Cambodia than with South Vietnam. The neutrality of Laos and Cambodia was an indirect gain for India in as much as it won two more adherents to the Indian policy of non-alignment. Indian diplomacy and participation in the ICC were both employed in limiting outside interference in the two states and in encouraging their governments in following the policy of non-alignment. Soon after the Geneva Conference, Cambodia's fears of China and the DRV had led Sihanouk to seek a military alliance with the United States. From the time of his visit to India in March 1955, however, Sihanouk gave up his quest for military alliances and instead opted for neutrality. In the following month at Bandung, Nehru brought Sihanouk and Chou En-lai together, where the latter promised non-intervention in Southeast Asia and began a friendship with the Cambodian prince, which has lasted to this day. All this watered down the strength of the US-Khmer military agreement of May 1955.[47] Sihanouk continually consulted Nehru for direction in foreign policy. He stopped in the Indian capital on his way from Europe and before each of his visits to Peking. And indeed, the ICC's work in Cambodia became the best success story of the work of the peace keeping agency.[48]

V

Laos was also helped by India to maintain its neutrality until its pro-west alignment in mid-1958. Once again Nehru's mediation at Bandung inspired the DRV's open promise not to interfere in the internal politics of Laos, including the political settlement with the Pathet Lao. Further, the efforts of the Indian delegation on the ICC were primarily instrumental in arranging meetings between the Royal Laotian Government (RLG) and the Pathet Lao (PL), in Laos and Burma leading to the agreements of 1956 and 1957. Souvanna Phouma's visit to Peking and Hanoi in 1956, arranged through Indian mediation, was designed to secure Chinese and North Vietnamese guarantees of the settlement with the PL. Until mid-1958, India certainly succeeded in inspiring Laos and Cambodia to think that a moral commitment from China and the DRV based on the Panchsheel, rather than a military alliance with a distant outside power, was the most feasible asurance of preservation of peace in the region.

While India was able to instil confidence in the Laotian and Cambodian leadership on the efficacy of the Panchsheel, she failed in her relations with South Vietnam. The issue that strained the relationship most, at least until mid-1956, was India's consistent advocacy of the territorial integrity of the three states of Indo-China as provided for in the Geneva Agreements. The Indian stand while it benefited the non-communist party in Laos, it favoured the communist position in Vietnam, which demanded national elections and re-unification of Vietnam by July 1956. Throughout 1955, undeterred by a government-supported attack on the Indian and Polish delegations in Saigon in July 1955, India advocated holding a conference between North and South Vietnam to decide on nation-wide elections. India rejected the South Vietnamese government's argument that it was not responsible for obligations assumed by its predecessor French administration under the Geneva Agreements. Matters were complicated by the complete withdrawal of French troops from the country in April 1956.

India's efforts led to the Co-Chairmen's conference in London in April-May 1956 to discuss the Vietnam question. India suggested the postponement of the projected elections for a short time. United States and Great Britain were, however, most apprehensive that the communists would win the elections by a large margin. The Soviet

Union and China did not want to precipitate a crisis. Russia, therefore, acquiesced with the other Co-Chairman in an agreement to postpone the elections in Vietnam indefinitely, thus tacitly accepting a divided Vietnam. India bowed to this east-west accord on the *status quo* in Vietnam and continued to serve on the ICC.

The Indian attitude towards Vietnam changed radically after the London talks. The Co-Chairmen's agreement indicated a communist desire for peace in Indo-China at all costs. India was no longer solicitous about the DRV's demand for the reunification of Vietnam, although she continued to believe that in the long run such a solution would be the best for lasting peace in the region. In October 1956, India recognised the *de facto* government in both North and South Vietnam and a year later played host to the heads of state of both the States. Thereafter, until 1962, India treated both the governments in Vietnam on an equal basis. India abandoned her condemnation of South Vietnam for the latter's dependence on the SEATO; India also stopped advocating the reunification of Vietnam.

A major weakness of the Indian policy was that it was governed by global considerations rather than being predicated upon the immediate interests of the region itself. In this respect India reacted as the major powers did, being concerned less with the territorial integrity of Vietnam and Laos for their own sake than with the wider implications affecting the peace of the world. The indefinite postponement of the re-unification of Vietnam, the lack of facilities afforded the Commission's terms in the inspection of war material imported into South Vietnam, and the suspension of the joint commission of the two high commands consequent to the dissolution of the French Union High Command—all these were far-reaching modifications of the Geneva Agreements. A situation had been created which could have been resolved by a new settlement on a new basis. Instead, India acquiesced, with the great powers, in the acceptance of divided status for Vietnam and stayed on as an ineffectual chairman of the commission. From 1956 to 1959, when the seeds of subversion in South Vietnam were sown by the North, the commission continued its frustrating existence without either authority or initiative.

The success of Indian foreign policy in the mid-1950's in Southeast Asia seems to have resulted in a feeling of complacency in the Indian Ministry of External Affairs and its consequent neglect of the region's military and political needs. This complacency was manifest even nearer home. In 1957 and 1958 intelligence reports of the Chinese construction of a highway across the Indian territory of Aksai Chin did not alarm the Indian government sufficiently for it to take the Indian public into confidence or to step up the defence of the country. In fact, the years 1957-58 are notable for a relative slackening of Indian activity in international affairs. For a change, Nehru seemed more occupied with domestic politics, which assumed importance with the States' reorganization and the general elections of 1957. It was a period when the Chinese diplomacy and trade relations subtly but assuredly made gains in Southeast Asia, largely at India's expense. Chou En-lai followed up his Bandung meetings with several visits to Burma, Cambodia and Indonesia; after 1955, Nehru failed to return the courtesy of the visits of dignitaries from Southeast Asia to India.

More importantly, the neutrality of Laos and Cambodia was vitiated in mid-1958 by American policies, which seemed at the time, part of an aggressive diplomacy to draw the two countries into the pro-west orbit. It was a multi-pronged effort that succeeded in ousting neutralist premier, Souvanna Phouma and assisting the pro-West CDNI (Committee for the Defence of National Interests) to form a government in Laos. The CDNI promptly acted against the Pathet Lao, nullifying the set of agreements arrived at in 1956-57 between the Royal Laotian Government and the Pathet Lao. In Cambodia, Sihanouk's government alleged pressures from the CIA as well as from border disputes with the American-backed traditional enemies of Cambodia, namely, Thailand and South Vietnam. At the same time, not coincidentally, Canada demanded the dissolution of the International Control Commission in Laos and Cambodia. This would make it easy and safe for the Americans and pro-west elements to play their game. In July 1958, the Laos government asked the ICC to fold up its activities in the country. With that, the Indian influence in Laos was practically reduced to nothing because since the very beginning of Indian diplomatic intercourse with that country, the ICC had been made the principal instrumentality for pursuit of Indian foreign policy aims in Laos. In the next three years, India, therefore, found herself insisting along with the communist countries upon the revival of the ICC, for restoration of the pre-1958 political stability in Laos based internally on agreement with the Pathet Lao and externally on non-alignment with either bloc. Only thus, could Indian influence be restored in Laos and peace guaranteed in the region.

In this test of the neutrality of Laos and Cambodia, the limits of India's policy of non-alignment were sorely tried. Whereas Laos moved closer to the west, Cambodia strengthened its ties with communist China. What role could India play in these circumstances? As a non-aligned country, she had considerable influence with the super-powers which could be used to resolve major crises in international affairs. Yet, she lacked adequate leverage with minor pro-west states, even less so in disputes between a non-aligned country and a member of either bloc. On the diplomatic plane, India was unable to do much to help Cambodia. Indian efforts to sponsor investigations of the Khmer-Vietnamese border dispute by the ICC proved vain in the face of Canadian delegation's refusal to cooperate. On the other hand, China offered Cambodia moral and material support in the dispute wth Thailand and South Vietnam. After 1959, Cambodia's relations with India remained correct, but those with China grew increasingly cordial.

VI

At this point, a comment or two on the ICC's role as a peacekeeping agency may not be out of place particularly in the later context of American-North Vietnamese negotiations for a reconstructed ICC for Vietnam. India was sought to be excluded according to some because of the American wrath over India's action in Bangladesh, in 1971. India herself had strongly resented the South Vietnamese Government's cancellation of visas of the Indian personnel of the ICC. It is forgotten that several years ago, in February 1965, the DRV had disclaimed any responsibility for the safety of the ICC's teams in North Vietnam and requested their withdrawal. How much reliance should have been placed by India on the ICC as a peace-keeping agency and as an instrument for the purusit of its foreign policy aims in the countries of former French Indo-China? In my opinion, India exaggerated the importance of the ICC as a peace-keeping agency. The Geneva mandate gave the commission authority to investigate, recommend and report, but none to enforce implementation of its recommendations. The ICC's investigations depended upon the military commands of both sides for logistic support, which could be so long delayed as to render the investigations of questionable value. Further, the Geneva Agreements were expected to be implemented within a specific period of time; two years in Vietnam and less in Laos and Cambodia. In the latter country, the goals were achieved in time; but in the other two countries, the commission's prolonged existence gave it an aura of permanence. No sovereign state can be expected to endure for long the presence of an external agency that has recommendatory powers in regard to functions ordinarily within the sphere of responsibilities of the state. Periodic attempts to remove the ICC— by the South Vietnam government in July 1955, April 1956, April 1958 and late 1972; by the DRV in February 1965 and by the RLG in May 1958—were indicative of the reluctance of each country to tolerate a foreign supervisory body on its soil for a prolonged period.

At the same time, one would need to acknowledge that despite meagre personnel and a weak mandate, the ICC's achievements were substantial. These were: the separation of forces and transfer of population in Vietnam; the transfer of power in Hanoi; the withdrawal of the Vietnam from Cambodia ensuring the freedom of former resistance workers and successful intervention between the two parties in Laos, leading to the agreement in 1957. But most of these results were expected and were the direct result of the conciliatory atmosphere between the east and the west at Geneva that had produced the Indo-Chinese settlement itself. The success or failure of the ICC must, therefore, be attributed not so much to the member countries as to the existence or extinction of the political atmosphere that had facilitated the signing of the Geneva Agreements in 1954.

But as soon as the "Geneva Spirit" showed signs of erosion, the ICC experienced difficulties. The cooperation of the local parties declined; the amity and unanimity that had characterized the ICC's deliberations gave way to acrimonious legal arguments based on partisan interpretations of the articles of the agreements. In this context it would have been more practical to have a commission consisting only of neutral countries instead of subjecting it to the strains of rival efforts determined by inter-bloc relationships. References to the "Co-chairmen" failed to evoke replies or assistance in handling the deadlocks. The Geneva Conference had provided for no permanent machinery that could be invoked in such circumstances. Of the "Co-chairmen," Great Britain openly disclaimed any greater responsibility than that of a postal clearing agency for the ICC's reports. Repeated references to all the Geneva Powers would not have been practicable. Only the major powers could goad the local governments in Indo-China into guaranteeing cooperation with the ICC. And of these, the United States was actively engaged in sabotaging the implementation of the agreements in Vietnam after 1955. It would have made greater sense in this context if the United States and the Soviet Union had been the Co-Chairmen of the Geneva Conference with continued authority for revision.

Participation in the ICC was not an unmixed blessing for India. The appointment to the chairmanship of such an important body on China's southern frontier was certainly an achievement and an advantage from strategic and diplomatic viewpoints. Yet, a point is soon reached when the returns from such a position diminish. In fact, it soon became a disabling factor in the pursuit of diplomacy, as the chairmanship precluded India from any independent approach apart from the non-partisan stand enjoined by the chairmanship. Until 1958, when all the major parties to the agreement continued to support the preservation of peace in the region, there was no need for the expression of any independent opinion apart from insistence upon the strict implementation of the Geneva Agreements. But with the reintroduction of the cold war in Vietnam and Laos and revival of the hostilities in the region, the ICC became the scene of an intense struggle between the east and the west. Pressures on India from either side mounted. Consequently, the ICC became almost completely stalemated; when it made any decisions at all, these were immediately met with charges of partisanship and—most important—were hardly respected. And India was blamed without any reason and without any corresponding compensations from either super-power.

Should India have withdrawn from the ICC? There were junctures in the Commission's history when such a withdrawal would have been appropriate and perhaps even fruitful. As argued earlier in this paper, the situation that had given the commission its aura and sanction in 1954 had lapsed on a number of occasions. North Vietnam's role in the subversion of South Vietnam and the latter's factual military alliance with the United States had completely altered the situation. In the other two countries, the ICC's tasks had been completed: in Cambodia, by mid-1955; and in Laos, according to the ICC's own report to the Co-Chairmen, all the provisions of the Geneva Agreements had been fulfilled by May 1958. In the Vietnamese situation, India should have insisted upon a meeting of the Geneva Powers to redraw a settlement and to afford a legal basis for the cooperation of the South Vietnamese Government in the ICC's work. If not, India should have indicated her readiness to withdraw from the ICC. Such a move could have had at various times a dramatic if not definitive impact upon the situation.

VII

If after mid-1958, Indian achievements in Laos and Cambodia had been seriously compromised by American policies, by the middle of 1959 the very basis of Indian foreign policy in the region was undermined by China. The simultaneous occurrence of hostilities on the Sino-Indian border on the Himalayan heights and in Laos in 1959 were manifestations of the abandonment by China and the DRV of the restraints imposed by the Panchsheel and the Geneva Agreements. Some critics have accused Nehru of naivete in believing that the Panchsheel would provide a permanent pedestal upon which to build the edifice of foreign policy. To him, as to most observers, the Chinese behaviour was incomprehensible. Some Indian leaders ascribed it to India's granting asylum to the Dalai Lama. In 1959 they thought it was a temporary aberration of an otherwise well-based relationship. Nehru refused to put Indian foreign policy in the melting pot simply because the Chinese had violated the Panchsheel. In the background, there still lingered a hope of reconciliation and the revival of better relations with China.

Politicians do not have the advantage of a historian's hindsight. Three years and a half later, in February 1963, China disclosed that her dispute with India marked the beginning of the Sino-Soviet rift. In October 1962, Nehru confessed that his policy of friendship with China had been a blunder. In an appeal to his countrymen, he said: "I want you all to realize the shock we suffered during the last week or so. We were getting out of touch with the realities of the modern world. We were living in an artificial atmosphere of our own creation and we have been shocked out of it."[49] Even after this realisation, however, India was slow to trim her sails to the Chinese winds of change. Nehru characterized the Sino-Indian

dispute as a part of China's global policy of "wars of liberation."
But instead of logically bringing the new framework of Sino-Indian
relationship to bear upon India's foreign policy in a wider context,
he sought to isolate the dispute. There were certainly some advantages in doing so, and indeed there were certain diplomatic compulsions that could not be disregarded. Among these were the pressures
from the Soviet Union[50] and the United States[51] not to abandon non-
alignment. Since late 1962, Indian foreign policy has operated in
two worlds: the narrow area of the Sino-Indian conflict; and the
wider area of international affairs, where India continues to adhere
to non-alignment.

This dualism in foreign policy has tended to distort Indian
attitudes towards the problems of the Indo-Chinese states, particularly in regard to the Vietnamese conflict. In 1962, a series of
decisions by the ICC in Vietnam reflected a belated Indian understanding of the changing political and military situation in Vietnam.
These decisions related to the increasing introduction of American
military personnel and material into South Vietnam and the alarming extent of subversion in that country. In June 1961, the Indian
and Canadian delegates resolved that the commission was competent
to investigate incidents of subversion. A year later they held the
North Vietnamese government responsible for subversion in the
south. At the same time, India and Poland considered the existence
of a large number of personnel and so much material from the
United States as being in effect the creation of a military alliance,
which was prohibited under the Geneva Agreements.[52]

In the last two years of Nehru's stewardship of Indian affairs, the
policy of non-alignment had lost part of its former strength, morale
and initiative. Non-alignment did not help India to avert humiliation
at China's hands in 1962. It could not, therefore, inspire the lesser
states of Asia and Africa to look to India for protection and leadership. Then too, the retention thereafter of the non-alignment policy
by India was not entirely owing to her own ability; it was partly
determined by the conjunction of Soviet and American attitudes
towards China.[53] If the road of neutralism or non-alignment had
always been slippery, needing extreme caution in normal times, it
became an even more treacherous path in the new context of dependence upon the west for arms aid and the desire to retain Soviet
friendship as well. In the remaining part of the Nehru era, his
personal stature and the momentum gathered by Indian diplomacy

in a decade and a half did help India remain in the vangaurd of global politics, but she could not operate any longer from the lofty vantage position of leadership.

It is a truism that one's real friends are discovered in days of adversity. However, when big nations are in distress, the small states find themselves incapable of being of much assistance. The fact of Sino-Indian conflict and its outcome caused anxiety among many states in Southeast Asia. Thus, after 1959, when India had reported Chinese occupation of Indian territory, the smaller states on China's periphery had become wary of China's motives and unsure about the effectiveness of the policy of non-alignment. As an observer commented, the Southeast Asian states developed "sudden jungle fears," adding that the proposition that Peking would not hurt a neighbour that trusted her and stood aloof from the cold war was the greatest casualty of the Himalayan war.[54] The question was: if India failed, would the smaller uncommitted nations be able to hold the line? Of the six non-aligned nations that met in Ceylon in December 1962, in an effort to resolve the Sino-Indian dispute, three were from Southeast Asia: Burma, Cambodia and Indonesia. They all agreed with the Prime Minister of Ceylon, Mrs. Bandaranayake:

The border dispute between India and China, which we are about to discuss is the greatest challenge which non-alignment and Afro-Asian solidarity has had to face....

In the Sino-Indian dispute...I see a situation which is a threat both to our way of life and to the future of mankind. The threat to non-alignment is not merely confined to the fact that there has been a negation of the agreed principles of Pancha Shila. The Sino-Indian border conflict has also afforded an opportunity for the power politics of the 'cold war' to penetrate as it were into the affairs of the Afro-Asian world....

We have all been accustomed to regard India as the foremost champion of non-alignment. None of us can deny the great contribution which India, led by her distinguished leader, Prime Minister Nehru, has made in this respect. The concept of non-alignment and its moral force today is due after all in large measure to the powerful advocacy of India and the personal example set by the Indian Prime Minister in his tireless efforts to promote the idea of non-alignment throughout the world. We should, therefore, make it our joint responsibility and a moral obligation which we owe to the cause of non-alignment to see that non-alignment is preserved.[55]

Although there was tremendous sympathy and concern for India, none of these countries was prepared, even indirectly, to offend China. Therefore, they preferred to adopt a neutral, non-committal attitude on the substance of the conflict on the pretext of not prejudicing a mediator's role. The most cautious were Burma and Cambodia. Norodom Sihanouk's words on the occasion reflected the helplessness, fear and the realisation of the magnitude of the problem of the non-aligned nations:

> My delegation admits with due humility its inability to suggest any compromise solution likely to assist in bridging the gulf fixed between the positions adopted respectively by India and China....
>
> Our role seems to be limited, therefore, to an appeal to the noble sentiments of our two great friends exhorting them to consider the most grave danger threatening the future of their respective peoples and that of the peoples of the Afro-Asian group and of the whole world ....[56]

As could be expected, the pro-west states of Southeast Asia—Thailand, the Philippines and South Vietnam—sympathised with India. And the DRV, whose cause had been consistently espoused by India, came out completely on the side of China. From 1959 to mid-1962, the DRV had followed the Moscow line and maintained a neutral attitude in the Sino-Indian dispute. But ever since India had voted with Canada in the ICC's special report of June 1962, condemning North Vietnam's role in the subversion of South Vietnam, the DRV had been chafing at India. It had overlooked the Indian position in the International Control Commission, condemning the United States' military help to South Vietnam. The DRV's reaction toward India in October 1962 was very sharp. It condemned the Indian "expansionist group" for colluding with the western imperialists in attacking China.[57] But in the aftermath of the Cuban episode and the Soviet Union's announcement that its military aid to India would continue, the DRV adopted a cautious approach. It was rather with the intention of not alienating the Soviet Union than with that of pleasing India that Ho Chi Minh softened his criticism of India and urged on November 24 that the

Indian and Chinese leaders settle the dispute through negotiations.[58] Ho, however, maintained that China's terms were reasonable and that India should accept them. Despite attempts to improve the mutual relationship between the two countries, Indo-North Vietnamese relations remained less than cordial for the remainder of the Nehru era. Even the effectiveness of the staff of the Indian Consulate-General in Hanoi was reduced as increasing curbs were placed on their movements by the North Vietnamese government.

Does this mean that Nehru's perceptions of international affairs in Southeast Asia were erroneous? Ironically enough, even as the Sino-Indian pedestal of the Panchsheel doctrine was cracking beyond any hope of diplomatic repair, the solutions that the Indian Prime Minister had prescribed for peace in Southeast Asia were being increasingly advocated by others. Among these solutions was a multi-national guarantee of the sovereignty and territorial integrity of the Southeast Asian states by the principal powers. Thus, in 1961, the enlarged Geneva Conference strained itself to leave no loophole in the drafting of the protocol for the complete neutralization of Laos. In Cambodia, Prince Sihanouk continued his demand for the neutralization of his country. And in 1963, President de Gaulle made the first western proposal for the neutralization of Vietnam. On the international plane, particularly in relations between the United States and the Soviet Union, the concept of co-existence came to be accepted not only as morally feasible but as the only practical basis of international relationship in a thermo-nuclear age. And today, twelve years, thousands of American lives, hundreds of thousands of Vietnamese lives, and over a hundred billion dollars after, broadly speaking, the same solutions that Nehru advocated for bringing peace in war-torn Vietnam and for reduction of tensions in the region twenty years ago, still hold good.

K. SUBRAHMANYAM

Nehru and the India-China Conflict of 1962

IN DEALING WITH Jawaharlal Nehru's concepts regarding national security and his policy one is faced with a tremendous disadvantage. We are all aware that the break up of the fourth Indian army division in Kameng in 1962 was such a blow to Jawaharlal Nehru that he probably never really recovered from it. Unlike other aspects of his policies we deal here with a failure which led to a considerable dimunition of his image. Secondly, we deal with an area where a large number of myths have been developed in the last eleven years. Lastly, it is an area where correct and full information is rather difficult to come by. The records for the period 1947-64 have not yet been made available to the public.

I may start my analysis on a note of personal involvement. I joined the Ministry of Defence formally as a Deputy Secretary on November 14, 1962, but had been working informally as a Deputy Secretary with the permission of the outgoing Defence Minister Krishna Menon since October 27, 1962. My charge included all General Staff directorates, excluding the Directorates of Military Intelligence, Military Operations and Staff Duties. But as Deputy Secretary in charge of Joint Intelligence Organisation I was also a member of the Joint Intelligence Committee during the year 1963 and 1964. In early 1963 I had an occasion to analyse for the then Defence Secretary, P.V.R. Rao, all intelligence that came in during 1962 before the Chinese attack. I am also familiar with the entire re-equipment programme from 1963 to 1965 since equipment selection, procurement, both from indigenous and foregin sources, budgeting and foreign aid were dealt with by me for the whole of the period and others for a part of the period. This gave me an opportunity to go into developments in the period 1959-62. It would not be proper to give out any information which is classified; but it may be appropriate to draw the conclusion (when in the course of this presentation arguments are supported from published literature) that to my knowledge there is nothing in the classified area to contradict them.

I have also had ample opportunities of discussing the events of the 'fifties and early 'sixties with some of the prominent actors of the period; notably the late Lt.-Gen. B.M. Kaul, B.N. Mullik, the former Director of Intelligence Bureau and Maj. Gen. D.K. Palit (retired) who was the Director of Military Operations. I had these discussions during 1970-71. More recently, I had opportunities of discussing these events with a number of retired officers of the foreign service. What struck me was the absence in them of an integrated view of international developments at various levels of the government in spite of Prime Minister Nehru's own uncluttered perception of them.

I am not mentioning this as a criticism, but only to emphasize the need for a scholarly study which would benefit the present and future decision-makers. A major difficulty one comes across, while dealing with this subject and the relevant events of this period is that though there is a wealth of detail, yet most of the people concerned were unable to put it together into a comprehensive hypothesis. This has resulted in anecdotal accounts and mutually contradictory versions which one comes across in Lt.-Gen. Kaul's *The Untold Story*, Brig. Dalvi's *Himalayan Blunder*, S.S. Khera's *India's Security Problem*, Neville Maxwell's *India's China War* and B.N. Mullik's *Chinese Betrayal*. The process of understanding is further complicated by the fact that most of the authors had been either relying on their own memories or the memories of others who had given them the information. Others, who have relied on documents, had access to them or preferred to use them only selectively. It is a great pity that the Government of India has not thought it fit to commission a comprehensive study on the events of 1962 and the developments leading up to them. This may be partly because the people who take the decision not to release the documents, have themselves no comprehensive idea of the developments and the value of these documents to students of history and the furtherance of knowledge. It is quite likely that most of our decision-makers had not studied Neville Maxwell's book or Mulliks trilogy, *My Years with Nehru* and other relevant literature. The current decision appears to be an *ad hoc* response of people who want to "play safe."

There also appears to be some element of parochial interest involved, since the bureaucracy, both military and civil, perhaps fears that a dispassionate study of the developments of the 1950s and the events of 1962 might show them up in a bad light and might highlight some of the grave deficiencies in our decision-making structures and processes, which probably still exist. In fact, my purpose in this paper is to discuss how, in spite of Prime Minister Nehru's correct perception of the international situation and developments, there was a very wide gap between his understanding and that of the bureaucracy, and there were so many shortcomings in our decision-making structures and processes, which led to the debacle of 1962. One may, of course, hold the Prime Minister ultimately responsible for those shortcomings, but at the same time one must also take note of the fact that these shortcomings were probably part of our political culture and they may be there even today.

II

With these preliminary observations, I propose to analyse Jawaharlal Nehru's perceptions regarding India's national security problems. First, let me deal with the popular myth, namely that Nehru's Gandhian background and liberal Fabian internationalist outlook had conditioned him against contemplating the use of force as an instrument of policy in international relations. As early as 1934, while discussing Gandhi's article "Doctrine of the Sword," Nehru clarified his own position in his autobiography:

> We were moved by these arguments, but for us and for the National Congress as a whole the non-violent method was not and could not be, a religion or an unchallengeable creed or dogma. It could only be a policy and a method promising certain results, and by those results it would have to be finally judged. Individuals might make of it a religion or an incontrovertible creed. But no

political organisation, so long as it remained political, could do so.[1]

The Congress Working Committee declared in October 1940 that "free India would, therefore, throw all her weight in favour of world disarmament and should herself be prepared to give a lead in this to the world. Such a lead would invariably depend on external factors and internal conditions, but the State would do its utmost to give effect to this policy of disarmament."[2]

Writing in the *Discovery of India,* Jawaharlal Nehru talked of war in the following terms:

Much as I hated war, the prospect of a Japanese invasion of India had in no way frightened me. At the back of my mind I was in a sense attracted to this coming of war, horrible as it was, to India. For I wanted a tremendous shake-up, a personal experience for millions of people, which would drag them out of that peace of the grave that Britain had imposed upon us, something that would force them to face the reality of today and to outgrow the past which clung to them so tenaciously....Out of death, life is born afresh and individuals and nations who do not know how to die, do not know also how to live. 'Only where there are graves are there resurrections'[3]

Speaking in the Constituent Assembly on March 8, 1949 Pandit Nehru discussed the conflict in the minds of the followers of Gandhi who were exercising authority at that stage. He said:

We cannot and I am quite positive that our great leader would not have had us behave as blind automations just carrying out what he had said without reference to the changes in events....It was a curious thing that we who carried on the struggle for freedom in a non-violent and peaceful way should immediately have had to be confronted with violence of the intensest form, civil violence as well as, what may be called, military violence, or that we should have had to undertake a kind of war in a part of the country....And in that difficulty of spirit I went—as I often did—to Mahatma Gandhi, for his advice. It was not natural for him to give advice about military matters. What did he know about them? His struggles were struggles of the spirit. But listening to me, if I may with all respect say so, he did not say 'No' to the course of action that I proposed. He saw that a government, as we were, had to follow its duty, even military obligations, when certain circumstances arose. And throughout those few months, before he was taken from us, I conferred with him on many occasions about Kashmir and it was a great happiness to me that I had his blessings in the steps we took.[4]

Nehru not only was not averse to using force in Kashmir, Hyderabad and Goa, he was even prepared to lend Indian troops to the United Nations to carry out military operations in the Congo to end the Katangan secessionist movement. As soon as China entered Tibet in 1950 he extended a unilateral security guarantee to Nepal, and in the same year warned Pakistan that any attempt to interfere in the affairs of Kashmir would lead to a general war between the two countries.

On February 23, 1950 Nehru declared in Parliament: "For my part, I would like to devote myself chiefly to the particular issues of Bengal and Kashmir which, as I have said, are linked together in my mind. If the methods we have suggested are not agreed to it may be that we shall have to adopt other methods."[5]

On August 11, 1951 Nehru declared: "I have ruled out war as a measure for the easing of Indo-Pakistan relations, but I cannot rule it out independently or unilaterally. Since the other party brings it in and talks and shouts so much about it, I have to be perfectly ready for it." In the same speech, deprecating civil defence measures, the Prime Minister said: "Trenches are dug for people who expect an invasion. Whatever happens, India is not going to be invaded. Even if there is war, do you imagine that we will wait idly to be invaded? Certainly not."[6]

What happened in 1971, when India had to take military action, when millions of refugees were pushed out of East Bengal, had been anticipated by Jawaharlal Nehru in 1950 when he talked of resorting to "other methods." As the tension between India and Pakistan grew in 1950-51, India moved its forces to the border. The Prime Minister also made it very clear that if there was going to be a war, he was not going to fight a defensive war.

On the whole, Nehru's attitude must be summed up as of one who wanted to avoid war, who abhorred it, yet who would not hesitate to fight to defend his country's interests. In this he was like many western liberal statesmen and thinkers.

III

We now turn to the second myth built in this country that it was Prime Minister Nehru's "Hindi-Chini bhai-bhaism" which was responsible for our inadequate preparedness against China. Recently, in his book, *My Years with Nehru: The Chinese Betrayal* B.N Mullik disclosed that from the very beginning Jawaharlal Nehru had his reservations about China. More recently, Frank Moraes in his book, *Witness to an Era,* has written that in 1952, when he went as a member of a cultural delegation to China, Nehru in his briefing had said: "Never forget that the basic challenge in South-East Asia is between India and China. That challenge runs along the spine of Asia. Therefore, in your talks with the Chinese keep it in mind. Never let the Chinese patronize you."[7]

In his book, *The Guilty Men of 1962,* D.R. Mankekar stated that at the time of his visit to Peking in 1954 during his discussions Pandit Nehru had said "that some day or other these two Asian giants, were bound to tread on each others' corns and come into conflict, and that would be a calamity for Asia. That was an eventuality which we should all strive hard to avert."[8]

On November 27, 1950 Nehru disclosed in the Parliament that ever since the Chinese revolution India had to take note of this major fact and what this new China, was likely to be.[9] Subsequently, on December 9, 1959 he referred to the Border Committee, which was appointed in 1951, and said that since 1950 the picture of the two powerful states coming face to face with each other on a tremendous border had been before the government. They might have "differed as to the timings in our minds as to when that would happen; whether in five years, ten years, fifteen years or thirty years." These confirm Mullik's version that from the beginning Nehru had his reservations about China.

Against this background it is somewhat amusing to hear the assertions of various people that Nehru did not countenance any thesis regarding the likely Chinese hostility towards this country. What is perhaps not clearly articulated in these complaints, and what Nehru was not prepared to countenance, was the thesis of communist aggression and the argument for India taking an anti-communist posture, the reason mainly being that he did not want to antagonise the Soviet Union in addition to China. There is today ample evidence to show Nehru's perception of the Chinese threat from the early '50s. Those who claim that they warned him about the Chinese threat, but he did not take timely action have to substantiate their thesis with specific references to what exactly they had advocated. In those years, (and even today) there were "cold-warriors" in India who were keen on pushing India into the western camp, they included not only politicians, but several senior bureaucrats, both civil and military.

Further, as mentioned earlier, from 1959 onwards Nehru talked openly about the Chinese hostility in the Parliament and in the press. It is, therefore, very difficult to understand how the "Hindi Chini bhai-bhaism" of the period 1954-58 explains the unpreparedness of 1962.

IV

Recently much was made of a letter from Sardar Patel dated November 7, 1950 to Nehru. It was suggested that for some reasons Patel had a keener awareness of the Chinese threat than Nehru and that Patel's warning went unheeded. A careful reading of the Sardar's letter would show that the initiative for it presumbaly originated in the Intelligence Bureau. In fact, following the letter, the Border Security Committee under General Himmat Sinhji was set up and its recommendations, including the assignment of responsibility for external intelligence to the Intelligence Bureau, were acted upon. In these circumstances, it is very difficult to accept the thesis that Nehru neglected the Chinese threat. However, the fact still remains that the Prime Minister for various reasons, not readily understandable, did not directly and explicitly take into his confidence the bureaucracy, both civil and military, and his Cabinet colleagues in regard to the developing Chinese threat. We have to look for an alternative explanation for this attitude instead of merely relying on the conventional explanation that Nehru ignored the threat.

Before doing so, we have to analyse the evolution of Jawaharlal Nehru's ideas regarding India's national security. Here it must be conceded that he had given more thought to this than many others, including the so-called professionals. As early as 1931, Nehru discussed the defence of India in two issues (September 24 and October 1) of *Young India*. He felt then, that after India became free, the only threat to its security would be from the Soviet Union. He felt that the United States was too far away, Japan had its hands full with the new developments in China, and because of the latent and sometimes apparent hostility of the United States, China would have to face her own difficulties for a long time to come, and besides it was difficult to imagine that our relations with her would be anything but friendly. The countries of western Europe were too much involved in their hates and jealousies to trouble India. This was a typical balance of power analysis.

By 1944 Nehru had come to the conclusion that in the post-war world there would be only four great powers; the United States, the Soviet Union, China and India. Britain would be a fifth power if it managed to salvage part of its crumbling empire.[10]

By 1946 Nehru had very correctly assessed that the post-war world was likely to be divided into two blocs facing each other in a confrontation. In the San Francisco conference (on the founding of the United Nations), while the Soviet Union strongly supported the Indian nationalist claims, the United States chose to remain silent. Subsequently on September 7, 1946 in his first broadcast to the nation as the Vice-President of the Viceroy's Executive Council, when Nehru proclaimed the policy of non-alignment, he made a careful distinction between the United States and the Soviet Union. He stated: "We send our greetings to the people of the United States of America, to whom destiny has given a major role in international affairs. We trust that this tremendous responsibility will be utilised for the furtherance of peace and human freedom everywhere." One may take note of the prophetic scepticism underlying this statement about the role of the United States in world affairs. On the other hand, he said about the Soviet Union: "To that other great nation of the modern world, the Soviet Union, which also carries a vast responsibility for shaping world events, we send greetings. They are our neighbours in Asia and inevitably we shall have to undertake many common tasks and have much to do with each other."[11]

As early as 1946, when the Soviet newspapers uncharitably described Gandhi as a Hindu reactionary and Nehru as an imperialist stooge, Nehru had the foresight to envisage a mutuality of interests between India and the Soviet Union. He sent his own sister as the first ambassador to the Soviet Union.

The policy of non-alignment which was in the making at that time had two important components; to stay clear of the cold war politics and attempt to promote decolonisation. This was not an easy option since following the Cominform line laid down by Andrei Zhadnov, it was decided in the Calcutta conference of the Asian communist parties early in 1948 to initiate insurgencies in various countries of Asia; in Philippines, Malaya, Indonesia, Burma and India. This was also the time when India was experiencing considerable difficulties in regard to Kashmir, integration of princely states in the Indian Union and the rehabilitation of millions of refugees in the aftermath of the partition. There was considerable pressure in the country for India to join the western bloc.

In October 1949, in his reply to a message of greetings to the Indian Communist Party, Mao Tse-tung expressed the hope that "India would certainly not remain long under the yoke of imperialism and its collaborators. Like the Free China, free India would one day march into the socialist and people's democratic family. That day could be the end of the imperialist reactionary era in the history of mankind."[12] The tone of this telegram was very different from what Mao Tse-tung had written to Jawaharlal Nehru in July 1940 when he said: "Our emancipation, the emancipation of the Indian people and the Chinese, will be the signal of the emanicpation of all the down-trodden and oppressed."[13] This change in tone could not but have had its impact on Nehru's perception regarding China.

Faced with the hostility of China, the cold and indifferent attitude of the Soviet Union and the hostility of the United States and the western bloc which supported Pakistan, no Prime Minister of India could have remained indifferent to the considerations of national security; and certainly not Jawaharlal Nehru. In 1945, replying to Gandhi, who insisted on the "Hind Swaraj" model, for the future of India, Nehru said: "The question of independence and protection from foreign aggression, both political and economic, has also to be considered in this context. I do not think it is possible for India to be really independent unless she is a technically advanced country. I am not thinking for the moment in terms of just armies, but rather of scientific growth."[14] He, therefore, appears to have decided to adopt a policy which would contribute to India's national security by bringing about a mutually countervailing balance of forces in this part of the world. Given the geostrategic location of the United States, the Soviet Union and India, given the American predilection in favour of Pakistan and colonialist and neo-colonialist forces, Nehru seems to have deliberately decided to cultivate the Soviet Union as a countervailing factor. As mentioned earlier, this was explicit even in his first broadcast in September 1946.

Though one cannot be quite clear how far the emergence of a strong central government in China influenced the Soviet leadership, from 1950 onwards, there was a perceptible change in the Soviet policy towards India. The Soviet leadership advised the Communist Party of India to give up its insurgency.[15] It assisted India by making a goodwill gift of limited quantity of foodgrains which in turn triggered off a much larger American wheat loan to India.[16] In 1950, Prime Minister Nehru was to write to his ambassador in the United Nations, B.N. Rau, that for reasons which were entirely different, neither the western powers nor the Soviet Union would like India and China to come together.[17] One may recall that this was the period when China's relations with India were strained in view of the Chinese occupation of Tibet.

For the first time in 1952 the Soviet delegate to the United Nations spoke about the western designs over Kashmir. The Soviet Union expressed its support to the Constituent Assembly on the Kashmir issue and criticised United Nations' interference in the affairs of Kashmir. B.N. Mullik has recorded, how at that stage, when he discussed with Prime Minister Nehru the scope of his intelligence activities, Nehru told him not to worry about the Soviet Union. Towards the end of his life even Stalin's attitude towards India registered a thaw. He received Dr. S. Radhakrishnan, the Indian ambassador, and his successor, K.P.S. Menon. This change in Stalin's attitude was also acknowledged implicitly by Nehru when he paid a tribute to Stalin on his death. Ambassador Chester Bowles has recorded, how in 1951, Nehru told him that the Chinese-Soviet association was unlikely to last for more than a few years. He also foresaw then, the beginnings of a somewhat more liberal trend in the Soviet Union.[16]

V

Simultaneously, during this period, the western pressure on

India reached its peak. Pakistan was inducted into both CENTO and SEATO and a regular flow of military aid to that country at around 70 million dollars a year, commenced. The Sino-Indian border treaty of 1954, popularly known as the Panchsheel Treaty, followed shortly after Pakistan's induction into what Nehru described as "encircling alliances." India had to strengthen itself against a Pakistan, which was being armed by the west and against another developing threat, that from China. In retrospect, it appears that Nehru very correctly decided to buy time in regard to China, and at the same time initiated a series of measures to strengthen India's defences against a Pakistani attack. When Chester Bowles wrote an article in *Foreign Affairs* in October 1954 expressing scepticism regarding China living upto the treaty with India, Nehru had the article circulated among the foreign service officials.[19]

Simultaneously, Nehru tried to establish cordial relations with the Soviet Union. It would seem that as early as 1954 there had been Soviet offers of defence equipment and India was perhaps the first country outside the communist bloc to receive such offers. However, the offer was not accepted at that stage. It is difficult to say how far this decision to decline the Soviet offer was influenced by the western and anti-communist orientation of our bureaucracy. The entire programme of rearmament against Pakistan was thus carried out by purchases from the United Kingdom, France and the United States.

Harold Macmillan has recorded in his memoirs that even in 1954 when the Russians participated in the Geneva summit conference, they were dropping hints on their anxiety about the Chinese.[20] China appears to have raised its border claims with the Soviet Union as early as 1954.[21] It is difficult to believe that Jawaharlal Nehru, who had a number of friends in the British establishment, was not aware of the beginnings of the Sino-Soviet differences, indeed he had the rare perception to conceive of such a development much earlier. When he visited the Soviet Union in 1955 there must have been exchange of views between him and the Soviet leadership on matters of such import. Earlier, in 1954, when he visited China he had already discussed the issues of war and peace with Chairman Mao Tse-tung. It was during those discussions that Chairman Mao made his now famous remark that only half of humanity would survive and only the socialist half would remain even if the other half was destroyed in a nuclear war.[22] On his return from his visit to China, Nehru again emphasised the peculiarity of Chinese communism, which he described as not a full-blooded communism.

Michael Brecher, who spent several days with Nehru in 1956 and published his biography in November 1958, writes:

> With the Chinese occupation of Tibet, their interests met in the heart of Central Asia. A conflict of interests in these circumstances might well lead to a direct clash as it almost did over Tibet in 1950. But in its present position of weakness India is determined not to become embroiled in a dangerous conflict with its neighbour, unless its vital interests are openly threatened such as control over the Himalayan border states of Nepal, Bhutan and Sikkim....
>
> It should not be inferred, however, that Nehru is dominated by these assumptions or that unqualified trust is the basis of his China policy. Indeed, he is disturbed by the evidence of Chinese penetration into the Himalayan border states and has made abundantly clear that he considers them to be in India's 'sphere of influence'. Nor is he oblivious to the inevitable long-run rivalry between Democratic India and Communist China for the leadership of Asia. He knows full well, but never admits in public, that the ideologically uncommitted countries of the area are watching the contest between Delhi and Peking, particularly in the economic realm, to see which system can 'deliver the goods'. He knows that the fate of Asia hangs in the balance—and hopes that sympathetic Western statesmen will realise the implications of the contest before it is too late. Thus far he has been disappointed with the evidence of such imaginative understanding.[23]

It is in this context that one must re-evaluate Nehru's policy towards the Soviet Union and the way in which India voted on the Hungarian issue and the anxiety to develop and accelerate India's industrial development during the second plan period, particularly to establish the defence production base.

Non-alignment was not merely a moral stand. As Nehru himself explained to the Parliament, it was, in fact, also based on considerations of India's national interest. It was a strategy by which he was trying to derive out of the world balance of forces the maximum cover for

India's security. Given the long association with the English-speaking world and the western-orientation of our elite, he had to be very cautious in developing India's relationship with the Soviet Union. Even the non-alignment policy came under severe criticism from large sections of our elite who preferred an outright alignment with the west.

VI

In regard to the military preparedness, the Indian defence expenditure was of the order of 1.7 per cent of our net national product during 1949-50. It fluctuated between 1.8 and 1.9 per cent till 1956-57. Thereafter it started moving up to a little over 2 per cent in the period 1957-58 onwards. The strength of the Indian armed forces which was 2.8 lakhs in 1949-50 went up to 5.5 lakhs by 1962. Similarly the Indian Air Force of seven combat squadrons at the time of partition was expanded to eighteen fighter, fighter-bomber and bomber squadrons by 1962. During this period, India acquired—through imports—the following items of major equipment:

For the Air Force
230 Vampire aircraft produced under licence from UK in India
104 Toofani aircraft from France
182 Hunters from UK
80 Canberras from UK
110 Mysteres from France
55 Fairchild Packets from USA
16 AN-12s from the Soviet Union
26 Mi-4 helicopters from the Soviet Union
For the Navy
3 R class destroyers
3 Hunt class destroyers
2 Cruisers
3 Leopard class frigates
3 Blackwood frigates
2 Whitby class anti-submarine frigates
1 Aircraft carrier
For the Army
180 Sherman tanks

over 300 Centurian tanks
160 AMX-12 tanks

These purchases indicate that Nehru was aware of the need to keep India's defence in good shape to deal with such threats as might arise. A detailed analysis of the purchases would reveal that as and when a major acquisition of weaponry by Pakistan was foreseen, India reacted to it quickly and adequately by resorting to import of weapons. It is necessary to emphasise this because of the accusation that the armed forces were generally neglected during this period. On the other hand, all reasonable requests of the armed forces were adequately met. The equipment which was acquired was mostly modern, and was able to stand up to the challenge of the American weapons supplied to Pakistan until 1965.

Simultaneously, with the acquisition of these weapons, the Government of India launched a programme of expansion of the defence production base in the country by acquiring technology along with the equipment. This effort was a wide-ranging one from manufacturing of self-loading rifles to the development of supersonic aircraft. Licences to manufacture in India were obtained from foreign countries for the following:

Gnat interceptor aircraft from UK
HS-748 transport aircraft from UK
Allouette helicopters from France
MiG interceptors from the Soviet Union
L-70 anti-aircraft gun from Sweden
Vijayanta tank from UK
Shaktiman truck from Germany and Nissan one ton truck and
Jonga-jeeps from Japan
Brandt mortars from France
106 mm recoilless guns from USA
Sterling carbines from UK
Wireless sets from different countries

Above all, research and development effort in defence was initiated and built up from 1958 onwards. Efforts were made to develop an indigenous self-loading rifle, an indigenous mountain gun, a whole series of wireless equipment and supersonic aircraft.

Explaining the equation of defence in the Lok Sabha in 1956

Nehru said: "In what lies the strength of a people for defence? One thinks immediately about defence forces—army, navy and air force. Perfectly right. . . . How do they exist? What are they based on? The more technical armies, the navies and air forces get, the more important becomes the industrial and technological base of the country. . . . The equation of defence is your defence forces plus your industrial and technological background, plus, thirdly, the spirit of the people. . . . The Five Year Plan is the defence plan of the country".[24] The outline for the entire defence production base that exists in this country today—from Ishapur rifles to MiG 21— was developed during the stewardship of Prime Minister Nehru.

Looking back on that period now, it would appear that most of those who ran down the efforts for self-reliance and the develop- ment of a defence production base in the country were, in fact, advocating an alignment with the West. At least one author has levelled the charge that the delays in the production of the Brandt mortar and Ishapur rifles were attributable to late General Thimayya's preference for alternative equipment, namely the American AR-15 rifle, which came under severe criticism subse- quently in Vietnam, and the Israeli Tampella mortar. It may also be recalled that the then Chief of the Air Staff was not very keen on the country going in for the Gnat aircraft. Nor was the decision to sign an agreement for the production of the MiG-21 aircraft under licence hailed with any great enthusiasm. In fact, the Air Chief at that time preferred the ill-fated American Starfighter, F-104. But for the sense of purpose with which the development of defence production base was pursued by Nehru and Menon, we would not be today where we are in regard to our capability to meet our own defence requirements. In this respect, Nehru was certainly far ahead of many of his professional advisers.

The effective countering of the Chinese threat did not call for the acquisition of very sophisticated weapons and equipments. On the other hand, preparedness against the Chinese, called for the development of an adequate and effective road network all along our borders, stationing of our men on high altitudes and getting them acclimatised, provision of adequate clothing and shelter in those altitudes, communication equipment and rifles, carbines machine guns, other mortars and light mountain artillery. The provision of this equipment was not a very costly proposition. It was also not the case that our capability at that stage to have

stationed enough number of men within the manpower availability
of the army on the northern borders was inadequate for the needs.

VII

But the development of roads and the creation of a communication infrastructure were time-consuming tasks. From 1950 when
the Indian administration in the Arunachal Pradesh was introduced
and began its consolidation, efforts were being made to develop
road communications. Earlier the Military Engineering Service was
entrusted with the responsibility to construct roads in these areas.
Because of inadequate progress the project was later taken away
from them and entrusted to the Public Works Department, but it
was found by 1958-59 that they also could not cope with this challenging task. At that stage a Border Roads Development Board
was created with the Prime Minister as Chairman and the Defence
Minister as Vice-Chairman. The acquisition of Fairchild Packets,
AN-12 aircraft, Mi-4 helicopters, engineering and other equipment
from the United States and the Soviet Union followed. When the
Chinese attack came in 1962, the border roads organisation was
just getting into stride. In fact, it should have been created some
four years earlier.

Even at that stage there was no clear conception among various
people about the nature of the threat we were expected to face
from the Chinese. There were many who advocated that the Indian
defence against China must be organised along a line which was
about 50-100 miles south of the McMahon line. The conception
behind this might perhaps be derived from what General Thimayya
wrote in an article in July 1962. He said:

Whereas in the case of Pakistan I have considered the possibility
of a total war, I am afraid I cannot do so in regard to China.
I cannot even as a soldier envisage India taking on China in an
open conflict on its own. China's present strength in manpower,
equipment and aircraft exceeds our resources a hundred-fold
with the full support of the U.S.S.R., and we could never hope
to match China in the foreseeable future. It must be left to the
politicians and diplomats to ensure our security....
The country is a mass of mountains right up to the highest ridges

of the Himalayas. The passes are practically impossible of crossing for over six months of the year except for men and animals, and that too with difficulty. China is, therefore, deprived of the use of its overwhelming superiority in heavy equipment of every kind, i.e., tanks, heavy-calibre artillery etc. This is where we should make full use of our manpower and light equipment which indeed we are doing....

If the Chinese do attack us with the intention of recovering territory which they believe to be theirs, we must meet them in those regions with commandos and highly equipped and fast-moving infantry. If the Chinese penetrate the Himalayas and are able to reach the plains and foothills, we must be in a position to take advantage of our superior fire power and manoeuvrability to defeat them and at the same time continue to harass their lines of communications by the use of commandos and guerillas.

To summarise our requirements for the defence of the India-China border, they are as follows:

(i) Large numbers of lightly equipped infantry, with the following role:

    (a) to give early warning and to defend approaches into our territory; and

    (b) sufficient reserves which should be mobile to move across the country if necessary.

(ii) A strong, organised force with heavy fighting equipment including tanks, armoured cars, artillery etc. to defeat the enemy after he has penetrated the Himalayan main ranges.[25]

It is obvious from the above statement of General Thimayya that the Indian Army staff was under the impression that China in its confrontation with India would be fully supported by the Soviet Union. Secondly, the Chinese were to be met in the mountain regions with only lightly equipped commandos and fast moving infantry. After they penetrated the Himalayas and came down to the plains we were to take advantage of our superior fire power to defeat them and at the same time harass their lines of communications by use of commandos and guerillas. Nehru also occasionally spoke about the possibility of an India-China war escalating. It would appear from all this that the expectation was that the confrontation with China would either be limited to patrol clashes, or a large scale war which would involve the Chinese coming down to the plains. Strangely enough at about this time Sardar Panikkar published a book in which he cast serious doubts on the Chinese penetrating the Himalayas and coming down to the plains. In all these arguments the possibility of the Chinese launching a very carefully controlled limited operation, with very limited political objectives, appears to have been overlooked altogether, both in the services and political circles, including the Prime Minister. The problem of fighting at high altitudes evidently was not given adequate thought. Otherwise, there would have been no attempt at moving the troops from the plains to the high altitude regions in the Kameng division in a hurry at the eleventh hour. They should have been there earlier. As Air Chief Marshal Arjan Singh later pointed out there was an insufficient appreciation of the problems of operating aircraft from high altitude airfields.[26] If those problems had been thought through then there would not have been as much reluctance to use Indian air power in support of our operations in 1962 as there was. Nor had the significance of the Sino-Soviet rift, the withdrawal of the Soviet technicians from China and the very difficult position in which the Chinese air force had found itself at that time been appreciated in India. What is quite evident today is that in spite of Nehru's references to the possibility of a war with China for over three years,—from the fall of 1959 to the fall of 1962— much professional thought had not been devoted to the problem of war in the Himalayas.

In December 1961 the Goa operations had revealed that the Indian Army's logistics were not quite up to the mark. Our soldiers did not have the necessary clothing items or equipment when they marched into Goa. The railway schedules in the western and mid-western part of India were considerably dislocated for the movement of troops. And all this to carry out an operation which involved one division and that too in the plains. A dispassionate assessment of the Goa operations and an attempt to draw lessons from them might have helped in avoiding the terrible mistakes that were committed in the logistic management of the 1962 operations.

VIII

Now we come to the issue of the Sino-Soviet rift to which I have already made a passing reference earlier, and its possible impact

on the Sino-Indian confrontation. It is obvious from General
Thimayya's article that he had no clue about this growing rift.

From Lt.-Gen. Kaul's book, *The Untold Story*, it is obvious he
also had no knowledge of the Sino-Soviet dispute or its impact on
China. This is all the more surprising since Lt.-Gen. Kaul was
considered to be a favourite of the Prime Minister and close to him.
On the other hand, B.N. Mullik records in his book that Nehru
talked to the intelligence officers in the first quarter of 1961 and
referred to the relationship between Russia and China.[27] He felt
that it was very helpful for India to have friendly relations with
Russia because "of all countries of the world only Russia could
prove to be useful to India by its policy in regard to the Sino-Indian
dispute." America was far away. It could help India with arms,
aircraft etc. in the eventuality of a war. But America was in no
position to help India diplomatically against China. On the other
hand, though an ally of China, Russia's apparent neutrality in the
India-China dispute was definitely in India's favour politically.

Nehru had referred to the Soviet neutrality in the India-China
border issue in a speech in the Parliament on September 12, 1959,
when he said that the "issue of that statement (the Tass statement
of September 9) itself shows that the Soviet Government is taking
a calm and more or less objective or dispassionate view of the
situation considering everything. We welcome that."[28] The Chinese,
subsequently described this Tass statement of September 9, as the
first instance when the Sino-Soviet differences were exposed to the
eyes of the world.[29] Subsequently, the border dispute between India
and China became a matter of heated discussion between Khrushchev
and the Chinese delegate, Peng Chen in the Bucharest meeting of
June 22, 1960.[30]

The Soviet Union knew very well that India was buying from it
the AN-12 aircraft and Mi-4 helicopters and the engineering equipment to construct the border roads in areas which were in dispute
with China. The Chinese must also have taken note of this fact.

The Sino-Soviet dispute was being discussed in the communist
and leftist press in various parts of the world, including India.
There was a detailed interview given by the Indian communist
party leader, Hare Krishna Konar, to the *Link* magazine of
October 15, 1960 when he reported on the differences between
China and the Soviet Union in the light of his discussions with
Chinese representatives, who attended the third North Vietnamese

Party Congress in September that year. The withdrawal of the Soviet technicians from China was also revealed by Konar, which in turn was reported for the first time in the Soviet press in early January 1961. Even in 1960 there were indications of friction on the Sino-Soviet border.[31]

Khrushchev visited India in February 1960. It is extremely unlikely that he and Nehru did not exchange views on the relation of their countries with China. Subsequently, in April-May 1962 there were a number of border incidents on the Sino-Soviet border in Sinkiang.[32] According to the Chinese, several tens of thousands of Chinese citizens of Ili region were enticed into the Soviet Union. The Soviets charged the Chinese with more than 5,000 violations of Soviet frontiers in 1962. By this time the Soviets had already repudiated the treaty they had concluded with China on the development of nuclear weapons. This had happened as early as July 1959. In fact, one could see correlation in time between the Soviet repudiation of this treaty and their neutrality over the Sino-Indian border question. In the Lu-shan Plenum in August 1959 the pro-Soviet Chinese Defence Minister, Marshal Peng Teh-huai was dismissed. One wonders how far Prime Minister Nehru was aware of these developments. But there was certainly not enough awareness of these developments in the country, particularly among our military and civilian bureaucracy.

IX

One comes across statements made by a few officials, both military and civil, and especially the former, about their having warned Nehru about the developing Chinese threat. In retrospect, it is obvious that no one has left such a complete record of his appreciation about the Chinese threat as Nehru himself. Some claim (these include the Canadian author Lorne Kavic, Frank Moraes and Brig. Dalvi) that General Thimayya had put forward plans which were rejected by the government. Lt.-Gen. Kaul talks about his having prepared as many as eight memoranda between November 1961 and June 1962 and having estimated a requirement of Rs. 459 crores to build up the defences. At the same time, he is emphatic that before he submitted these plans there had been no previous plans.[33] When these plans were considered at a meeting of the secretaries, according to Lt.-Gen. Kaul, the Finance Secretary stated that if India had to have a defence programme of the magnitude asked for, it would be necessary to slash down the expenditure contemplated for the next five year plan, and therefore, suggested that a plan must be prepared and submitted to the government for approval. Though Lt.-Gen. Kaul has recorded that this was done, he has not given the details about the dates. B.N. Mullik says that this was done in June 1962.[34] It should be obvious that any action taken at that stage could never have produced the requisite equipment by October 1962. It is somewhat intriguing that Lt.-Gen. Kaul, who met the American Under-Secretary of State, Chester Bowles, in March 1962, and told him that he expected a Chinese attack between July and October of that year (this has been confirmed by Chester Bowles himself)[35] and submitted plans for acquisition of equipment in June'62, chose to be away on leave in September 1962. It is also not quite clear why the Chief of General Staff who had been expecting in the early months of 1962 a Chinese attack during the autumn of that year did not brief the Army Commander, the Corps Commanders and others concerned. This sequence of events, which is fairly well established now, tends to support the thesis of Mullik that there had been no failure in intelligence reporting, but the failure was in the intelligence assessment and utilisation of the intelligence for policy-making. P.V.R. Rao and General Chaudhuri have made it clear that in 1962 there was no intelligence failure.[36]

This grave failure on the part of the bureaucracy, both military and civil, needs to be analysed in some detail. P.V.R. Rao, who took over as Defence Secretary in November 1962, has recorded that the Joint Intelligence Committee, which was then a sub-committee of the Chiefs of Staff Committee, did not function. It would appear the various intelligence reports that flowed from the Intelligence Bureau were never assessed and made the basis for policy formulation. In the writings of Lt.-Gen. Kaul and others who appear to have derived their information from senior army officers, there is no evidence to suggest that the process of decision-making in regard to national security policy was well understood by them. There seems to have been individual *ad hoc* views about the Chinese threat and the timing of their attack, but there was no attempt to pool all this information by the Joint Intelligence Committee which had this responsibility and to derive an assessment regarding the nature and magnitude of the threat, the type of war that was likely to ensue, alternative scenarios and the likely timing. The responsibility for the failure of the Joint Intelligence Committee at that stage was that of the Chiefs of Staff. Without a threat assessment the proposals that were put forward to the government were merely *ad hoc* individual appreciations.

Having failed to get a proper threat assessment prepared, the Army Headquarters, and the ministries of External Affairs and Defence tended to confuse intelligence reports with threat assessments. The intelligence reports are meant to cover the current events while the assessments are not only about the current situation, but also meant to be extrapolated into the future. This confusion is aptly illustrated by the way in which both Army Headquarters and the External Affairs Ministry are reported to have acted when the so-called "forward policy" was being discussed. Very appropriately the question was raised as to what the Chinese response to that policy would be. This ought to have been referred to the Joint Intelligence Committee of which a Joint Secretary of the External Affairs Ministry was the Chairman at that time. Instead, the External Affairs Ministry chose to refer the matter to the Director of Intelligence Bureau. One of the elementary principles in intelligence assessments is that the reporting agency should never be asked to assess its own reports. Evidently this was overlooked.

Mullik stated that with reference to the past conduct of the Chinese it appeared that the Chinese intended to come up to their "claim line," but that they would keep away when the Indian troops were present, even if it were only a dozen men. Therefore, he suggested that the army should quickly move forward to fill the vacuum, or otherwise the Chinese were bound to do so within a few months. The External Affairs Ministry promptly endorsed this view to the Army Headquarters.[37] No one even asked the question: "What would happen if the future Chinese conduct presented a discontinuity from the past?"

After having committed the blunder of asking the Intelligence Chief for an assessment, after having sent that information without any further scrutiny to the Army Headquarters and the information not having been subjected to any further debate even in the Army Headquarters or in the Joint Intelligence Committee, the tendency now is to blame the only person who gave an opinion, namely B.N. Mullik. No one except P.V.R. Rao has raised the question about the External Affairs Ministry, the Army Headquarters, the Joint Intelligence Committee, and others whose primary duty it was to assess a threat and why they failed in their duty.[38]

X

There has been considerable discussion in this country about the wisdom of the so-called "forward policy." The critics of this policy put the blame mostly on the Prime Minister, and the Intelligence Chief, Mullik and, to a lesser extent, on the Chief of General Staff, Lt.-Gen. B.M. Kaul. A few, who have accepted uncritically Neville Maxwell's version, have even discovered that forward patrolling by Intelligence Bureau in October 1959 was perhaps in contravention of the Prime Minister's directive. A careful study will lead to the conclusion that such criticism is not valid. On September 13, 1959 the Prime Minister recorded this directive:

> The Aksai Chin area has to be left more or less as it is as we have no check-posts there and practically little of access. Any questions in relation to it can only be considered, when the time arises, in the context of the larger question of the entire border. For the present, we have to put up with the Chinese occupation of this north-eastern sector [of Ladakh] and their road across it.... I think it is unlikely that the Chinese forces will take up any aggressive line on this frontier, that is, try to enter into our territory any further. If they should do so, they will have to be stopped and the matter reported to us immediately for instructions.[39]

The Kongka pass where our police patrol was ambushed in October, 1959 is not in Aksai Chin, which is north-east of Ladakh, but it is due east, of Leh. Consequently, those who have criticised that sending in of the patrol parties to Kongka La was in contravention of the Prime Minister's directive have not cared to study the map properly.

It was decided in a meeting on November 2, 1960 that:

> So far as Ladakh is concerned, we are to patrol as far forward as possible from our present positions towards the international border. This will be done with a view to establishing our posts

which should prevent the Chinese from advancing any further and also dominating from any posts which they may have already established in our territory. This must be done without getting involved in a clash with the Chinese, unless this becomes necessary in self-defence.[40]

What the critics of the so-called "forward policy" miss is that the Chinese were constantly moving forward during the years 1959-61 up to their "claim line." They put forward at that stage two "claim lines"; the second one claiming more areas than the first. Given the fact that the Chinese were brazenly lying that they were already in occupation of this area, when the Government of India were aware that they were not, it would have been imprudent on anybody's part to accept that the second Chinese claim line was a final one. The second claim line cut across some of the river valleys of the Indus basin and into the trans-Karakorum area. They were quite at some distance from Aksai Chin and the Chinese roads to Sinkiang. The Chinese intentions, therefore, had to be tested by setting up a line of check-posts which, with the exception of a few posts, mostly fell somewhere between their old and new "claim lines," and then by watching what the Chinese were up to. This was the essence of the so-called "forward policy." In fact the more appropriate name would be intensive or continuous surveillance policy.

Those who criticise this policy have not suggested what alternative course the Government of India should have adopted. Do they suggest that the government should have left this area unpatrolled and with no check-posts at all? Was there any evidence in 1961 to show that the Chinese would stop even at their second claim line? Perhaps today, eleven years after the event, it is possible to say that the Chinese appeared to be satisfied by reaching up to their second claim line. But no one could be sure of this in 1960 or 1961.

The so-called "forward policy" was not a provocative one, as it has been characterised by Maxwell. It was a policy of patrolling our border in an area between the two claim lines of the Chinese. We had been patrolling further forward between 1958 and 1960. It was the only sensible policy available to test the Chinese intentions. Though we had to sacrifice a number of lives in the process, it appears in retrospect that the cost of a non-policy at that stage would have been far more disastrous.

The same considerations hold true in regard to our policy in Arunachal Pradesh as well. A nation has to fight at its border, if the border means anything to it. How it would fight a long drawn out war and ultimately defeat the enemy is a different matter. There, one could trade off territory for time or for a counter-attack at a convenient line. But there can be no two opinions when it comes to fighting at the border. We can debate about the possibility of holding the line at Sela or Bomdilla or somewhere else. But one is amazed at the criticism about fighting the Chinese at a line which we considered to be our border. Those who advocated the policy of giving up territory and not fighting at the border and only at a defensible line much farther below, have not explained what they would have done if the Chinese did not oblige them by coming down to that particular line and offering battle. Was it their intention to give up the territory in between permanently? A critical analysis of these views would show who had thought through the problems of national security and who had not.

So much for the "forward policy." Now let us come to the events of 1962. The Sino-Soviet border clashes have been mentioned earlier. According to Mullik, he obtained reliable information and transmitted it to the government early in June 1962, regarding the probability of a Chinese attack in the ensuing autumn. Subsequently, in the first week of August 1962, India concluded an agreement with the Soviet Union on the manufacture of MiG-21. This was a major event. The Soviet Union was licensing India for the manufacture of a very sophisticated equipment for which it had not licensed even China. This was also the first agreement for military hardware between the two countries and therefore, had an enormous military significance. Earlier purchases of AN-12 transport aircraft and Mi-4 helicopters were on behalf of the Border Roads Development Board. In the last week of August the Soviets informed the Chinese that they proposed to pursue the negotiations for the Partial Test Ban Treaty.[41] This the Chinese considered as a step directed against their development of nuclear weapons.

The Chinese crossing of the Thagla ridge took place on September 8, 1962. Between 24th and 27th September of that year was also the plenum of the Chinese Communist Party. On June 23, 1962 the Chinese had obtained an assurance from the United States at their Warsaw meeting that they would not support any Chinese nationalist attack on the mainland.[42] At present it is very difficult to trace all the links between these events. Nevertheless, these must be seen in the context of the Chinese decision to escalate the border situation in September and to launch a deliberate full-scale attack subsequently. Some American scholars, notably Harold Hinton, have also hinted at a time correlation between the Chinese attack on India and the confrontation between the Soviet Union and the United States over Cuba. The Chinese evidently were aware of the Soviet plans to place missiles in Cuba and the possibility of US-Soviet confrontation.

However, it is obvious, that at that stage, in India, neither Prime Minister Nehru nor Defence Minister Krishna Menon had any idea of the imminence of the Chinese action. Otherwise both of them would not have left the country in September. The Chief of the General Staff, Lt.-Gen. Kaul, was on leave. The Director of Military Operations was sent on the *Vikrant* cruise. All evidence points out to the high probability that the Chinese action was not a response to the alleged provocation of Prime Minister Nehru (such as his airport interview on October 12) but was the result of a deliberate decision taken in Peking well in advance to humble India. The Chinese forces could not have been assembled in such great strength to carry out the operations just within those few days. All that one can say is that the Government of India perhaps walked into a cleverly baited trap.

XI

Even then, in retrospect, one would say that those who fought in Ladakh and laid down their lives did not do so in vain. Nor could it be considered that the battles of Namkachu or Walong were fought to no purpose. But for those battles, Arunachal Pradesh would not have all been an Indian territory. When we come to the sequence of events of that fateful November in the Kameng Division we encounter that myths had been deliberately created to confuse the whole issue. The available evidence shows that in Kameng the Fourth Indian Army Division was not given a chance to fight by its own Commander, and the failure was entirely a local one. The Fourth Indian Division, contrary to the popular impression, was not out-weaponed. It had tanks and field guns which the Chinese did not have. It had enough supplies to hold back the Chinese for at least seven days. If it had done so it is doubtful whether the Chinese would have been able to sustain their campaign, and if it had held them back for those few days the history of the 1962 war would have been very different. In June 1972 General Chaudhuri himself expressed the view that available resources were not effectively utilised in 1962.[43]

Also incomprehensible was the decision not to use the Indian air force. The Chinese air force had very few MiG-19s then and it was not in a position to undertake air operations at that stage. In 1966 Air Chief Marshal Arjan Singh had recorded that the aircraft taking off from the high altitude air fields in Tibet would lose in their engine efficiency and consequently would have very limited weapon load and range. He also admitted that in 1962 we did not have much experience in these matters. If more attention had been paid to the course of the Sino-Soviet dispute, the impact of the withdrawal of Soviet technicians from China and if some effort had been specifically directed to assessing the operational capabilities of the Chinese air force, then it would have been evident in 1962 that there was no need to fear the superiority of the Chinese air power.

It is not necessary here to go into the details of the events that followed November 1962 which are now fairly well-known. Even at that stage Nehru had to fight hard against the forces which were anxious to move this country away from the path of non-alignment into the western camp. One may recall, in this connection, the request for the sharing of the "Voice of America" broadcast time, joint air defence exercises and so on. It is now part of history that in spite of our having fought a war with China, the United States was not willing to supply India lethal weapons. The American policy aimed at creating a tripwire force in India and keeping the decision-making in regard to the extent of their support in Washington. Our non-alignment policy came to our rescue, and it was possible to strengthen our military preparedness in the absence of any meaningful support from the United States.[44]

It is difficult to analyse what the Chinese were aiming to gain by their operations. However, the thesis that they acted in self-defence is absurd. In retrospect, the Chinese by their deep penetration into the Indian territory and thereafter withdrawing in Arunachal Pradesh, had validated the Indian title to Arunachal Pradesh. The long slice of land about 20 kilometres in width where they overran our check-posts and occupied in Ladakh was not worth the price of completely alienating India and triggering off a major Indian re-armament programme. Consequently, one should look for their motivation in political spheres. They may have aimed at toppling the Nehru government or at pushing India into the western camp in the hope of scoring a point vis-a-vis the Soviet Union in their ideological debate. In either case the Chinese appear to have failed in achieving their objectives. The Indian military humiliation was not a policy failure. The military Commander who failed had an excellent combat record and had been decorated earlier. This can only be characterised as one of those unforseeable random events of history.

This analysis would show that in the realm of broad concepts Nehru had an extraordinary correct assessment of the international situation, India's security situation and its requirements in terms of political and diplomatic support. He was farsighted in insisting on developing a defence production base in India. He had no emotional "blocks," as had been depicted popularly in the country, in regard to use of force in international relations. There is no reliable evidence to prove that he had ever stood in the way of any reasonable plans for augmenting the defence capacity of the country. Having said this, we must also look into the mistakes he committed.

Nehru talked of the equation of the defence and development, yet for reasons which are not clear, he permitted a dichotomy to be developed between defence and development and between "plan" and "non-plan" in this country; a dichotomy which appears to be purely bureaucratic in origin. He did not appear to have fully shared his perceptions regarding the international situation or the Indian security situation with his Cabinet colleagues or the bureaucracy (both civil and military). One cannot be sure whether these reservations originated because of his distrust of our elite with its avowed western orientation and his fears that his strategy of using the countervailing forces to ensure India's security would be thwarted by our elite. Considering the way in which our elite behaved in the months following that fateful October (1962), the way in which they denigrated Nehru's policies, and concealed the truth under an anti-Nehru propaganda barrage, one could perhaps see some justification for such fears on his part. Thirdly, he does not seem to have pursued vigorously the translation of his perceptions into policies and programmes. This particular weakness of Jawaharlal Nehru one comes across in other fields too, such as in the implementation of the five year plans, the organisation of the Congress Party, the administrative reforms and so on. It is quite possible that this fundamental weakness was perahps attributable to his being weighed down by the day-to-day burdens of his office and his own political and strategic thinking being far ahead of the main-stream of views in the country.

History will record that Jawaharlal Nehru's perception of India's problems of security was accurate. The policies he pursued were also perhaps the best under the circumstances. But he failed partly in their implementation and partly for reasons which could never have been anticipated, such as the local command failure in the 1962 war. If we take into account the magnitude of the crisis that India faced, it would seem that Nehru pulled her through it at a relatively low cost.

K. P. S. MENON

India and the Soviet Union

INDO-SOVIET COOPERATION is a comparatively recent development. Yet, some of its roots go back into the distant past. The first Russian, in fact the first European —for he preceded Vasco da Gama by a quarter of a century—to have come to India was one Afnasi Nikitin. After a journey which lasted three years—and not six hours as at present—he came to India and stayed in the Deccan for a number of years. He saw, observed, made notes, made friends, even made love and went back to Russia. To judge by his memoirs he was a humane and tolerant individual. He spoke of India with complete respect. He was a religious person, but he was tolerant and even appreciative of other religions. In fact, he forgot the date of Lent, when Christians are expected to fast, and so he decided to fast with the Muslims during their *Ramzan*. His memoirs conclude with the words: "God knows true faith, and the true faith is to know the one God and to call on his name in purity of heart in every place."

Afnasi Nikitin was thus very different from that breed of European adventurers, the Portuguese, who soon came to India with the sword in one hand and the Bible in the other.

In the 16th and 17th centuries, small colonies of Indian traders had settled on the ports of the Volga river. Peter the Great issued special decrees for the protection of Indian merchants; and Emperor Aurangzeb sent an elephant all the way to St. Petersburg as a present for Peter the Great. Thus, began, what a Pakistan newspaper called, "elephant diplomacy", when Jawaharlal Nehru sent two baby elephants, Ravi and Shashi, for the children of the Soviet Union. While sending them, Jawaharlal Nehru sent me a letter saying: "These are two Ambassadors of India to the Soviet Union, apart, of course, from yourself; only, they will be specially accredited to the children of the Soviet Union."

Some Indians seem to have done very well in Russia. There was one Mogun Mogundasov—a Russified form of his name, Mohan, son of Mohan Das—who settled in Astrakhan and had a large and lovely villa on the Caspian sea and a large fleet of sailing boats. I myself saw in Baku a fire-temple-cum caravanserai, where Indian traders have inscribed their names and addresses on the walls. In fact, in the eighteenth century, Indians were the carriers of a substantial part of the trade from India across the Persian gulf to the Caspian Sea and the Black Sea and beyond.

With the establishment of British dominion over India, all this intercourse came to an abrupt end. Then indeed an iron curtain rose between India and Russia, an iron curtain, established by Britain. Britain had good reason to keep India and Russia apart. Throughout the 19th century, one of the principal articles of British foreign policy was the so-called Russian bogey. Britain assumed that Russia, which began its march through Siberia to the Pacific Ocean in the 16th century and annexed even Alaska which an impecunious Tsar subsequently sold to the USA for seven million dollars; which reached the Black Sea and the Caspian Sea in the 18th century, and before which the decadent Khanates of Central Asia fell like ninepins in the 19th century, would not be content with anything less than dominion over India. It was to forestall this that Britain fought three wars against Afghanistan. And when in 1917, the Russian bogey put on the red cloak of communism, it looked all the more terrible; and it was thought essential to save India—and the British Empire—from what Churchill called "the foul baboonery of Communism." Hence the iron curtain.

Yet, across the iron curtain flowed ideas, the ideas of the Great October Revolution. Despite the iron curtain some remarkable men too went to the Soviet Union. One of them was Rabindranath Tagore who went to Russia in 1930 and waxed almost ecstatic over what he saw. Tagore was particularly impressed with the progress of literacy and education in the Soviet Union. Comparing civilisation with an oil lamp, he said that from time immemorial the lamp of civilization used to shed its illumination upwards. Only the upper tenth was lighted up; the remaining nine tenths, symbolizing what we in our superiority used to call the lower orders, remained in darkness. After the Great October Revolution, said Tagore, an attempt was being made to light up the entire lamp, that is, the entire society with the flame of knowledge. It is this passage from Tagore, which impelled me to call one of my books on Russia, *The Lamp and the Lampstand.*

Jawaharlal Nehru visited the Soviet Union in 1927. He was greatly impressed with some things which he saw and repelled by others. He felt convinced, however, that a great human experiment was being performed in Russia and that, in any case, Russia and India could not afford to be enemies. India, he said, was an Asian country. So was the Soviet Union, sprawling over Asia and Europe. "Between two such neighbours," said Nehru, "there can be amity or enmity; indifference is out of the question." And from the moment he became Prime Minister, he sought to establish amity between India and the USSR; and neither country has had reason to regret it.

As soon as Jawaharlal Nehru became Prime Minister and, in fact, even earlier, as soon as he formed the interim Government of India in September 1946, he sought to establish diplomatic relations with the USSR. The alacrity with which the Soviet government responded to his overtures and agreed to exchange diplomatic representatives even before India became formally independent showed that even at that time the Soviet government appreciated the potential, geo-political importance of India. Towards the Government of India itself, the Soviet government had, as we shall presently see, some reservations.

To Jawaharlal Nehru, amity with the USSR was part of his plan to establish amity with all nations, regardless of their ideological antipathies. These antipathies, and especially the antipathy between the United States and the Soviet Union had been kept well under control during the war with Germany. Now that the common enemy had been humbled, these animosities flared out afresh and took the form of an intense cold war.

Many factors contributed to this development. Communism overflowed into Eastern Europe. It was because of this fear that Chruchill wanted to launch the second front through the Balkans, "the soft underbelly of Europe," instead of through France, but was overruled by Roosevelt and Stalin. The United States government abruptly stopped all lendlease assistance to the Soviet Union though the USSR needed greater assistance for relief and rehabilitation than any other country, because it had suffered far more grievous losses. The Soviet army arrested sixteen emigre Polish leaders who had appeared on the scene with the blessings of the western powers to establish a "bourgeois" government in Poland. Instead, it helped the establishment of a communist government of Poland. Above all, America refused to share with Russia, its war-time ally, the secret of the atom bomb. In announcing the discovery of the atom bomb, President Truman took even God's name and thanked Him for having placed the secret in America's hands and not in the hands of its enemies. God, however, proved to be impartial. Before long He placed the secret of the atom bomb and the hydrogen bomb in Soviet hands also.

It was at this stage that India became independent. Jawaharlal Nehru knew that the cold war was but a passing phase in history, as confirmed by the recent rapproachement between the Great Powers. But he also knew that it was a dangerous phase and that, if it was allowed to escalate into a hot war, it might cause incalculable damage to civilization in this nuclear age. He, therefore, was determined to keep away from it and do whatever he could to assuage the bitterness of what he called "the mobilised antagonism" between the Soviet and American blocs.

On the eve of my departure for China as India's first Ambassador to that country, Nehru sent me a note dated January 2, 1947, for my guidance. It dealt with a variety of matters and also contained a broad enunciation of his foreign policy. Nehru wrote:

Our general policy is to avoid entanglement in power politics and not to join any group of powers as against any other group. The two leading groups today are the Russian bloc and the Anglo-American bloc. We must be friendly to both and yet not join either. Both America and Russia are extraordinarily suspicious of each other as well as of other countries. This makes our path difficult and we may well be suspected by each of leaning towards the other. This cannot be helped.

Our foreign policy will ultimately be governed by our internal policy. That policy is far from being Communistic and is certainly opposed to the Communist Party of India. Nevertheless, there is a great and growing feeling in India in favour of some kind of vague socialist order of society. There is much goodwill for

America and expectation of help from her in many fields, especially technical. There is also a great deal of sympathy for the work of the Soviet Union and the remarkable change that this has brought about among the people. The Soviet Union, being our neighbour, we shall inevitably develop close relations with it. We cannot afford to antagonize Russia merely because we think that this may irritate someone else. Nor indeed can we antagonize the USA.

Here, in a nutshell, was Nehru's foreign policy, which has come to be called the policy of non-alignment. From the beginning this policy was somehow distasteful to the United States of America, whereas the Soviet Union came gradually to understand it, to appreciate it and even to support it.

Not to start with, though. The diehards in the Soviet Union had grave misgivings as to how far India was and would remain truly independent; their misgivings were confirmed when India decided to remain in the Commonwealth. Soon after this decision was announced, Mr. Novikov, Soviet Ambassador to India, came and saw me and told me: "Today is a sad day for India and the world." But before long the Soviet Union completely changed its attitude towards India remaining in the Commonwealth.

II

A serious obstacle in the way of Indo-Soviet friendship in the early stages was the Soviet misunderstanding of the Indian struggle for independence and its leader, Mahatma Gandhi. Lenin himself had a juster appreciation of both. Lenin thought that Mahatma Gandhi was essentially a revolutionary leader. M.N. Roy, however, differed from him and argued with him that Gandhi must be reckoned not as a revolutionary but as a reactionary. In Roy's own words: "The role of Gandhi was the crucial point of difference between Lenin and myself. Lenin believed that as the inspirer and leader of a mass movement, Gandhi was revolutionary. I maintained that as a religious and cultural revivalist he was bound to be a reactionary socially, however revolutionary he might appear otherwise." After further arguments, Lenin said: "We are exploring new ground and we should suspend final judgment pending practical experience." Unfortunately, towards the latter part of Stalin's regime, it was M.N. Roy's view which prevailed.

Mahatma Gandhi was then described in the Great Soviet Encyclopaedia thus: "A reactionary who hails from the Bania caste—betrayed the people and helped the imperialists against them; aped the ascetics; pretended, in a demogogic way, to be a supporter of Indian independence and an enemy of the British and widely exploited religious prejudices."

In my first year in Moscow I used to go to the Foreign Office and protest against the Soviet attitude towards Mahatma Gandhi. I would ask them how they could expect the friendship of India as long as they held, the Father of our nation in such derision. Invariably the answer which I got was that for every single disparaging reference to Gandhi in the Soviet Union there were a hundred disparaging references to Lenin and Stalin in the Indian press. This, of course, was no answer, for while the Soviet press generally echoed the Soviet government's views the Indian press took delight in differing from the views of the government. However, it was no use arguing with the Soviet authorities. All one could do was, to put it bluntly, to wait in patience for Stalin to pass.

To say so, however, is not altogether fair to Stalin. Towards the end of his life Stalin himself appeared to relent towards India. He had declined to receive Mrs. Pandit, our first Ambassador to the USSR, but he readily received her successor, Dr. S. Radhakrishnan, and also myself.

Our attitude during the Korean war seems to have impressed Stalin. Throughout the war India showed that, by following a policy of non-alignment, she could be a factor for peace. At the same time, she showed that non-alignment did not mean neutrality or indifference to right and wrong. My own first encounter with the cold war was in Korea at the end of 1947, when I was appointed Member of the United Nations Commission on Korea and elected its Chairman. The task assigned to us was to try and unify Korea; and, in my report to the United Nations I made an appeal to the great powers to let Korea be united. If the unification of Korea is blocked, I said: "Korea may blow up, and that may be the beginning of a vaster cataclysm for Asia and the world."

In 1950, the first part of this dire prophecy came true. Korea blew up. When war borke out, India had no hesitation in voting in favour of the American resolution declaring North Korea the aggressor, for, from the facts at our disposal, we were convinced that it was the North Korean troops who had invaded South Korea. "This", said Mr. Loy Henderson, the American Ambassador to India, to Sir Girja Shankar Bajpai, "is the day I have been waiting for." Henderson assumed that, by voting for the American resolution, India had aligned herself on the American side in the world-wide contest between capitalism and communism. Before long, however, he was disillusioned. India's main concern was that the war should not assume wider dimensions. Nehru made an appeal to Stalin as well as to Truman and received a warm and forthright response from Stalin.

An opportunity for a peaceful settlement presented itself when General MacArthur cleared South Korea of the North Korean invaders; but, intoxicated by his victory and without authorisation from the United Nations under whom he was supposed to be acting, General MacArthur crossed the 38th parallel into North Korea and pushed towards the Yalu River, separating Korea and China. China then gave a warning that if General MacArthur proceeded further, China would have no alternative but to intervene. In fact Chou En-lai woke up K.M. Panikkar, our Ambassador to China, at midnight and conveyed this warning to him clearly to be communicated to the western powers, for at that time India was the only link between the east and the west in Peking. We transmitted this warning in all earnestness, but the Americans pooh-poohed it. Would China have the temerity to take on the mightiest power on earth? China did. Then there was a fierce outcry in the USA. There was even a demand for the use of the atom bomb. American troops were mown down in thousands and pushed south of the 38th parallel. The Americans suffered some 140,000 casualities, including nearly 50,000 dead, and John Foster Dulles comforted his countrymen by saying that if the American casualties had been heavy, even heavier were the Korean casualties: one out of every three Koreans, he said, was dead.

Even at this stage Jawaharlal Nehru used his influence to stop the war and to have a general conference for easing the situation in the Far East. Britain was favourably inclined to this proposal, but the United States wrecked it by bringing forward a resolution in the United Nations declaring China the aggressor. India voted against it, because in reality it was General MacArthur who was the aggressor in North Korea.

The war went on inconclusively for the next three years. India still strove to bring about a cease-fire in Korea. The final negotiations were held up over a hitch in the repatriation of prisoners of war. In order to remove this last hitch, Krishna Menon, our permanent representative to the United Nations, brought forward a formula which was accepted by the entire General Assembly with the exception of the Soviet bloc. Vyshinsky, the fiery representative of the Soviet Union, denounced India for putting forth this formula. "At best" he said, "you Indians are dreamers and idealists; at worst instruments of horrible American policy."

The fact is that there was a situation in which Stalin took a macabre pleasure. Here were Americans, Chinese, North Koreans and South Koreans merrily killing one another, and not a Russian soldier was involved. It was exactly the kind of situation which developed in Indo-China later. There, South Vietnamese, North Vietnamese and the Americans and their allies, Australians, South Koreans, Britishers and Philippinoes, were killing one another and not a Chinese was involved. But, soon after Stalin's death, the very formula which Vyshinsky had so fiercely denounced, was accepted and the war in Korea came to an end.

I have dwelt on the Korean war at some length because it was an acid test of India's foreign policy. The Soviet government now understood better, and recognised the policy of non-alignment as a factor for peace. The Soviet attitude was very different from that of the United States. The attitude of the American policy-makers was bluntly expressed by John Foster Dulles, who called the policy of non-alignment "short-sighted and immoral." In saying so he was practically overruling his own chief, President Eisenhower, who was perspicacious enough to see, and gracious enough to say, that non-alignment did not mean indifference to right and wrong and that it was after all a policy which had been followed by America itself for a hundred years.

George Washington, in his farewell address, had said: "Observe good faith and justice towards all nations and cultivate peace and harmony with all." He had also asked that the United States of America should refrain from "cultivating permanent inveterate antipathies against particular nations and passionate attachments for others." Jefferson, in his inaugural address, had defined American policy more succinctly thus: "Peace, commerce and honest friendship with all nations—entangling alliances with none."

The policy of John Foster Dulles was the very reverse of Washington's and Jefferson's. It was a policy of entangling alliances. How entangling alliances with weaker countries could be to both sides was shown both in Vietnam and in Bangladesh. In Vietnam there was the spectacle, which would have been comic if it had not been tragic, of the creatures of the USA in Vietnam seeking to dictate to the President of the United States and to plunging the whole country into a mess. The entangling alliance of the United States with the military dictatorship in Pakistan has not done Pakistan or itself any good. Pakistan lost half its territory and the USA lost a good deal of prestige by ranging itself on the wrong side in a war for freedom.

At the end of the Korean war the Soviet Union realized that India was determined to follow an independent policy even if it remained in the Commonwealth. Prime Minister Bulganin told me that he and his colleagues fully appreciated India's position in the Commonwealth and hoped that India would continue to remain in it. By that time, they realised that India would not allow her freedom of action to be curbed or hampered by her membership of the Commonwealth. On the contrary, India acted as a useful link between the communist and the capitalist blocs. Some Americans were worried over India's growing influence in the Commonwealth and in the world. There used to be a gibe in America at that time that Eisenhower followed Macmillan, Macmillan followed Nehru, Nehru followed Mao Tse-tung, and therefore Eisenhower followed Mao!

Another interesting development was the reassessment of Mahatma Gandhi by Soviet scholars and statesmen. I could hardly believe my ears when, at the 20th Congress of the Communist Party of the Soviet Union in 1956, Kekkonan, the veteran Communist leader confessed that the Soviet estimate of Gandhi was mistaken and that he was one of the great liberators of mankind. Before long the offending passage about Gandhi was deleted, and the sketches of other Indian leaders in the Great Soviet Encyclopaedia were also revised.

III

In other ways, too, the 20th Congress proved to be a landmark in the relations between India and the Soviet Union. Indeed, it should also have been a landmark in the relations between the east and the west, but for the stubbornness of John Foster Dulles and men of his way of thinking. At that Congress, peaceful co-existence was declared as the main goal of Soviet foreign policy. In order to ensure this, even some of the fundamental maxims of Marx were modified. Marx had laid down that war was inevitable. He had envisaged the future of mankind as a series of wars, each more terrible than the previous one, and a final cataclysm in which capitalism would be utterly destroyed and communism would triumph. And history seemed to confirm this view. As a result of the first world war a sixth of mankind went communist; and as a result of the second world war a fourth of mankind went communist. Why, all that was necessary was to have a few more wars and the world would be delightfully communist! In the meantime, an epoch-making event had occurred. Man had discovered the atom bomb. Man had discovered something which, if he was not careful, might be the engine of his own destruction. The Soviet government had the wisdom to realise the awful potentialities of an atom war and this, more than anything else, caused them to modify the old axiom that war is inevitable.

Another axiom used to be that violence was essential for the transformation of society. This theory, again, was modified. Perhaps the visit of the Soviet leaders to India in the autumn of 1955 might have had an effect on their minds. Here they saw a country which had proclaimed a socialistic pattern of society as its goal and was progressing, however, slowly and hesitantly, towards that goal, eschewing violence. The 20th Congress declared that not only was violence not essential to the attainment of socialism, but that in certain circumstances socialism could be reached through the parliamentary method.

All this had an effect on Indo-Soviet relations. In one sentence, it may be said that the 20th Congress removed the ideological impediments in the way of the free development of friendship and cooperation between India and the Soviet Union.

We have seen that during the first few years after independence there were various misunderstandings on the part of Russia. These were not confined to one side. Many Indians, too, had grossly distorted ideas of the Soviet Union and its policy. To some extent, this was a hang-over from the British period, when India was subjected to ceaseless anti-Soviet propaganda. It was also the outcome of the fear and hatred, on the part of the vested interests, of a country which was out to destroy capitalism and all forms of exploitation of man by man.

Let me mention an incident to show how the suspicion towards the Soviet Union was shared even by intelligent people. When I was Foreign Secretary the first trade agreement with the USSR was concluded. The draft of the agreement was prepared in our Ministry and sent to other ministries, including the Home ministry for their approval. In the draft agreement there was a provision for the exchange of experts and technical personnel. On receiving the draft H.V.R. Iengar, then Home Secretary, came into my room and said: "KPS, what have you done? Exchange of experts and technical personnel with Russia: under the cover of this clause hundreds of Soviet spies and saboteurs will enter India and wreck our entire economic build up." I told him that his fears were groundless. At that time the Home ministry was in charge of that man of iron, Sardar Patel. Nevertheless, our ministry had its way, and the clause relating to exchange of experts and technical personnel was retained intact. Since then thousands of Soviet experts and technical personnel have come and stayed and worked in India; and there has not been even the whisper of a suspicion that any of them has indulged in any undesirable activities. In fact, they were even prepared to acquiesce in our law of prohibition. How difficult that is for a Russian you can imagine.

Before very long, HVR's own eyes were opened to the realities of the international situation. In 1952 I was posted to Moscow and H.V.R. Iengar was transferred from the Home ministry to the Commerce Ministry as Secretary. I received a letter from him saying that he had been trying to get the services of a particular kind of specialist in steel for Tata's Steel Works. He had been going hat in hand to the British and the Americans, but without any result. Would I, he asked, approach the Soviet Government for the services of such and such, a steel specialist? I did so, and within a fortnight a Soviet specialist arrived in India. He did his work within the stipulated time and went back to the Soviet Union.

Before very long there came an offer from the Soviet government to build a steel project for us. It took the western world by surprise. The Delhi correspondent of the London *Times* sent a telegram to London saying that a "snap decision" had been taken by the Indian cabinet to accept the Soviet offer. In fact, it was not a snap decision, but a well considered decision on the part of Jawaharlal Nehru.

Nehru knew that steel was the barometer of a country's strength. He thought that it was essential for India to have a steel project. We approached Great Britain, the United States and West Germany, but none of them was interested. It was then that we approached the Soviet Union, and it was after the Soviet Union had made its offer to build a metallurgical plant at Bhilai that Britain came forward to put up one at Durgapur and West Germany at Rourkela. "If there had been no Bhilai", said Dr. V.K.R.V. Rao, "there would have been no Durgapur and no Rourkela."

Subsequently, in order to show our impartiality towards the Great Powers, we approached America for assistance to set up the fourth steel project at Bokaro. After months of shilly-shallying, the USA refused to help, because of its antipathy to the public sector. And then the Soviet Union stepped in and offered to build the project at Bokaro. The Bhilai metallurgical project, originally designed for one million tonnes, has been progressing impressively, and now it is proposed to expand it to seven million tonnes.

It had long been acknowledged that India had desposits of coal, iron and manganese which could last for a thousand years. It was, however, thought that India was deficient in oil. Some Indian scientists thought otherwise. We therefore approached western experts to explore for oil. They did so, or professed to do so, and reported that they could find no oil. We then approached the Soviet authorities and Soviet experts have found oil of good quality in abundant quantities in the very region which other experts had pronounced as bereft of oil.

Throughout India there are many monuments of Indo-Soviet economic cooperation. Suffice it to say that 30 per cent of India's steel, 35 per cent of our oil, 20 per cent of our electrical power, 65 per cent of heavy electrical equipment and 85 per cent of our heavy machine-making machines are produced in projects set up with Soviet aid.

In the cultural field, again, there were initial difficulties. The Communists held rigid views on art, particularly in Stalin's time. When the first delegation of Indian artists came to Moscow soon after I went there, a western colleague of mine told me that it was a very risky thing to have invited our artists to Moscow. Moscow he said, believed only in one kind of painting, the realistic type; all else was trash. Our Indian painters, on the contrary, belonged to all schools, realistic, surrealistic, impressionistic, cubist and so on. They follow no laws; they are a law unto themselves. Yet, the delegation had a most enthusiastic reception both at the hands of experts and the common people. I remember the remark entered in the visitors' book by a Soviet citizen. "This exhibition", he said, "is a breath of fresh air in a suffocating room."

Several cultural delegations came from the Soviet Union to India in 1953 and 1954. Then there appeared, in the London *Times*, a report from its correspondent in Delhi with the title "the Soviet Union woos India; the Soviet Union is making a cultural onslaught on India comparable to saturation bombing in conventional warfare." On the day on which that report appeared we happened to give a farewell dinner to a Soviet cultural delegation, which included that peerless ballerina, Plisetskaya. In the course of my toast I referred to this report and said that anyhow the Soviet "onslaught" on India would not cause such havoc as the bombing of North Korea was doing at that very moment; but I said, even the ballerinas might do some mischief: they might leave a few broken hearts behind.

I wonder what the *Times* and its correspondent could now think of the sustained "cultural onslaught" of India on the Soviet Union and vice versa. There is a comprehensive cultural exchange agreement, covering almost every field of human activity, on a state-to-state basis. There is also a more modest agreement between the Indo-Soviet Cultural Society in India and the Soviet-Indian Friendship Society in the USSR.

The cooperation between India and the Soviet Union was not confined to the cultural and economic fields, but extended to the political field as well. On all matters connected with colonialism, India and the Soviet Union have taken an identical stand in the United Nations. In matters affecting India's territorial integrity, the Soviet Union has stood by India. One remembers how furious the western representatives in the Security Council were when India, after fifteen years of patient waiting, integrated Goa into India with the merest show of force. Adlai Stevenson, the American representative in the UN made a particularly nasty speech. Indeed, the western powers would have dubbed India the aggressor but for the fear of the Soviet veto. In fairness it must be admitted that Adlai Stevenson later regretted his effusion in the Security Council. In *The Complete Speeches of Adlai Stevenson,* the speech which he made on Goa was left out.

The Soviet Union has stood by India over Kashmir and used its veto in the Security Council on more than one occasion. The Soviet Union had no hesitation in recognising Kashmir as an integral part of India, unlike China, which remained on the fence even in the *"Hindi Chini Bhai Bhai"* days.

India's gravest problem has been her relations with China. Here, throughout the fifties, the Soviet Union had to be cautious, because it was bound to China by a treaty of alliance. Moreover, "the monolithic solidarity of the communist camp was the rule. When the Soviet Union criticised China, it criticised Albania; and when China had to criticise the Soviet Union, it criticised Yugoslavia." Both followed the well-known Bengali proverb, "If you want your daughter-in-law to behave, beat your daughter."

The first blood on the Sino-Indian frontier was shed in 1959, when seven Indian policemen were shot by the Chinese. At that time, the rift between the Soviet Union and China still lay below the surface. All that the Soviet Union could say and did say was that it hoped that "fraternal China" and "friendly India" would settle their problems amicably without external interference. The Chinese were furious because, for the first time, a communist State had equated a communist and a non-communist country. Strangely enough, some people in India were also annoyed, or pretended to be annoyed. After all, they said, China was a brother to the Soviet Union whereas India was only a friend; and blood was thicker than water. If things became worse, they predicted, the Soviet Union would willy nilly be on China's side. In saying so, they forgot the common experience of a man often preferring a friendly stranger to a cantankerous relation.

The controversy at that time reminded me of an interesting incident in the life of Sir C. Sankaran Nair, who presided over the Indian National Congress in 1897 and was Education Member of the Viceroy's Council during the first World War. One of his portfolios was "ecclesiastical affairs", which dealt with the Christian church in India. On the first anniversary of the outbreak of the first World War, the Education Secretary, Sir Edward Maclagan, submitted to Sir Sankaran Nair, the draft of a prayer to be read in all the Christian churches in India. It implored Jesus Christ to bestow victory on the Allies and to crush the enemies. Sir Sankaran Nair said that he knew something of Jesus Christ. Jesus Christ was not the man who would take sides in a war. It was Jesus Christ who said: "He who taketh up the sword shall perish by the sword." He therefore refused to sign the draft prayer. Thereupon, the Secretary exercised his right of taking the matter up to the Viceroy. The Viceroy, Lord Chelmsford told Sir Sankaran Nair that he had always been interested in ecclesiastical affairs; would Sir Sankaran mind if he took up the ecclesiastical portfolio? Sir Sankaran said that he had no objection whatever. There was, however, a curious sequel. The Roman Catholic Archbishop of Simla wrote a letter to the *Statesman* objecting to the Viceroy handling ecclesiastical affairs and saying that any day he would prefer "a cultured Hindu rather than a bigoted Protestant." Similarly, I felt certain that the Soviet Union would prefer a cultured India to a bigoted China.

IV

We have glanced briefly at the growth of the cultural, political and economic relations between India and the Soviet Union. A comparatively later development has been their cooperation in the military field. China's wanton attack on India in 1962 convinced India of the need for strengthening her defences. Hitherto, India had proceeded on the assumption that she had no enemies. Indeed, at a great banquet in the Kremlin in 1955, during Jawaharlal Nehru's historic visit to the Soviet Union, Nehru said so in reply to the toast of Prime Minister Bulganin. "Mr. Prime Minister", said Bulganin, "we, Soviet people, if we are friends, we are friends unto death; and if we are enemies we are enemies unto death." Nehru warmly reciprocated his sentiment of friendship and added, "We, Mr. Prime Minister, have no enemies". Since then we have had some lessons in the play of power politics.

China's attack in 1962 had opened India's eyes to the need for strengthening her defences. India first turned to the USA for help. Y.B. Chavan, the then Defence Minister himself led a mission to America. To his surprise, America was unresponsive. Instead of giving the arms and equipment which India so sorely needed America preached a homily that India's first concern must be to strengthen her economic position and that nothing should be allowed to deflect India's energies in this respect. They also said that American naval equipment was too delicate to be handled by Indians; and that if any jet planes were to be supplied they would have to be paid for in dollars. Chavan then went to Britain. There too he met with a cold reception. Britain would not supply even an old submarine of which we were in need. The fact is that Britain and the United States were afraid of hurting the sentiments of their ally, Pakistan. Chavan then proceeded to the USSR and got all that he wanted—and more. Not only did the Soviet Union supply the MiG aircrafts but it has also helped India to set up a plant for their manufacture.

The fact that we, unlike Pakistan, could ourselves make many kinds of arms and equipment made all the difference during the war with Pakistan in 1971. What enabled us to score so decisive a victory over Pakistan was not merely the superior strategy of our Generals and the heroism of our soldiers, but the fact that industrially we were stronger than Pakistan. In our industrial development we have had assistance from many countries. Soviet assistance, however, was directed precisely to those vital sectors which would make India strong and self-sufficient.

Why has the Soviet Union helped India so readily and ungrudgingly? Not because of altruism. One cannot expect any country to regulate its relations with other countries on the basis of altruism. The simple reason is that the Soviet Union needs India, and India needs the Soviet Union. The friendship of the second largest state in Asia is of value to the Soviet Union, especially because of the antipathy and the hegemonistic ambitions of the largest state in Asia, China. Moreover, friendship for India was implicit in the Revolution of 1917. The objective of the Great October Revolution was to establish communism. Communism, however, could not be established without eliminating capitalism; and imperialism, as Lenin said, is "the highest stage of capitalism." Anti-imperialism, therefore, lay at the root of Soviet policy.

The keynote of the Indian struggle for independence, too was anti-imperialism. By the time India became independent, imperialism was already on the run. After that, within a decade almost all countries in Asia and Europe freed themselves politically from the clutches of imperialism. Politically, but not economically. In some countries the former imperialist powers have managed to stage a come-back through economic means; and all countries have to be on their guard against the machinations and instrusions of what may be called economic imperialism. Indeed, India herself has had to struggle against it in various fields, such as the development of her oil resources.

Lenin, the architect of the Revolution of 1917, stipulated that it would be the duty of the Soviet state to help other countries to stand on their own feet. In his instructions to the first Soviet Ambassador to Iran and Afghanistan in 1921 he said: "Our eastern policy remains diametrically opposed to that of the imperialist countries. In our eastern policy we strive to promote the independent economic and political development of the eastern peoples and shall do everything in our power to support them in this respect. Our role and our mission is to be neutral and disinterested friends and allies of peoples struggling for a completely independent economic and political development." In helping India, successive Soviet governments, regardless of changes in personnel, have been acting in accordance with Lenin's views.

The common aversion to imperialism on the part of India and the Soviet Union found expression during the Bangladesh crisis. It is sometimes forgotten that imperialism need not be necessarily white; it can be black or brown and equally ruthless. Rabindranath Tagore, who was a great admirer of ancient Japanese civilisation, deplored the conduct of Japan in imitating western imperialism and subjugating Korea and trying to subjugate China. In strong words he cried out against Japanese imperialism, saying that "Japan showed that the bloodhounds of Satan can be kennelled not merely in Europe but domesticated in Asia and fed with man's miseries."

In 1971, in Bangladesh, there was staged the latest act of arrogant colonialism, which even had racial overtones. When seventy-five million Bengalees, who had been discriminated against, humiliated and exploited by West Pakistan to its own advantage or rather, to the advantage of its notorious twenty-two multi-millionaire families for quarter of a century, rose in revolt, the Government of West Pakistan let loose an orgy of repression of Hitlerian proportions. Some three million Bengalees were murdered in cold blood, 300,000 women were assaulted and raped; and ten million people were forced to leave their homes and flee to India. And the world looked on. One great power not only looked on, but seemed to abet and assist Pakistan; another great power started making noises across the Himalayas; and two great powers chose to sit on the fence. India seemed almost isolated. It was at that time that the Soviet Union came to the rescue, and we signed the Treaty of Peace, Friendship and Cooperation. Though it was signed at a critical hour, the foundations for the Treaty had been laid during the period covered by this article.

V

Such has been the story, I nearly said the saga, of Indo-Soviet relations. It is an offshoot, the finest offshoot, of the Indian policy of non-alignment. Though this policy has an enduring value, it was devised at a time when the world was divided into two military-political blocs, led by the two super-powers which had come into being after World War II. But by the end of Jawaharlal Nehru's life cracks had already begun to appear in the blocs. France, under De Gaulle began to walk on a path of its own choice; and Pakistan, began to veer towards China, against whom the CENTO and SEATO Pacts (of which it professed to be a loyal member) were designed. President Ayub Khan spoke of Pakistan's "triangular diplomacy"—this tight-rope walking between China, the USA and the USSR. Some of our own people used to think that Pakistan's diplomacy was much more adroit than ours. The net result of Pakistan's diplomacy, however, was that Ayub Khan lost his job, Yahya Khan lost his freedom and Pakistan lost half its territory.

China's onslaught on India in 1962 robbed the policy of non-alignment of some of its magic. To start with, the policy of non-alignment was so successful that it lulled us into a sense of security. We began to think that we had only to be good to others for others to be good to us. We now realised that the law of the jungle still prevailed in international relations; and this has instilled greater realism into our foreign as well as defence policies.

Does this mean that non-alignment is no longer valid? What, after all, is non-alignment? Basically it means the right of a country to ask itself, whenever it is confronted by an important international issue, not who is right, but what is right. All countries would like to put this question to themselves, but not all countries are in a position to do so. From whichever point of view you look at India, whether from the standpoint of size, location, population, resources or tradition, India must have this right and continue to exercise it.

The refusal of India to align itself with this or that philosophy or system is entirely consistent with her immemorial tradition. We have never believed in the concept of a "jealous God." We have never believed in an exclusive revelation. Let me quote two *slokas* from the Gita, which strike the keynote of our internal policy, known as secularism or non-discrimination towards people following different religions and our external policy, called non-alignment.

> *ye'py anyadevatābhaktā*
> *yajante 'sradhayā' nvitah*
> *te' pi mām ev kaunteya*
> *yajanty avidhipūrvakam*

There Krishna says that even a man who worships alien gods, though this is contrary to the scriptures, will come to Me, provided he worships in good faith.

Again,

> *yāvān artha uḍapane*
> *sarvataḥ samplutodake*
> *tāvān sarveṣu vedeṣu*
> *brāhmaṇasya vijānatah*

That is, a man who thinks that all truth is contained in the Vedas is like a man who thinks that all the water of the world is contained in a pond, when the whole countryside is flooded.

How can we, who do not feel that even the Vedas are the sole repository of truth, believe that all truth is contained in the Bible, the Koran, Karl Marx or John Stuart Mill? How could we have joined, or professed to join, the holy crusade of John Foster Dulles to save Christian civilization from the ungodly creed of communism, or vice versa? No: that would have been out of tune with our entire philosophical background. It is a matter for satisfaction that the Soviet Union, at any rate, has understood, appreciated and even reinforced our policy.

SURJIT MANSINGH

India and the United States

IF A MAP of the world is projected with India in the centre, the North American continent appears as two narrow strips along the extreme eastern and western circumference. A map like this illustrates the geographical fact that India and the United States of America are at opposite sides of the globe, and the psychological fact that one barely impinges on the consciousness of the other's population. Contacts between them are the result of human endeavour rather than natural circumstance. Intimate involvement is inhibited by mutual ignorance or stereotyped images of each other which are mostly negative. Different histories, cultures, and life styles sharpen the variance of perspectives on the world gained from their respective geographic locations.

Notwithstanding the recent use of "patriotic" world maps in Indian and American schools, educated adults of both countries probably studied standard Mercator projections centred on the Greenwich meridian, from which the expressions of America as west and Asia as east are derived. Links of language and political institutions, once again derived from Britain and adapted in America and India to local needs, foster the belief that interchanges and cooperation between the two peoples are mutually desirable. Occasionally it is urged that India is vital for American security, or that the United States is vital for Indian development. In 1963-64 there was even brief talk of an alliance between them. Yet both countries survive the indifference or the near-hostility which became obvious in 1971-72.

No consensus of opinion exists on an "optimum" or "normal" relationship between India and the United States of America. Neither State has been able to gain from the other its maximum, if unstated, demands. Americans would have liked an uncritical, undemanding ally in India, internally stable and providing an open profitable market for private American enterprise. Indians have wanted from America friendship without attempted dominance or pressure, support for India's international aspirations and large scale assistance without political or emotional strings attached. Each government has adjusted to having expectations from the other unfulfilled, but not without expressing disappointment Their moments of forthcomingness have not always coincided. Thus, any survey of Indo-American relations is obliged to take into account fluctuations and frustrations. There has been an enormous verbal output, published and unpublished, attempting to explain why the two countries have failed to achieve harmony, or how their real cooperative achievements could be extended. Many Indians and Americans share an assumption that they are committed to common goals in the world and that only the methods pursued by their governments towards these goals differ, and have created misunderstandings. Others challenge such an assumption, finding good reason to doubt US commitment to peace or Indian commitment to democracy. A great number of people in both countries are essentially isolationist and are willing to write off continents on the opposite side of the globe as unimportant to their lives.

The fact remains, however, that in the latter half of the twentieth century objective conditions preclude the possibility of India or America ignoring each other. This was obvious after the Seocnd World War when the two states were growing into new positions in the international community—the US as a superpower, and India as the largest nation to gain independence from European colonialism. Their dealings with each other in these early post-war years began tentatively, developed in content and intensity during the early 1950's, and soon acquired emotional overtones which remained despite the establishment of strong links in the late 1950's and early 1960's. By the time of Jawaharlal Nehru's death in 1964 the international scene, India, and the United States had all changed considerably from what they were in 1946 when he headed the Interim Government and ambassadors were exchanged between

New Delhi and Washington. But subsequent events demonstrated that Indo-American relations continued to be as multifaceted and unpredictable as they had been during the Nehru Era with which this paper is concerned.

II

The Indian side of the equation was dominated by Nehru. He was the architect and chief executive of Indian foreign policy and enjoyed an unusual freedom in constructing its main pillars. Nehru had been the acknowledged spokesman for the Congress on international problems since the mid 1930's; his views on the world and India's place in it were not disputed by Cabinet colleagues or career diplomats after independence and were criticised in Parliament or the press for specific applications rather than their general sweep. His foreign policy of non-alignment, anti-colonialism, racial equality, and peaceful solution of conflicts was widely supported in India, being consistent with its national movement and desire for international recognition. Nehru's ambiguous feelings about the United States too were representative ones. For example: warm friendship for individuals was combined with fastidious distaste for Americans as a group; admiration for American dynamism and technology was coupled with mistrust of their ability to use power and disdain for their flaunting of wealth; curiosity about the American achievement was accompanied by the desire to have Indian achievements admired too.[1]

Nehru recognised his loss in not having got to know the country and common people of America as a young man; more, that he had been constrained from visiting President Franklin D. Roosevelt in 1942. He referred to that as a "great opportunity" which he had allowed to pass and regretted so many times since.[2] Undoubtedly, because in that year Roosevelt ceased his efforts to persuade the British Prime Minister, Winston Churchill to satisfy the demands of Indian nationalists and did not replace his personal representative Louis Johnson in Delhi, and concentrated entirely on accelerating the Allied war effort, including stationing America's troops in India. Nehru was well aware of American contribution to the Cripps mission negotiations and the effect of Gandhi's statements on the war and the Quit India movement in the United States; American public opinion towards the Indian national movement was transformed from sympathetic support to open opposition.[3] Nehru's disappointment at this first shattering of expectations from the US can perhaps be gauged from the fact that he did not publicly speak of it in America even when discoursing on his experiences before independence.

While it is difficult to assess accurately psychological influences on state policy, there is little doubt that Nehru was not his most charming self when first meeting important Americans. There seems to have been a certain defensiveness of manner, a reserve, which made him "prickly" and inhibited his frankness. A desire to preserve personal dignity and forego the initiative was, of course, most obvious in the matter of requesting or acknowledging any kind of assistance. Nehru was also sensitive to political atmosphere, especially anything that smacked of militarism or fanaticism. He visited the United States first in 1949 when fears of "communist infiltration" were becoming a public issue. He was there again in 1956 and must have witnessed the power of what President Eisenhower depicted as the "military-industrial complex." And at the time of his last visit in 1961, the Bay of Pigs (Cuba) scandal was still fresh. With the wisdom of documented hindsight we can surmise that Nehru instinctively reacted against the obsession with national security in American politics.

High placed Indians, knowledgeable about the process by which a British trading company had created an Empire, were suspicious about the nascent imperialism of large corporations investing in underdeveloped countries and of military bases abroad, for both loomed large in American foreign relations. Periodic statements of intent of progressive socialization were issued from India, and some industries were reserved for the public sector; but the Government of India also tried to attract American capital by promising equal treatment, full remittance of profits, and fair compensation in case of eventual nationalisation.[4] This ambivalence in theory could also be seen in personal attitudes towards Americans in India—a mixture of envy and resentment. Indian hostility towards American military bases in Asia was unequivocal. They were regarded as provocative to Russia and China; through Pakistan they brought the danger of direct American intervention to India's doorstep. The Indian government openly criticised smaller Asian States who had succumbed to what was considered in Delhi to be a modern equivalent of "subsidiary alliances." American motives were questioned.

Despite the cultural preferences of a westernised elite in India, its ties were with Britain rather than America. Nehru's closest adviser on foreign affairs, V.K. Krishna Menon, took perhaps a more radical view of the US than he did, and K.M. Panikkar wrote a critical history of western dominance in Asia in terms of sea power and trade. Girja Shankar Bajpai served in Washington before becoming Secretary-General of the Ministry of External Affairs, but is not known to have influenced more than the conduct of diplomacy. Of India's ambassadors to the US. Mrs. Vijaya-lakshmi Pandit was probably most comfortable in her position and arranged her brother's first visit to that country—with disappointing results. G.L. Mehta was as aware of American shortcomings as of strengths,[5] having personally encountered racial discrimination during his tenure. And after a successful term as negotiator of economic collaboration with the US and the World Bank, B.K. Nehru experienced to the full the frustrated hopes that characterised Indo-US relations of the Kennedy-Johnson years, during which Jawaharlal Nehru died.

Among political parties, Congress dominance was assured in Nehru's lifetime, and early criticism of foreign policy came mainly from the left-wing parties. Conservative groupings were predictably disinclined towards close relations with the Soviet Union, but the Jana Sangh and supportive Hindu organisations could hardly favour Pakistan's big ally and source of military strength, the United States. The Swatantra Party, formed by a distinguished secular leadership in 1959, was too preoccupied with building a popular base on domestic issues to formulate an alternate policy to Nehru's non-alignment. Thus, while many Indians thought they understood the west, and a great number were willing to study and earn livelihood in America, there were few political apologists for American policy. The surge of goodwill which followed prompt US support in the China war of 1962 ebbed rapidly during the conflict with Pakistan in 1965.

III

American policy formulators in the administration or Congress tended to judge India through Nehru. They saw in him qualities they admired or disliked and made decisions accordingly. They found him personally difficult to deal with, but recognised his crucial role in modern India.[6] They probably never understood his complex personality or his philosophy of action; they were confused by his statements, irritated by them, and paid more attention to his words than his deeds. It was easier for them to take umbrage at alleged anti-Americanism than to concede the possibility that Nehru's interpretations of Russian or Chinese intentions, for example, might be correct; or that non-alignment (termed by them "neutralism") was a tenable posture. Numerous public laudings of India's democratic political system notwithstanding, few Americans believed in it. They over-estimated the British contribution to India and under-estimated the ability and independence of Indians. They discounted the domestic imperatives on Indian policy—foreign or economic— assumed both government and society to be authoritarian, and attributed shortcomings of performance to "softness".

Nehru was often described as "aristocratic," "intellectual," or "introspective," and, however apt the epithets, the implication was that he would not be able to deliver the goods for poverty-stricken India. To the extent that national images are personalised, Americans saw India as a helpless woman, vulnerable to seduction from communism, and foolishly rejecting the husbandly advances of the west. Independent India, Nehru's India, appealed almost exclusively to liberal Americans like Socialist Norman Thomas, One Worlder Harris Wofford, or New Dealer Chester Bowles; but there were very few such liberals with political influence in the United States between 1946 and 1961.

At the end of the Second World War there existed in America a profound ignorance of Asia in general, and India in particular. Secretary of State Dean Acheson's persistent childhood illusion that "if the world is round, the Indians must be standing on their heads"[7] represented the vagueness prevailing even among educated Americans. Pictures of a vast chaotic Asian landmass, far away and different, filled with millions of dark skinned, mysterious, "heathen" people, bristling with fantastic insoluble problems, writhing in hunger and disease, occasionally illuminated by "holy men" and Taj Mahals, had been scratched on their minds[8] by a narrow range of prose, movies,[9] or churches. Neither wartime experiences nor rapid tours on which some Americans first came to India were conducive to depth of understanding. In any case, little in their background could prepare the average American for the shock of first encounter with the sights, smells, and physical discomforts of Indian cities like Calcutta. American investment and scholarship was absent from British India; American missionaries were more numerous in China than in India; it was difficult for Indians to obtain residence in the United States and almost impossible for them to become citizens until the US Immigration Act was amended in 1946 and 1965.

Thus, the most effective means of spreading awareness of India, through a large number of knowledgeable persons, was lacking. A handful of respected Indian residents, a few American Indic scholars, and some officials, returned from Indian assignments, attempted to educate the American public. Voluntary organisations were formed, and over the years have built up an impressive record of disseminating information. Two or three newspapers and news services assigned permanent staffs to India. But there was no India "lobby" in the United States. During the period under review for most Americans the world remained western centred, their attention on Asia focussed on the Far East. For them historic Asia was insignificant, "emergent" or "resurgent" Asia either irrelevant or dangerous. Distinctions between India and other Asian countries were hard to make except in terms of reaction to America, which is one reason why simplified slogans like "ally", "neutral", "communist" were used to identify different nations. Neither the Truman nor the Eisenhower administration had men in high places who were familiar with or sympathetic to India. Eisenhower himself was concerned that India survive as a democratic state and was the only American President to visit India; but he looked at South and Southeast Asia almost exclusively in terms of possible "power vacuums." In the Kennedy administration, Democratic adviser John Kenneth Galbraith became Ambassador in New Delhi and Bowles served briefly as Under Secretary in the Department of State. The President's admiration for Nehru was well-known, but he did not feel that India would play an important role in world affairs for some time to come. There were a few spokesmen for India in the Congress, notably Senator John Sherman Cooper of Kentucky, but on the whole legislators reflected the interests of their constituents, and India was not one.

One of the few serious books on India written by an American before the war was the muckraking *Mother India* by Katherine

Mayo. The other side of the picture was rarely presented except in terms of ancient art and philosophy. The study of social, economic and political problems is relatively recent. For the problem-solving, present-conscious Americans filled with the illusion of omnipotence, India was impossibly frustrating to contemplate, partly because they were not invited to tackle India's problems on their terms, and partly because they saw themselves making but small dents through the limited roles of helpfulness assigned to them.

IV

Impressions of subconscious attitudes among large numbers of people appear oversimplified if not unjust when reduced to paper, but their importance in the Indo-American relationship should not be underestimated. In the first place, during the Nehru era there was no conflict of real interests between the two states; their differences of opinion were ideological or concerned with relations with third countries. Their economic and cultural cooperation was growing; yet their verbal disputes, often commentaries on each other's policies, overruled their tangible relationship. Next, the two states did not confine themselves to a dialogue between executive heads who would be expected to be informed and rational. They inter-acted on a variety of planes in which the opinions of legislators, businessmen and pressmen counted as well as those of officials. Because most of their business was conducted in public and in English, it was impossible to isolate the different planes. Thus, speeches of V.K. Krishna Menon at the UN (on Korea) could and did affect Congressional consideration of surplus grain sales to India; remarks of Secretary of State, John Foster Dulles in Portugal (on Goa) could and did antagonise Indians against his entire foreign policy.

Apart from predictable conflicts, many unhappy incidents were attributable to misunderstandings between the two governments. The Indian diplomatic style was not to spell out advice or future intentions in words of one syllable, but to speak obliquely, and to expect understanding. At times the United States paid insufficient attention to hints from New Delhi and then over-reacted to events, as on the occasion of Chinese entry into the Korean War, or, most notably, on the subject of Goa in 1961. Similarly, the hard hitting, constantly proferred American advice on Indian problems was not always received in New Delhi without suspicion of motive—such as on China, Kashmir, or on agricultural development. Absence of respect and lack of trust are more often based on an individual's judgements than on objective facts. Finally, the beneficial results on both countries of a large scale economic programme harnessing American resources to Indian development were frequently endangered by negative psychological effects of the relationship; a conspicuous example was when the American Congress virtually cancelled assistance to the public sector steel mill at Bokaro in 1963 and the Indian government withdrew its request.

India and the US developed relations for the first time when they were each assessing the nature of the post-war world and evolving new ideas on their roles in it. Their separate perspectives determined their commentaries on each other's global policies and so affected their dealings with each other in the United Nations Organization and elsewhere.

V

During the years 1946-49 the Truman administration developed the thesis that Europe, the eastern Mediterranean, indeed, the world, was threatened by imminent danger from international communism directed by Moscow. The thesis gained credence because of the strength of the communist parties in France and Italy, the take-over of Czechoslovakia and Poland by communist governments, Soviet moves on behalf of the Azerbaijan rebellion in north Iran and towards a Mediterranean sphere of influence through Turkey and Greece, the Berlin blockade of 1948, and, of course, the communist victory in China (popularly referred to in America as the "loss of China"). Ambassador George Kennan predicted from Moscow that the Soviet Union would take every opportunity of weakening the west and use every means of probing existing spots of vulnerability. Western leaders saw as an "iron curtain" the hard line ideology adopted by the communist movement in 1946 postulating confrontation between capitalism and communism.

The men in Washington, looking out at the world, were decisively influenced by their awareness of the contribution made to Nazi and Fascist expansion by the Anglo-French "appeasement" policies as well as by American isolationism and neutrality which resulted in World War II. They were determined to avoid making the same mistake with regard to another enemy, communism, Therefore, the strategy they gradually evolved was essentially an uncompromising one of demonstrating western strength on all fronts. It included rebuilding the productive capacities of war-torn Europe through a massive transfer of goods and capital—the Marshall Plan; American support in pursuing specified European interests, such as those of Britain in West Asia and France in Indo-China; the welding together of western Europe and North America in comprehensive alliance—the North Atlantic Treaty Organisation; attempted application of counter force against any possible point of Soviet expansion—the famous "containment" policy; and, as an underfinanced after-thought, an effort to pre-empt the Marxist appeal to poverty by making American achievements available for the improvement of the underdeveloped countries—the "Point Four Program" of President Truman.

Since every item of these ambitious programmes involved consider-able expenditure, and a bipartisan foreign policy appeared neces-sary, each stage of the strategy had to be presented favourably to the US Congress and public. Every tactic of the administration, including friendship or aid to India, had to be justified in terms of immediate benefit to US global strategy. Almost inevitably, an apocryphal view of a world in urgent need of American leadership to save it from chaos became popular. Policy was articulated in the sweeping and highly moralistic terms of "assisting free peoples to defend themselves" from a fate presumably worse than death: communism. It was but a short step to the view that the United States was a world policeman on the side of law and order and righteousness, and that all criticism against it was communist inspired.

VI

In New Delhi after 1947 a different world perspective prevailed. The shattering of Europe meant the liberation of colonial peoples. India wished to act as the spokesman for all subjugated peoples and the leader in a revolt against economic exploitation, racial dis-crimination and warfare. The United States was initially regarded as a natural ally in dismantling European empires, and its failures in this respect were seen as a "betrayal" of its own revolutionary heritage. Nationalism was seen as a far stronger force in Asia than any other "ism", and western resistance to it—albeit in the guise of anti-communism---a threat to independence which must be resisted. Further, the main tasks of former dependencies was seen as one of social and economic modernisation leading to the uplift of the masses. Preservation of a feudal order or external bolstering of autocracies was regarded as an insult to nationalism and a long-term disservice to the freedom of the peoples concerned. No credibility was attached to "free world" definitions which excluded the nationalistic forces of major countries like Egypt and Indonesia, but included minority governments like those in South Africa and Taiwan. For informed Indians the great events of the post-war era were Indian independence and the resolution of the Chinese civil war. These were read as signs of a "resurgent Asia" as Nehru called it, where nations were at long last capable of acting as subjects and not objects in the international system. India pressed for international recognition of the importance of this new Asia.

Indian observers saw the concentration of preponderant power in the hands of two huge and mutually hostile States as an unwelcome condition of international life because it distracted attention away from the colonial problem and because it threatened to erupt into nuclear war. Drawing on the mainsprings of Indian culture, Gandhi had taught that all conflicts could be resolved peacefully, that non-violence could prevail over military force, that ideas were more influential than wealth or arms, and that independence grew out of self-respect and self-reliance. Out of these ingredients also was fashioned the posture of non-alignment. As Jawaharlal Nehru never tired of explaining, it was a declaration of independence from alien control of external relations; it was an assertion by India, warning both militant power blocs, that it would not commit itself in advance to supporting the diplomatic tactics of either. Further, it was accompanied by a willingness to serve as a channel of communication or a mediator between the two sides and a conviction that merely by remaining uncommitted India helped to reduce the chances of war.

Nevertheless, the absence of tangible power was galling to Indians. Nehru reacted to India's peripheral influence on international events on the one hand by building up the image of India's prestige, and on the other hand by disclaiming any intention of seeking "spheres of influence" or leadership of any "third bloc". A heavy burden was thus placed on moral principles and hortatory statements. Familiar as they were with Anglo-American liberal ideals, Indian officials often represented the Indian peaceful perspective as the higher self-interest of all countries, and the voice of India as that of mankind's conscience. Such a stance was especially obvious in UN discussions on world disarmament. The glimmer of truth in India's claim, and the sense of their own lost innocence, made such a perspective unacceptable to western powers, whose national interests were heavily engaged.

The world seen from India displayed another characteristic, the unequal distribution of economic resources among nations. The productive capacity of underdeveloped countries needed to be built up almost from ground level to rectify this hideous inequality. India, in particular, was periodically faced with food shortages, and early plans to build a million ton grain reserve depended on cheap purchases abroad. The Nehru government deliberately abjured methods of domestic coercion to raise the national income as had been done elsewhere in recent history, but tried to enlist regulated foreign capital and technology in its development plans. The rhetoric of the United Nations agencies and the United States government encouraged the expectation that international assistance could be so harnessed without prejudice to national sovereignty. India was an early participant in schemes and institutions to make this possible around the world, and itself became their major beneficiary.

National perspectives and personal attitudes became established during the Nehru era and decisively influenced Indo-US relations. The two countries interacted on every subject of importance to them, sometimes positively and at other times negatively. Broadly speaking, their areas of interaction pertained to: US security interests *vis-a-vis* the Soviet Union; Indian territorial interests; and bilateral economic and cultural relations. One reason why over the long-run and in any given year the tone of the relationship was liable to vary was that the uppermost issue of the moment set that tone, but distinctive patterns of behaviour evolved in each category and continued to affect it.

VII

The diplomacy of the Korean War 1950-53 was the proving ground for Indian non-alignment. As a member of the UN Commission on Korea and a non-permanent member of the Security Council, India was committed to the United Nations resolutions supporting the Republic of South Korea, which was attacked from the north in June 1950. India voted for the resolution of June 25 naming North Korea as aggressor and calling for withdrawal of its troops below the *de facto* boundary of the 38th parallel. Weighing the prospects of an expanded conflict against the necessity of checking aggression, India hesitated before finally accepting the resolution of June 27 calling for collective UN action; it contributed an ambulance unit rather than combat troops to the UN cloaked American force. In July India took the initiative in Washington, New York, and Moscow, proposing steps for a peaceful settlement in Korea which would include seating the representative of the Peoples Republic of China in the United Nations, a ceasefire along the 38th parallel, and eventual unification and independence of Korea. Nehru followed with identical letters to Joseph Stalin and Dean Acheson; predictably, they were rejected by the latter and accepted by the former.

The United States of America and India consistently disagreed on China's membership in the United Nations. And when the UN forces, led by General Douglas MacArthur, took the offensive in October and pressed northwards, India's distance from the US side became apparent and remained so for the rest of the war. India's diplomats, fed by information from Ambassador K.M. Panikkar in Peking, often defended China's entry on the side of North Korea as "defensive", and criticised the militancy of American policy in Asia. India abstained from or opposed several US sponsored UN resolutions including those naming China as aggressor and the "Uniting for Peace" resolution of September 1950.[10] India refrained from signing the Anglo-American Peace Treaty with Japan in 1951.[11] At the United Nations the Indian delegation formed an informal grouping of Asian and Arab delegations for purposes of mediation.

By late 1951 India had established her identity as an independent non-aligned state in the international community—but at the cost of considerable loss of support in America and without marked gains in Moscow or Peking. A kind of military equilibrium prevailed

in Korea and for about a year peace talks were conducted between
the two sides at Panmunjon. In 1952, India resumed its diplomatic
intervention on the problem of repatriating the prisoners of war.
The intricate task of charting a course between the western and
communist positions fell to Krishna Menon. Drafting skill matched
with painstaking work in consulting other UN delegations went
into the Indian draft resolution of November 17, ultimately passed
on December 3. This detailed proposal tried to find the centre point
between the announced stands of either side through a formula
of "non-forcible repatriation" to be carried out by an impartial
body of "neutral" states. The Soviet Union initially rejected the
proposal which gained western support, but after Stalin's death
in March 1953, China signified its acceptance. A five nation
"Neutral Nations Repatriation Commission" was established with
India's General K.S. Thimayya in the decisive position of chairman.
A small Indian custodian force was responsible for holding the
prisoners in their assigned camps, arranging their interviews, and
deciding on their final disposition within ninety days. This delicate,
even dangerous task came under conflicting demands of both sides,
neither of which was pleased by the decisions taken, but had to
recognize their impartiality and courage. However, because of
South Korean and US opposition, India was not included as a
member of the conference held on Korea in Geneva in 1954; Krishna
Menon made informal contributions to that conference's agreement
on Indo-China since none was reached on Korea.

The Korean War episode illustrates several aspects of the Indo-US
relationship on cold war issues. India established its non-alignment
by moving away from the west, not from Russia; the US did not
welcome this dimunition of the majority support it had hitherto
enjoyed in the UN and was angered by what it saw as a favouring,
or at best, an even balancing of the Soviet position. While India's
power to affect American actions was limited to its diplomatic
persuasiveness, the power of Indian leaders to comment on American
actions was unlimited; Americans reacted badly to both. Krishna
Menon's voting and speeches during the UN debate on the Hungarian Revolution of 1956 demonstrated identical concerns as in
Korea—and left even deeper scars on American public opinion.
Similarly, when expounding on the Berlin crisis of August 1961
in the Indian Parliament, Nehru suggested that western access to
that city was a "concession" by the Soviet union and not a treaty

right; Washington "raved".[12] So it did on the many occasions when India pointed out that responsibility for the nuclear arms race rested at least as much with the US as with the Soviet Union.

On the whole, Nehru restrained his comments on specific manifestations of the cold war in Europe except when world peace seemed to be involved. Not so, when American-Soviet rivalry was played out in Asia, as in Korea, Indo-China, or West Asia. He consistently made a distinction between China and Russia even before their rift became obvious, and persistently opposed military alliances and direct intervention in Asia. When the United States identified its own national interest with regimes India considered non-nationalistic, as in Vietnam, there was a divergence of views between Delhi and Washington.

On occasions, however, America was willing to utilise Nehru's prestige and active Indian participation to circumvent confrontation with the Soviet Union in an international crisis—as in the UN backed solution of the Suez crisis of 1956, the Lebanese incident of 1958, negotiating agreement on neutralisation of Laos in 1962, and most concretely, during the UN Congo operations after 1961. In short, cooperation in third countries occurred when India and the United States converged their divergent global policies.

VIII

India too had its disputes involving national honour and integrity. They were with Pakistan over Kashmir, with Portugal over Goa, and with China over large areas in Ladakh and NEFA. The US was in a position to influence the outcome of each dispute and certainly did not refrain from commenting on India's approaches to its security problems. American policy towards them was not uniform, however, and is hard to generalise about unless one adopts the doubtful hypothesis that it was inimical to Indian power on the subcontinent *per se*. More reasonably: America looked at Indian disputes through the distorting prism of national attitudes and perspectives, weighed India's demand for support and assistance against the claims of the declared allies of the United States and in no case completely identified its own vital interest with either side.

In the case of Goa, for example, Dulles statements in 1955 about overseas colonies belonging to Metropolitan Portugal, US diplomatic efforts in December 1961 to postpone Indian military action for six months,[13] and the unprecedented storm of anti-India feeling expressed in Adlai Stevenson's UN speech and the American press after the "liberation" of Goa do not alter the fact that Portugal was not assisted in remaining in Goa. The US government acquiesced in the Indian action without allowing it to interfere with the process of increasing cooperation.

As a permanent member of the Security Council, the United States was involved with the question of Kashmir from the time India first submitted it to the United Nations in January 1948 requesting assistance in the peaceful settlement of the dispute. A large number of Americans served in UN forces stationed on the cease fire line and in the UN Commission on India and Pakistan; a UN mediator, Dr. Frank P. Graham, was an American as was the appointed plebiscite administrator, Admiral Chester W. Nimitz. Thus early UN efforts in Kashmir took on the character of an American operation and later moves by Pakistan (in 1957, 1962, and 1964) to revive the Kashmir question in the Security Council succeeded because of American backing. Indian frustration over the UN slurring of the fundamental issue of Pakistan's aggression was inevitably vented against the United States; most Americans regarded India—specifically Nehru—as the stumbling block to any settlement in Kashmir.

Without attempting to retell the oft-told story of Kashmir, a few aspects of its importance in Indo-US relations must be stressed. At the time of partition an image of "Hindu" India and "Muslim" Pakistan was created in America which no subsequent talk of Indian secularism has yet eradicated. Therefore, the logic of Pakistan's case, first brilliantly presented in the United Nations by Zafrullah Khan, was *ipso facto* more appealing to the US government and public alike than India's legalistic and sometimes inconsistent terminology. Second, the repeated pledges made by Indian spokesmen, including Nehru, in 1947 and 1948 that the matter of Kashmir's accession to the Indian Union would be decided in accordance with the wishes of the people through plebiscite or referendum struck a sympathetic chord in the west. Accompanying mention of preconditions for a peaceful plebiscite were ignored, and later Indian assertions that the 1954 ratification of accession by the Kashmir Constituent Assembly signified the wishes of the people were disbelieved. Thus UN mediators drew up plans for phased withdrawals of both Pakistani and Indian troops and the United States criticised India for not permitting a plebiscite in the Kashmir valley; India complained of insufficient differentiation between itself and the aggressor state and increasingly reacted defensively toward any mention of third party mediation or plebiscite.

Third, the US as a global power was probably interested in Kashmir as an area of strategic location to itself and did not easily adjust to the idea of continued disturbance there, or absorption in India. In fact, after 1953, the Kashmir question reverted to bilateral negotiation between India and Pakistan, and adjustments of relationship between Kashmir and the rest of India; possible UN intervention was effectively blocked by the Soviet veto exercised in India's behalf. Most important of all, the United States government signed a military alliance with Pakistan in early 1954 after having given serious attention to its possibility since 1951.[14] Vigorous objections from the Indian government and several high placed Americans had been over-ruled by the Eisenhower administration. In addition to the well publicised objectives of American alliances of the time, some in the government, such as Vice-President Richard Nixon, were motivated toward Pakistan as a useful counterforce to Nehru's neutralism.[15] Balance of power on the subcontinent became an assumption of American policy on which practice was based.

Despite assurances from Eisenhower to Nehru in 1954 and 1958, when the US-Pakistan alliance was renewed, that the build up of Pakistan's armed forces would not be used aggressively against India, despite efforts by both the Indian and the United States governments to avoid jeopardising all cordial relations between themselves, there is no doubt that Indian security interests were adversely affected by American military assistance to Pakistan amounting to about 1.5 billion dollars by 1966.[16] In the long run the alliance made possible two more armed conflicts on the subcontinent, and in the short run it vitiated the climate of India's relations with both the United States and Pakistan. American Congressmen were wont to suggest making economic aid to India conditional on settlement of the Kashmir dispute so as to obviate financing an arms race; India almost automatically hardened against remedies for reducing Indo-Pakistan tensions suggested by Americans—such as "joint defence" or "good offices" of prominent personalities. Nevertheless, it is well to remember that Pakistan also criticised America bitterly for lack of full support on Kashmir, and that no American administration has been willing to use more than words to try and alter the *status quo* in Kashmir favouring India.

A convincing thesis has been presented that the US mortagaged the possibility of good relations with India for the use of a top secret intelligence bases in north west Pakistan.[17] Events of the last few years of Nehru's life bear this out. Maturing of their global outlooks in both the American and Indian governments brought greater toleration for each other's policies; US economic aid to India reached its highest level; increasing intellectual and cultural exchanges created a bridge between the two peoples. But the United States discouraged Indian attempts to purchase and manufacture sophisticated American aircraft and missiles for a modernised air force, while proceeding with deliveries of F.104 fighter planes and Sidewinder missiles to Pakistan in 1961. Subsequent Indian-Soviet agreement on MiGs was critically observed by Washington.

The breakthrough of Chinese forces into Assam in October 1962 provided cause for an unparalleled deepening of the Indo-US involvement. Washington responded to Nehru's world-wide request for military assistance within twelve hours, and in November a military agreement was signed between the two countries to strengthen India's mountain defences against China with an indication that America would give Indian cities air protection if necessary.[18] Negotiations for a long-term aid programme ensued over the excited objections of Pakistan. But Britain also became a partner in supplies and watered down discussion of Indian defence needs. More important, in response to Pakistan's complaints, the British and US governments put heavy pressure on New Delhi to reach a settlement on Kashmir in territorial terms. Indo-Pakistan talks did open in December 1962 with intermediaries Duncan Sandys of Britain and Averell Harriman of the United States in attendance, and were continued in 1963. Their failure surprised no one. By the time of Jawaharlal Nehru's death in 1964 Indian gratification at American support had turned into irritation with its qualifications. Liberal Americans saw that a great opportunity for bringing India into close working association with the west had been dulled over by deference to US allies, especially Pakistan. 1965 saw another slump in Indo-US relations.

IX

The economic ties established between India and the United States provided a productive contrast to their political dialogue. Controversies were less evident between the two governments than between the American administration and Congress where debates reflected uncertainties about purposes and quantity of economic assistance. The result in the United States was an over-burdening of the aid programme with motivations ranging from pure humanitarianism to crass materialism. The size and complexity of the subject defies brief comment.[19] Suffice it to say here that the 1951, wheat loan was the first substantial American assistance to India but it did not inaugurate a Marshall Plan like programme—Chester Bowles' efforts notwithstanding. In the mid 1950's developments produced greater US involvement in the Indian economy.

During India's second five year plan the theory that large-scale government to government transfer of funds could facilitate a "take off" into self-sustained growth gained popularity in both countries. Initial Soviet assistance to Indian heavy industry promised in 1955, and a communist electoral victory in Kerala in 1957, aroused American competitive instincts in global strategy. An unanticipated shortage in foreign exchange reserves spurred Indian efforts to obtain greater outside assistance. The Nehru-Eisenhower talks in December 1956 were exceedingly cordial and made possible expanded collaboration between the two countries.

In 1957 the United States established a Development Loan Fund to provide loans repayable in rupees for procurement of essential capital goods in America. In 1958 the World Bank, on American initiative, formed an Aid-India Consortium which made heavy commitments to the Third Five Year Plan. In 1960 the US made the largest single contribution to the Indus Basin Development Fund. And in 1964-65 the wheat transferred to India under US Public Law 480 amounted to one fifth of the total American crop. US aid focussed on agriculture, rural progress, and infrastructure projects such as production of electric power; a thirty year agreement on cooperative development of atomic power plants was signed in 1963 beginning with Tarapur near Bombay. With very few exceptions in the private sector the United States declined to invest in or assist Indian heavy industry.

Though burdened with psychological difficulties and verbal

disputations on priorities and methods, Indo-US economic relations gradually improved in the Nehru era to an impressive record. Disillusionment and decline set in only later. Allowing for over-simplification, the same comment may be applied to the relationship as a whole.

J. BANDYOPADHYAYA

Nehru and Non-Alignment

THERE ARE TWO apparently contradictory views on Jawaharlal Nehru's personal contribution to the policy of non-alignment. One of these, which tends to minimize his personal role in the formulation of this fundamental and long-term strategy of India's foreign policy, has been expressed, understandably, by Nehru himself in his own words:

It is completely incorrect to call our policy "Nehru" policy. It is incorrect because all that I have done is to give voice to that policy. I have not originated it. It is a policy inherent in the circumstances of India, inherent in the past thinking of India, inherent in the whole mental outlook of India, inherent in the conditioning of the Indian mind during our struggle for freedom, and inherent in the circumstances of the world today. I come in by the mere accidental fact that during these few years I have represented that policy as Foreign Minister. I am quite convinced that whoever might have been in charge of the foreign affairs of India and whatever party might have been in power in India, they could not have deviated very much from this policy. Some emphasis might have been greater here or there because, as I said, it represents every circumstance that goes towards making the thought of India on these subjects.[1]

The other view, expressed by Michael Brecher, tends to ascribe the conception, formulation and implementation of the policy of non-alignment almost entirely to Nehru. Brecher wrote:

> In no other state does one man dominate foreign policy as does Nehru in India. Indeed, so overwhelming is his influence that India's policy has come to mean in the minds of people everywhere the personal policy of Pandit Nehru. And justifiably so, for Nehru is the philosopher, the architect, the engineer and the voice of his country's policy towards the outside world. This does not mean that he operates in a vacuum, for the aspirations discussed earlier provide the framework within which policy must be devised. Nor is he entirely free from the influence of individuals and institutions in India. It does mean, however, that he has impressed his personality and his views with such overpowering effect that foreign policy must properly be termed a private monopoly....It was he who provided a rationale for India's approach to international politics since 1947. It was he who carried the philosophy of non-alignment to the world at large. And throughout this period he has dominated the policy-making process.[2]

It is my purpose in this paper to reconcile these two apparently conflicting opinions, and to show that Nehru and his biographer are in fact looking at the same reality from two different points of view. While certain basic determinants of India's foreign policy and environmental contingencies did in fact make non-alignment the only rational choice of strategy, it required the personality of Nehru to transform the rational into the real.

II

Geopolitical considerations, which are often basic to a state's foreign policy, indicated the rationality of an independent and important role in world affairs on the part of India. Emerging as the seventh largest state with the second largest population in the world, with a relatively large stock of natural resources, India in 1947 had the power potential necessary for influencing, to some extent, the course of contemporary world politics. It would have been irrational for her to be oblivious of this geopolitical reality and to restrict her freedom of action in the international field by being politically or militarily aligned with one of the two blocs of power into which international politics had come to be divided. Nehru perceived this geopolitical reality when he said:

> I can understand some of the smaller countries of Europe or some of the smaller countries of Asia being forced by circumstances to bow down before some of the greater powers and becoming practically satellites of those powers, because they cannot help it. The power opposed to them is so great and they have nowhere to turn. But I do not think that consideration applies to India.... India is too big a country herself to be bound down to any country, however big it may be.[3]

The strategic geopolitical location of India between the east and the west has also a great significance for her role in international relations, and Nehru was one of the first to perceive this aspect as well. In his own words: "...India becomes a kind of meeting ground for various trends and forces and a meeting ground between what might roughly be called the East and the West."[4] The geographical insularity caused by the Himalayas and the Indian Ocean, which has made India very different from most of the European countries, for example, from the geopolitical point of view, also enabled her to stay away, to a certain extent, from the political and ideological crusades of the mid-twentieth century. Nehru recognized this geographical condition for non-alignment when he said:

> I do not say that our country is superior or that we are above passion and prejudice, hatred and fury. But as things are, there are certain factors which help us. First of all, we are geographically so situated that we are not drawn into controversies with that passionate fury that some other countries are. This is not due to our goodness or badness, but is a matter of geography.[5]

India's abysmal poverty made rapid economic development a categorical imperative of domestic policy, and made it necessary to link the broad orientation and strategy of foreign policy closely with those of domestic economic policy. As Nehru said as early as 1947: "Ultimately, foreign policy is the outcome of economic policy, and until India has properly evolved her economic policy, her foreign policy will be rather vague, rather inchoate, and will be groping."[6] The vast and rapidly growing population made economic development in per capita terms an extremely difficult task and called for a massive programme of capital investment within a short period of time. On the other hand, the geopolitical environment, especially the emergence of a hostile Pakistan, made it equally necessary to invest a sizeable proportion of our resources in defence. The emergence of a potentially powerful (and later on actually hostile) China further increased our security requirements and, therefore, also defence expenditure. This inevitable conflict between the needs of development and the needs of defence placed a serious limitation on the investment of resources in economic development.

The constraints of a democratic political set-up, as embodied in the Indian Constitution, set definite limits on the extent to which the power of the state could be utilized to mobilize the manpower and resources of the country. Nor was there any voluntary mass mobilization programme for socio-economic reconstruction, as advocated by Gandhi. Under the circumstances, relatively heavy dependence on foreign aid became inevitable. It was the natural function of foreign policy to ensure not only the availability but also the maximization of the quantum of such aid. It was also the function of foreign policy to avoid political pressure from the aid-giving States. These politico-economic objectives of foreign aid could be achieved only through a policy of non-alignment since such a policy alone could ensure the diversification of the sources of aid as well as prevent the exercise of political pressure by one of the super powers. Nehru perceived this logical connection between non-alignment and foreign aid when he said: "Even in accepting economic help... it is not a wise policy to put all our eggs in one basket."[7]

III

The compulsions of a developing economy also indicated the manner in which foreign policy could be utilized for safeguarding the country's security. In spite of her relatively large stock of natural resources, India could not expect to become a first rate industrial power within a short period of time. The low level of her technological development and the wide and widening gap between the technological levels of the developed and the developing countries made it impossible for India to make a defence effort that would meet all possible external contingencies through military means. It was, therefore, necessary to replace military defence by political diplomacy to a considerable extent, as Nehru often emphasized.[8] Nor was it possible for India to play the role of a big power in international politics, and, as such to adopt the attitudes and policies of a big power.

Political diplomacy, moreover, could not be expected to serve the needs of India's security if such diplomacy meant alignment with a power bloc. A policy of alignment with one of the two power blocs might have undermined both internal and external security in the long run in a variety of ways. In a newly independent Asian state with strong nationalist traditions and values, the national aspirations and global outlook are markedly different from those of the older European or American States. Military alignment with a power bloc by such a state may look to large sections of its people as a betrayal of the national revolution and promote insurrectionary propensities among them. Such a situation had developed in Kuomintang China and might as well have developed in India in the post-independence period, if a policy of military alignment with a super power had been followed. Moreover, India's bigger military partner might not have approved of her politico-economic system or trends, and might have encouraged directly or indirectly forces and tendencies within the state, which would have, in the long run, undermined the state system established by the will of people. The fact that few of the new states of Asia which have joined military alliances have achieved domestic politico-economic stability and viability, cannot be treated as a mere accident of history.

External security might also have been compromised through a military alliance in a number of ways. A military alliance is likely to affect the external sovereignty of a state especially with regard to treaties, bilateral and multilateral relations with other states outside the alliance, the structure and orientation of foreign trade or voting at the United Nations, not to speak of the mere invisible constraints. While such matters may not be of any great significance for the national interests of the European states, they are vital to the very international personality and even survival of the Asian and African states. Secondly, India might have been involved in a regional or even global war resulting in serious internal economic and political dislocation. Finally, military alliance with a big power might have undermined the morale of the armed forces and seriously weakened the will of the people to defend their sovereignty against external attack or interference.[9]

There is no escape from the conclusion that, given the economic compulsions and the constitutional and political set-up, the only rational stance for our diplomacy could have been one of avoidance of war to the best of our ability. Peace is a minimum pre-condition for our economic development, not only because a military preparation, which would be adequate for our security in all contingencies, would in fact be beyond our economic capability, but also because, even when we are not directly involved in a war, a war elsewhere would inevitably dislocate our foreign trade, reduce, if not eliminate the inflow of foreign aid, and thus upset our programme of development. Therefore, even if we leave aside the possibility of self-extinction by involvement in a major war, local wars must also be avoided at all costs, unless of course war is imposed on us by an aggressor. In other words, it was necessary for India from the beginning, for the sake of her economic development, if for no other reason, to avoid entanglement in the world-wide bipolar (or poly-centric) power conflict, and to play such a role in international politics in general and the United Nations in particular, as would minimize the chances of war, global, regional or local. From the security point of view, non-alignment alone could, therefore, be the diplomatic supplement to our defence effort.

IV

The political experience of the Indian national movement and the political and ideological thinking of the nationalist elite in the first half of this century, both of which were represented by the Indian National Congress, were one of the important determinants of Indian foreign policy. This experience and thinking was informed and inspired by a high degree of political idealism, inherited from the Indian renaissance of the nineteenth century, which had re-ordained Ashoka rather than Kautilya as the model of India's political aspirations. This idealism manifested itself, first, in an idealist view of politics and power. Gandhi, for example, defined politics not in the usual sense of the art of capturing and managing governmental power, but as the "transformation of social relationships" in terms of certain ultimate values. He was severely critical of power politics and advised his followers to stay away from "power politics and its contagion." His ultimate values had an essentially inward or subjective quality, and the "transformation of social relationships" in terms of these values had to be inalienably non-violent. The only desirable and enduring form of power, according to him, was what Vinoba Bhave has called the Third Power, namely, the non-violent power of the masses as opposed to the power of violence on the one hand and the power of the state on the other; and he wished to apply this power, as is well-known, to both national and international politics. Rabindranath Tagore, in whom, according to Albert Schweitzer, "modern Indian thought makes a noble attempt to get really clear about itself", seems to have given poetic expression to this romanticist view of India's role in world affairs when he said:

> Men of feeble faith will say that India requires to be strong and rich before she can raise her voice for the sake of the whole world. But I refuse to believe it. That the measure of man's great-ness is in his material resources is a gigantic illusion casting its shadow over the present-day world—it is an insult to man. It lies in the power of the materially weak to save the world from this illusion, and India, in spite of her penury and humiliation, can afford to come to the rescue of humanity.[10]

The idea of One World, and of an Asiatic Federation as a prelude to it, haunted the Indian National Congress and its leaders, includ-ing Gandhi, almost from the beginning, and the intellectuals, philosophers and poets of India in the first half of this century. No rational Foreign Minister in India could completely ignore this tradition in the making of foreign policy, even in a world dominated by states which are materially strong and by thinkers who are dedicated to the concept of material power.

Nehru did not entirely accept this romantic idealism of modern Indian thinking on national and international politics, and certainly introduced a large measure of objectivity into the formulation and implementation of Indian foreign policy. But he constantly referred to the influence of the Gandhian tradition on India's political behaviour, particularly international behaviour, and to the ideal of One World as a basic goal of Indian foreign policy. The logical outcome was a foreign policy which would steer clear of the contemporary power balance and open up a new dimension of international relations. This was precisely the function of non-alignment.

The ideological thinking of the Indian national movement, which grew largely out of India's own historical experience of western imperialism and racialism, developments in the Soviet Union and contemporary international relations in general, was represented by equal rejection of both western capitalism and Soviet communism as guidelines for India's national development. The western politico-economic system was rejected because it was believed inevitably to breed exploitation, economic inequality, imperialism and racialism. But the Soviet model of development was also rejected because it was believed to be based on violence and dictatorship, which were alien to the ideals of the Indian national movement. By the early 'thirties the Indian national movement stood firm on its own ideological ground, and was not only determined to follow an autonomous ideological course involving the rejection of both western democracy and communism, but also confident of building a new set of political and economic institutions which would steer clear of the unwanted features of both the systems and break new ideological ground for the future course of human progress. This urge for a new ideology of the future was clearly expressed by Mahatma Gandhi during the Second World War when he said: "Between Scylla and Charybdis, if I sail in either direction, I suffer shipwreck. Therefore, I have to be in the midst of the storm."[11] The resolutions of the Indian National Congress since the Karachi Congress of 1931 on both political and economic issues clearly reflected this ideological autonomy of Indian nationalism. In 1947 the Congress gave clear expression to this ideology when it resolved:

Our aim should be to evolve a political system which will combine efficiency of administration with individual liberty, and an economic structure which will yield maximum production without the creation of private monopolies and concentration of wealth.... Such a social structure can provide an alternative to the acquisitive economy of private capitalism and the regimentation of a totalitarian state.[12]

In a world divided in two powerful blocs which coincided with the two dominant ideologies, both of which were repugnant to nationalist

Indian thinking, the only rational strategy for foreign policy could be that of non-alignment. Nehru clearly perceived this ideological base of Indian foreign policy from the beginning of his career as Prime Minister and foreign minister, and often referred to it in explaining the rationale of non-alignment. In 1956, for example, he stated in the Indian parliament:

> The world seems to be divided into two mighty camps, the communist and the anti-communist, and either party cannot understand how anyone can be foolish enough not to line up with itself. That just shows how little understanding these people have of the mind of Asia. Talking of India only, and not of all Asia, we have fairly clear ideas about our political and economic structure. We function in this country under a Constitution which may be described as a parliamentary democracy. It has not been imposed upon us. We propose to continue with it.... We intend to function on the economic plane, too, in our own way....We have no intention to turn communists. At the same time, we have no intention of being dragooned in any other direction....We have chosen our path and we propose to go along it, and to vary it as and when we choose, not at somebody's dictate or pressure; and we are not afraid of any other country imposing its will upon us by military methods or any other methods.... Our thinking and our approach do not fit in with this great crusade of communism or crusade of anti-communism.[13]

The socio-political aspect of the domestic milieu has also an important bearing on the foreign policy of a state, and this was particularly true of India during the Nehru era, when the problems of national integration and state building were rather acute.

V

The regional, political, economic, linguistic, religious and other socio-cultural diversities posed greater problems for state building in India than probably in any other country in the modern world. A generally acceptable and dynamic foreign policy which made India an important actor on the international stage could provide a common focus for the nation as a whole and thus help the difficult process of national integration and state building. Of utmost importance from this point of view, needless to say, is the balance of political forces in a newly independent state. While the Indian National Congress represented the mainstream of Indian thinking on political and ideological issues, there were segments of political opinion and organization on both the right and the left, inside the Congress and outside, which could have been seriously disaffected by India's alignment with one of the two power blocs, to the point of threatening the internal security of the state. Such alignment or even the suspicion of it would also have seriously antagonized the other power bloc. Only a policy of non-alignment could have prevented the acute polarization of the domestic political forces and thus created one of the essential conditions for state building. That Nehru recognized this compelling influence of the domestic milieu on foreign policy and *vice versa* was evident when he said: "The internal policy and foreign policy of a country affect each other. They should, broadly, be in line with each other, and have to be integrated. By and large, there has been in India an attempt at this integration."[14]

Last but not the least, the international milieu in which the newly independent India found herself was a major determinant of the broad orientation and strategy of Indian foreign policy. Indeed, the term "non-alignment" assumed meaning and significance only in the context of the cold war. In the late 'forties and early 'fifties, not only were more and more States being drawn into two antagonistic blocs of power sworn to mortal combat, the rapid development of nuclear weapons with almost infinite destructive power by both the blocs posed a real danger of the cold war exploding into a universal holocaust. To India and other newly independent states, the choice during this period was limited to two broad alternatives. On the one hand, there was the choice of participating in the cold war, inevitably including military alliances and counter-alliances, possibly compromising to a considerable extent the newly-won sovereignty, contributing through conscious and deliberate design to the psychology of war both at home and abroad, and probably also sliding inexorably into the vortex of a totally destructive third world war.

There was the choice, on the other hand, of keeping out of the bi-polar confrontation, preserving the newly won sovereignty and playing an independent role in international politics, concentrating on domestic economic development and state building, and endeavouring to reduce tension and control conflict situations by all possible means. From the point of view of the national security and national development of the emergent states like India, as well as from that of promoting a workable international order (which is the minimum necessary guarantee for the free and full development of the international personality of a state, just as the existence of a national political order is the minimum necessary precondition for the free and full development of the individual), the only rational choice was the second one, namely, that of steering clear of the bipolar confrontation or, in other words, non-alignment. The emergence of Asia and Africa and the coming into existence of the United Nations as a stronger and more viable international organization than the League of Nations created external conditions for the practical implementation of such a policy.

VI

It would thus appear, the policy of non-alignment was indicated by the realities of India's geography, economic development, recent political and ideological tradition, domestic milieu and international milieu. It was more or less a logical corollary of the given basic determinants of foreign policy. In this sense it is correct to say, as Nehru did, that the policy of non-alignment was not the inspiration or creation of anyone individual, that it was rooted in India's history and geography and the outcome of many given conditions. But Nehru's self-effacing statement regarding his personal role in the formulation of Indian foreign policy is quite wrong in the equally important sense that what was logical in the given situation was not inevitable. It has never been so in the history of international relations, which is replete with instances of irrational decision making in foreign policy. The provocations were often great enough in India for adopting a different policy from what Nehru adopted. In the initial phase, the open hostility of the Soviet Union, its refusal to regard India as an independent country, its open call for armed insurrection by the Communist Party of India (which resulted in the uprisings of 1948-49) and its unwillingness or inability to meet even a fraction of our urgent economic needs, posed serious problems for India, which were further aggravated by the equally hostile attitude of the Communist Party of China and subsequently of the People's Government of China, until the signing of the Panchsheel Treaty in 1954. There were also strong elements within the Congress and the Foreign Office which would have preferred a pro-western policy from the beginning. A mediocre foreign minister might easily have been tempted, in this situation, to seek security in the embrace of the western powers.

Subsequently, Pakistan's membership of the western military alliances seemed to upset the world balance of power against India and to endanger her external security seriously, especially in the context of the Kashmir dispute. There was again the temptation to reply to this challenge by a military alliance with the Soviet bloc, to which the common run of statesmen might have succumbed. It required the wisdom of Nehru to interpret the logic of the basic determinants of India's foreign policy correctly and to take a long view of India's national interest and of international relations as a whole.

The main reason for Nehru's sound grasp of the basic determinants of foreign policy and his ability to formulate a rational policy in terms of these determinants, is the fact that he was a child as well as a leader of the Indian national movement; he had grown with it and lived its inner experiences, urges and aspirations. His deep study of India's history, philosophy and culture gave his life experience a depth and meaning which very few other Indian leaders possessed. Long before the independence of India he had pondered deeply on problems of foreign policy, and played a decisive role in shaping, if not actually originating, the foreign policy of the Congress. He thus knew and understood the basic conditions and problems of India's foreign policy better than any other Indian leader in the post-independence period.

Nehru also shared in some way in the collective unconscious of the Indian people which accepts diversity in the cosmic scheme of things, and particularly in human society, almost as a law of nature, and refuses to think in terms of a polarization of ideas and forces. In his own words:

... our whole culture testifies to our understanding of the variety of humanity laying stress always on the unity, but also on the variety and diversity.... Whatever we may do in our limited outlook and failings, we have had a type of philosophy which is a live-and-let-live philosophy of life. We have no particular desire to convert other people to any view or thought.[15]

What other world-view could be a better philosophical foundation for a policy of non-alignment?

Added to this life experience was a profound history-consciousness which heightened Nehru's awareness of the broad forces of contemporary international politics and the actual and potential role of India on the world stage. In a land traditionally deficient in history-consciousness, Nehru was one of the very few modern exceptions. His *Autobiography*, *Discovery of India* and *Glimpses of World History* are all primarily essays in understanding and interpreting the history of India and the world. It is this historical perspective which enabled him to view India's national interest in the broader context of world history, and to say that "so far as India was concerned, placed as she was historically and geographically, it would have been quite astonishingly foolish to fall into this business of the cold war, either on grounds of principle or on grounds of expediency."[16] Historical perspective enabled him to see the futility and destructive potentiality of the cold war and impelled him to work out a new dimension of international relations.

But perhaps the most distinctive characteristic of Nehru's personality as a statesman was his persistent endeavour to combine idealism and realism in the formulation and implementation of policy and to conciliate the two into a state of equilibrium according to his own lights. Nehru was powerfully influenced by the idealistic tradition of the Indian renaissance and the national movement, especially by Gandhi. In emphasizing the need for adopting the right means in the relations among nations he often referred to the legacy of the Mahatma and explained that his basic approach to world politics in general and Indian foreign policy in particular had been profoundly influenced by the Gandhian tradition.

Nehru's relatively idealistic view of internationalism is also proved by his frequent reference to the ideal of "One World" his dedication to the United Nations and his constant, almost monotonous theme of world peace. He justified idealism in international relations by saying that realism as such "leads to incessant conflict" and that the realist "looks at the tip of his nose and sees little beyond; the result is that he is stumbling all the time." At the same time, however, he defined idealism as the "realism of tomorrow" and observed that the question of foreign policy ought to be approached "in a spirit of realism." "It is easy to lay down principles," he said, "but the difficulty comes in when high principles have to be acted upon."[17] At times he even adopted an approach to foreign policy which would delight the most diehard realist. As early as 1947 he said, for example: "Whatever policy we may lay down, the art of conducting the foreign affairs of a country lies in finding out what is most advantageous to the country.... In the ultimate analysis, a government functions for the good of the country it governs and no government dare do anything which in the short or long run is manifestly to the disadvantage of that country."[18] Nehru attempted to achieve a synthesis of idealism and realism in Indian foreign policy when he said that "we propose to look after India's interests in the context of world cooperation and world peace, in so far as world peace can be preserved."[19]

The realist in Nehru understood Indian geopolitics and security problems, but the idealist in him saw the tremendous human problem of India's poverty, and the damage militarism could do to India's political institutions and values. He assigned higher priority to economic development than to military preparation. He shared the idealistic urge of the Indian national movement, but tried to give it a less romanticist and more historical outlook and the humanitarian content of Marxism. The realist in him saw the limits of the practical experiments with Marxism and identified himself with the mainsteam of ideological thinking in the Indian national movement. The realist saw the destructive potentialities of nuclear war, and the idealist tried to look beyond the immediate sphere of political and ideological crusade for a tomorrow of peaceful co-existence, and even to dream of One World. "The truth is", as Nasser once said, "Nehru is not only the exponent of the dreams deeply nestled in the hearts of the people of India. He is also the expression of the human conscience itself...."[20] "In this critical moment of human history," Bertrand Russell wrote in 1959, it would be Nehru who "will lead us out of the dark night of fear into a happier day."[21]

I have argued elsewhere that Nehru did not always succeed in achieving a rational synthesis between idealism and realism in the detailed implementation of his foreign policy.[22] But this synthesis was largely achieved in the broad policy of non-alignment which constituted the very foundation of his foreign policy. There can be little doubt that the striving for the "realism of tomorrow" in international relations, without sacrificing India's immediate interests, was one of the most important reasons why, he alone of all the Indian political leaders, could have projected the idealist tradition of modern Indian political thinking into Indian foreign policy without sending it on a fourth dimensional flight into metaphysics.

K. B. LALL

Nehru and International Economic Cooperation

WE ARE TODAY so familiar with the theory and practice of international economic cooperation that it is difficult for us to realise
how recent this phenomenon is, and how much it owes among
others to Jawaharlal Nehru. As far back as 1929, in his presidential
address to the Lahore Congress, Nehru declared: "India today
is a part of a world movement." He proceeded to utter a warning:
"If we ignore the world, we do so at our peril . . . . Civilization has
had enough of narrow nationalism and gropes towards wider cooperation and inter-dependence. Having attained our freedom,
I have no doubt that India will welcome all attempts at world
cooperation."

However, Nehru was not thinking of cooperating within narrow
political limits alone. In April 1936, he told the Lucknow Congress:

> I work for Indian independence because the nationalist in me
> cannot tolerate alien domination; I work for it even more because
> it is an inevitable step to social and economic change . . . . I should
> like the Congress to become a socialist organisation and to join
> hands with other forces in the world who are working for the
> new civilisation.

Paradoxically, Nehru struggled for the political independence of
India so that she might be free to promote international cooperation.
He told the Constituent Assembly on January 22, 1947: "If we

seek to be a free, independent, democratic Republic, it is not to dissociate ourselves from other countries, but rather as a free nation to cooperate in the fullest measure with other countries." Immediately after assuming office as Prime Minister, he sent his greetings to the nations and peoples of the world and "a pledge to cooperate with them in furthering peace, freedom and democracy."

It is important to recall that little thought had been given in the nineteen thirties or early forties to international economic cooperation. Economic competition and autarchial development were regarded by most countries as the panacea for national ills. To beggar one's neighbour had become the usual objective of national policy. Economic confrontation was one of the contributory causes of the Second World War. Out of its harrowing experience came the first glimmers of international economic cooperation.

It is remarkable that at a time when few people in the world at large, let alone those in an India, fettered and bound, recognised the need for cooperation, Jawaharlal's voice should have been raised so consistently, so forcefully, in such impassioned tones for a greater and greater measure of cooperation, between the nations of the world in all fields of human endeavour. It is remarkable that at a time when the preoccupation of most nationalist leaders was only with the freedom of their own country, Nehru should have perceived the vital inter-connection between national freedom and international cooperation. It is remarkable too, that so long ago, Nehru was able to see that economic change in India was bound up with India's economic cooperation with other nations of the world. If today, we have a great deal of literature on economic cooperation, if today no statesman in the world can afford to ignore its importance in the affairs of nations the credit must go partly to Nehru who was never tired of urging the nations of the world, even at a time when they did not listen to him, to sink their rivalries, to base their policies on cooperation, and not on confrontation or domination.

If I have ventured to quote so freely from Nehru's speeches of a by-gone era I have done so for two reasons. Firstly, to refer to the political and economic urges of the people of India, to the economic content of the Indian struggle for Independence, and to Nehru's vision of a world power structure based not on domination but on cooperation. Secondly, to draw attention to Nehru's role in conceiving the idea of economic cooperation, in adapting it to meet the needs and urges for social and economic progress, not only of India, but also of all the emerging nations of the world. Nehru thus helped to start and carry through a process of change in international economic relationships, not merely for the benefit of India, or of the emerging nations, but of the world as a whole.

II

Once the process of political consolidation was completed with the coming into force of our Republican Constitution, Jawaharlal Nehru had the political base for promoting economic and social change within India and for putting forward his ideas for a restructuring of the world economic order.

Nehru would have been the first to deny that his vision of India's role on the world stage, sprang only from his own imagination. His imagination drew deeply upon the millennia of India's history, her culture, and her traditions. The transition from a tradition-bound, disparate "dependency" into a modern, united and industrially developing nation was in a great measure a response of the people of India to Nehru's urges, ideas and policies.

In the early years of our independence, in the fifties, economic cooperation with the nations of the world was an urgent need, if economic freedom was to be achieved, if the leeway of centuries in the social and economic sectors of our polity was to be made up rapidly. We needed peace for our progress: hence, the policy of non-alignment with military blocs or big powers.

When Nehru surveyed the scene in 1947, what did he find? India needed new markets besides the old ones; she needed new technology in addition to what had been imported to enable the British to fight the war; she needed new sources of capital besides the sterling balances. Hence, the policy to forge new links, and to transform-not destroy old ones. It was called a policy of non-alignment which meant in fact, a policy of being aligned to every nation of the world in friendship on a basis of equality and for mutual benefit.

To Nehru, international economic cooperation provided an acceptable means of furthering the economic progress of India. As far back as December 4, 1947 he remarked, in a speech to the Constituent Assembly, that foreign policy ultimately was the "outcome of economic policy." That he had already started for-mulating an economic policy can be seen in the resolution which he had moved at the Karachi Congress, as early as 1931. It was then, that the concept of planning had begun to take shape. Seven years later the National Planning Committee came into existence and was headed by Nehru himself.

In his speech to the Constituent Assembly on December 4, 1947, Nehru argued that "in the long distant future," self-interest itself demanded a policy of cooperation with other nations. "External Affairs," he said, "will follow internal affairs." The linkage between the economic situation of a country just freed from colonial domi-nation and international cooperation as a major plank in that country's foreign policy could hardly have been put more clearly.

What was the content of international economic cooperation Nehru was setting out to seek? He had observed in 1929: "Our economic programme must be based on a human outlook, not merely the internal programme, but also the external programme." The key thought in this quotation, to my mind, is the relevance of a human outlook in elaborating both internal and external pro-grammes. It is to this humanistic approach of Nehru that we can trace, at the internal level, the adoption by India of a socialistic pattern of society as a frame for socio-economic progress; and at the external level, the adoption at his insistence by the international community of the objective of restructuring the international econo-mic order in which the poorer nations may occupy a position in keeping with their human and material resources. In the combination of self-interest, a human outlook, and international cooperation Nehru saw a possible solution of the problems that developing countries encountered in their relationship with the developed world. The birth of United Nations Commission for Trade and Development (UNCTAD) was implicit in Nehru's approach to internal and external problems of economic development.

Nehru did not omit from his purview the role of rich industrial nations. He dealt with it in his address to the Canadian Parliament on October 24, 1949: "There can be no security or real peace if vast numbers of people in various parts of the world live in poverty and misery; nor can there be a balanced economy for the world as a whole if the under-developed parts continue to upset that balance and drag down even the more prosperous nations." He spelt out the connection between international security and international economic development. If under-development was not overcome, the prosperity of prosperous nations itself would be in jeopardy. These concepts of Nehru have formed the basis for wide ranging debates, discussions, and negotiations in UNCTAD I, UNCTAD II and UNCTAD III. When the International Development Strategy was debated in the General Assembly of the United Nations in 1970, different views were expressed on the relationship of the development of impoverished parts of the world to the industrial nations. It was with some difficulty that a consensus could be reached on the view that such development would be conducive to the benefit for all the nations of the world.

Nehru's basic ideas on international economic cooperation, had been, as explained earlier, formed during the days of the Indian struggle for independence. The dawn of India's freedom provided the opportunity for launching them on the world stage. Nehru realised, however, that unless India was able to help herself, it would not be possible for her to serve as a launching pad for ideas to reshape the world economic order.

During the early years of independence, Nehru sought to transform and strengthen the Indian economy, and to develop a purposeful pattern for India's external relations. He had thought deeply on economic development and its practical implications. These implications included in the first place his grafting of a process of planned development on a democratic system; he said, "I shall show to the world that political democracy and economic progress can go together." Secondly, there was his mix of ideology and pragmatism. "One has to remember," he said, "that the primary function of a growing society is to produce more wealth; otherwise, it will not grow. We must not imagine that we have grown up because we have satisfied some text-book maxim of a hundred years ago. The essential thing is that there must be wealth and production.... There must be equality of opportunity and the possibility for every one to live a good life." To him, economic growth was inextricably intertwined with social justice. Third, in importance was the role of science and technology. Fourth, was Nehru's integrated view of economic endeavour, embracing simultaneous and inter-acting development of agriculture, industry, power, socio-economic infrastructure, and also combining an expanding public sector with thriving private enterprise. Fifth was his positive concept of non-alignment, to disentangle international economic relationships,

industrial collaboration, commercial exchanges, financial cooperation, and technical assistance from the coils of the cold war and
ideological confrontation.

This five-fold path, in Nehru's opinion could help India
to break out of economic bondage and also furnish a flexible pattern
for the differing circumstances of other emerging nations.

There is no doubt that it was during the nineteen fifties and early
sixties when the foundations of India's modern economy were laid.
We are familiar with the "Industrial Policy Resolutions" of 1948 and
1956; steel plants and hydro-electric dams, the setting up of heavy
industry in the public sector, the application of scientific techniques
to agriculture, the development of small-scale industries, and our
early endeavours to locate petroleum, start petro-chemical industries
and develop nuclear energy, the Five Year Plans the growth of the
public sector and its extension to the field of external trade and
the simultaneous expansion of entrepreneurial skills and private
enterprise.

In our preoccupation with the problems that we are encountering
today we are apt to forget or overlook the peaks we scaled in India
in the Nehru era. We owe to his vision and to his labours our present
capacity to build many things from a pin to an aeroplane, even to
make machines to build machines. We have now the technical
competence to grow enough food to meet our requirements and to
convert our raw materials to meet rising levels of consumption.
We are also in a position to share the fruits of our experience and
of our labours with other countries, who, like us had suffered from
arrested development. With increasing sophistication our own
problems have in the meanwhile become more complex. The concepts
of international economic cooperation evolved by Nehru have
some relevance to our current efforts to advance to the next stage
of our progress.

III

Most of these concepts have grown out of Nehru's efforts to diversify
India's external economic relations. Great Britain was, of course,
the starting point. To a lesser man than Nehru the first thought on
the attainment of freedom would have been to cut off the chains
that bound India to the economy of the United Kingdom. Indeed

some Indian leaders were arguing and thinking in those terms. But Nehru had not conceived of independent India in a constricted frame. He did not, denounce the agreement of 1935. Nor did he ask for a new agreement with the United Kingdom. He succeeded in transforming the old relationship and placing it in a new perspective. The old agreement, particularly its principles of preference, became an important element in our economic relationship with the Commonwealth.

The industrial development of India converted the agreement of 1935 into a balanced relationship between the two countries, equally advantageous to the development and the developed partner. In 1962, when the United Kingdom attempted to join the European Economic Community, Nehru told the Commonwealth Prime Ministers: "It is only lately that duty-free imports into the United Kingdom and preferential arrangements over the Commonwealth as a whole have helped us to build up a sizeable trade in our manufactures, a trade which has proved beneficial not only to ourselves but also to the United Kingdom." He put the dilemma of the developing countries before the Conference thus: "In order to avoid the barrier erected by the Community, the United Kingdom is seeking to join the Market, but in the case of developing countries like India, whose need to increase exports is greater and whose difficulties in increasing exports are manifold, it is proposed to erect a tariff where none existed before." In a prophetic vein he proposed a structural change in international commercial relationships as a solution for the problem of developing countries. He went on to say: "The solution to the problem which concerns not only India but other developing countries in and outside the Commonwealth lies in extending duty-free treatment to as wide a list of items as possible and to lower the tariff on the rest. I do not see how else this problem can be solved."

Not destruction, but transformation, a concept from Indian philosophy, transplanted by Nehru to the realms of diplomacy and economic relations—was the cornerstone on which Nehru erected the new structure of Indo-British relations. This applied equally to the field of finance, industrial and modern technology, with the result that economic contact and cooperation between the two economies is now much wider and closer than in the past and is based on equality and mutual benefit.

The role of the United States in the world economy is well-known.

It was natural for the two democracies—India and America to think of friendly cooperation with each other. While economic relations grew between the two countries, difficulties were experienced in negotiating a treaty of friendship, commerce and navigation. The standard draft of these treaties was inherited from the old order. When applied to relations between a weak and a strong partner the standard provisions did not meet the needs of an under-developed country struggling to overcome the weaknesses of the colonial past. The beneficial aspects of the provisions were explained to us from time to time; our difficulties and our apprehensions were explained, by us politely but firmly. Efforts were made to discover mutually satisfactory solutions. It was in 1958 that I went to the United States, it was not possible to conclude a trade agreement. A joint statement—at a somewhat low level—was issued. This defined the commercial relationship between the two countries and made it possible for trade between them to expand and for industrial collaboration to grow. At the same time important arrangements in the field of development assistance and financial cooperation were discussed and put into effect. It can be said in retrospect that, despite difficulties, ways and means were found for the United States to make an important contribution to our effort to diversify our economic relations, to seek new markets and to secure access to new sources of finance and technology.

India did not have any significant trade with the Soviet Union before 1947. In fact, all socialist countries, at the end of the 1940s and even in early 1950s were living in a state of seclusion. Their seclusion set limits to Nehru's urge for diversification of our economic relations. The first trade agreement with the Soviet Union, for a period of five years, was signed on February 2, 1953. I was associated with the negotiations. Payments were envisaged to be made in rupees. But the solution to the problems of the currency policies pursued by socialist countries and the "strangulation effects" of our own currency shortages was still to be found. The trade between the two countries expanded, but at a slow pace during the period of the first agreement.

The first industrial cooperation agreement with the Soviet Union to set up a steel plant at Bhilai, was concluded in 1955. The difficulties posed by the differences in our respective economic systems in achieving a mutual expansion of trade to the full limit of our needs and possibilities, however, persisted. I was sent to Moscow in search of a solution. It was clear that we would have to think in terms of solutions without the conventional frames to which we or the rest of the world, or even the Soviet Union, had been used to. There was need for ingenuity and innovations. Widely differing views were held by experts on both sides. It was not easy to assess the full implications of some of the solutions that were discussed. Nehru's vision was clear. His boldness overcame the hesitation of sceptics. In 1958, a new mechanism of payment was devised: it provided for all commercial and noncommercial payments to be made in non-convertible rupees. Technical credits and settlement of outstanding balances through additional exports were expected to take care of lags and leads. In view of the lack of practical experience, it was informally agreed that in case the new arrangement led to unforeseen results it could be reviewed. No need has so far been felt for second thoughts. Within a year, means were found to make it possible, by relating the rupee to its gold content in terms of the International Monetary Fund norms, for socialist countries to supply investment goods to India on long-term loans at a low rate of interest repayable in Indian goods over a period of ten to twelve years.

The new mechanism became the keystone of our economic relations with socialist countries. However, we ran into trouble with the International Monetary Fund and the General Agreement on Trade and Tariff. We were accused of acting in violation of the agreements to which we had subscribed. Year after year we were asked to explain our digressions from accepted modes and to pledge our loyalty to them. We tried to defend ourselves. We argued that our payment arrangements should be viewed as a substitute for the traditional liquidity of gold and for convertible currency settlements. We asked for alternative modes to service economic contacts with countries which did not subscribe to the IMF and the GATT. We urged that bilateralism was unavoidable relations with countries which did not practise multilateralism. The pressure on us to conform to accepted norms was maintained, but gradually the argument that the experience of bilateral trading might eventually extend and strengthen multilateralism began to tell. Even the western countries striving to develop their trade with the socialist countries found it necessary to resort to some form of bilateral adjustments. When the history of this period is studied in some depth, it may be found that their compensatory arrangements owed much to Nehru's initiative in forging new links with the socialist world. These links have been of great benefit to India, to some other developing countries and to the Soviet Union. They also helped to initiate the process of bringing the socialist countries into the mainstream of the world economy.

Economic cooperation with the Soviet Union and other socialist countries made it possible for us to have access to a new source of finance and technology, to acquire experience of socialist techniques of planning, industrial development, and market management. In consequence, a sort of competition between two different systems was set up within our geographical boundaries.Evidence of its beneficient impact can be seen throughout the length and breadth of our country. The two systems have in their own way contributed to a successful "mix" of our economy. We may yet succeed in evolving out of their methodologies and experiences a third way, the Indian way, of combining economic growth with social justice. In any case, the synthesising strand in the Indian ethos seems to have helped Nehru to impart a constructive content to his concept of non-alignment.

In his effort to diversify India's external relations, Nehru also sought to build contacts with the free market economies of Western Europe. These countries were recovering from the ravages of the war, and did not have much interest in India, which had for long been regarded as an appendage of the British Empire. Nevertheless India concluded trade agreements with Switzerland, Finland, West Germany and Austria in 1949, with Sweden in 1950 and with Norway in 1951. Later, two economic groupings, the European Free Trade Area and the European Economic Community came into being. I had opportunities of leading trade delegations to some of these countries. Previous agreements were revised or fresh agreements were concluded to take care of the evolving situation, notably with Italy, Switzerland, France and the Federal Republic of Germany. I also paid a visit to Brussels, the headquarters of the European Economic Community.

By 1961, Britain had decided to apply for admission to the European Economic Community. Nehru decided that India should have direct access to this emerging Colossus. Early in January 1962, I presented my credentials to the President of E.E.C's Council of Ministers and the President of the European Economic Commission. The Indian Mission to the Community was charged with a two-fold mission: first, to protect the interests of India in the British market in the event of Britain joining the Community and secondly, to develop contacts with the European Common Market.

At the height of the negotiations between the E.E.C. and the United Kingdom, the Commonwealth prime ministers met in London in September 1962. Addressing the conference, Nehru put forward the case of the developing countries of the Commonwealth: "The developing countries are struggling hard to raise the standard of living of their people and the levels of production. It is impossible for us to import machinery and capital goods necessary for our development plans unless we can increase the level of our exports. We are grateful for the foreign aid which is largely in the shape of loans and credits. These have to be paid back with interest. We can pay them back only through increase in our exports. There is no other way." He went on to say, "We are terribly anxious to modernise our agriculture and develop our industries. This is a problem of urgent need and importance to us.... Even the developed countries in affluent circumstances must realise that the poorer countries must grow and be provided with wider markets." He urged that "firstly any agreement made must help in the wider context of the world, and, secondly, it is essential generally from the world point of view to develop industrially the countries that are not developed today."

The British negotiations to enter the E.E.C. failed. The Indian effort to develop closer relations with the Community and its member-states, however, was pressed on. The Community could be persuaded to suspend or scale down the import duties on some of our products, particularly tea. An organisation for popularising tea drinking was set up in Brussels. The European Parliament was invited to send a delegation to India. On its return, the delegation urged closer economic relations with India. The movement, however, was slow and sectoral. Considerable expansion, nevertheless, took place in the field of industrial collaboration and financial cooperation. Most of the member states of the Community were persuaded to become the members of the Indian Consortium.

Britain joined the E.E.C. on January 1, 1973. The opportunity for building India's economic relations with the enlarged Community on the lines envisaged by Nehru was thus at hand. Inter-state relations inside the Community are no longer governed by mutual rivalry and internecine conflict. These rivalries had led in the past to mercantilism, colonialism and imperialism. The fact that the nations of Western Europe are coming together in friendship and in cooperation, means that they can no longer maintain the exclusive horizontal relationships they had developed in the past with individual countries in Africa and in Asia. The time has indeed come for building a new relationship between Western Europe, on the one hand, and India and the developing countries of Asia and Africa, on the other. The new relationship will inevitably be based on inter-regional cooperation. In the wake of Indian Independence, the political aspects of colonialism were liquidated during the 1950s; its economic aspects are likely to be transformed in the coming years. It is thus that Nehru's ideas on relations between Western Europe and the developing world may be expected to reach their fulfilment.

IV

It would be useful to examine Nehru's contribution to the development of new relations amongst the developing countries themselves. On March 23, 1947, in a speech to the Asian Relations Conference called to discuss the Indonesian situation, Jawharlal Nehru observed: "As European domination goes, the walls that surrounded us fall down and we look at one another again and meet as old friends long parted." Placing his observations in the wider perspective of international economic cooperation, he went on to explain: "We have no designs against anybody; ours is the great design of promoting peace and progress all over the world. Far too long have we, of Asia, been petitioners in western courts and chancelleries. That story must now belong to the past. We propose to stand on our own legs and to cooperate with all others who are prepared to cooperate with us. We do not intend to be the playthings of others."

Even in those early years Nehru was dreaming of one world and of Asian regional cooperation as Asia's contribution to it. Many countries of Asia, however, soon found themselves entangled in the coils of the cold-war. SEATO AND CENTO appeared on the Asian scene, as an extension of the NATO. The creation of Pakistan had been expected to enable the peoples of the sub-continent to live and develop in peace and freedom. But India and Pakistan got involved in bitter controversy and armed confrontation. China attempted to nibble at the north-western and north-eastern frontiers of India. Bloody wars ravaged the fair lands of Laos and Vietnam. Nehru had to bide his time to fulfil his dream, and yet, he struggled manfully. He tried to apply to the Asian continent the policy of non-alignment and the principles of peaceful co-existence. He went on to assert that "we would rather delay our development, industrial or other, than submit to any kind of economic domination by any country."

Nehru widened the sweep of his ideas to include Asia and Africa. When the heads of state and of governments, African, and Asian, met in Bandung in 1955. Nehru described the Conference as essentially an experiment in co-existence . . . "a meeting together in a friendly way and trying to find what common ground there is for cooperation in the economic, cultural and political fields." The Bandung Conference declared its "conviction that...cooperation in the economic, social and cultural fields would help bring about the common prosperity and well being of all" in Africa and in Asia.

The meetings of ECAFE and its subordinate bodies were used to develop common thinking and further regional cooperation. In 1962, I was called by ECAFE to head a group of "3-wise men" to elaborate a regional project for trade expansion and for mutual cooperation in economic development. Nehru granted an interview to this group. A scheme for the setting up of a Council of Ministers was proposed. But it ran into difficulties. Many years later, the project was revived in another form. An Asian Council of Ministers on Regional Cooperation has since come into being, and has met several times. At the meeting held in Kabul in 1970 the scheme for the establishment of an Asian Clearing Union was approved and directions were given for the further processing of other schemes. This is a hopeful beginning but Nehru's dreams on Asia, remain to be fulfilled.

While advance on the multilateral front proved to be halting, Nehru's efforts to intensify India's economic relations with Asian and African countries met with a measure of success. Besides the treaty with Nepal in 1950, agreements were negotiated with Burma and Ceylon. New contacts were forged with Indonesia. Towards the end of the 1950s the difficulties experienced by Nepal in implementing the provisions of the 1950 treaty caused Nehru much worry. The Trade and Transit Treaty between India and Nepal was signed on September 11, 1960; it provided Nepal with transit facilities for the development of its trade with overseas countries and set up a frame for the two countries to develop in mutual cooperation their respective economics in accordance with their own views and interests.

The Commonwealth arrangements and contacts provided facilities for the expansion of our relations with many developing countries. It was also found possible over the 1950s and in the early 1960s to introduce some new elements in our economic relations with other developing countries. The inadequacy of our foreign income to support our development needs had obliged us to impose drastic restrictions on the import of consumer items. Afghanistan's economy however, was partly dependent on the export of fresh and dry fruits to India. In 1957, a bilateral arrangement was entered into with that country, providing a special procedure for the maintenance and development of Afghanistan's trade with India. Similarly, special arrangements were made to facilitate the import of dates from Iran and Iraq.

An interesting pattern of trade was developed with those countries of Africa and the Middle-East which were in a position to meet our requirements for industrial raw materials. The import of raw cotton from Egypt, Sudan and Uganda was used for the development of a two-way trade with these countries. A somewhat similar arrangement was evolved with Jordan for the import of phosphate rock. Green tea from India was introduced to Morocco and Tunisia; we bought phosphates in return. Special efforts were made to develop our economic relations with the Arab countries.

An effort was made to break the isolation of India from Latin America. A trade agreement was concluded with Chile and discussions were held with representatives of Argentine, Brazil, Mexico, Peru and Columbia.

The first agreement with Yugoslavia was concluded as far back as 1948. The introduction of the rupee trading system from 1962 helped India and Yugoslavia to widen their economic contacts, especially in industrial collaboration and shipping.

There is one country in Asia whose rise to economic prominence on the international horizon was foreseen by Nehru even in early fifties. He thought it could serve national and wider purposes if good economic relations could be developed with Japan. A series of agreements have been concluded since 1958. The Japanese government particularly appreciated our willingness to accord full GATT treatment to their exports. India and Japan undertook to expand trade, to strengthen economic relations and to further the exchange of scientific and technical knowledge. A beginning was also made with financial cooperation and with arrangements by the State Trading Corporation of India to supply raw materials needed by the Japanese steel industry.

V

While engaged in diversifying India's external economic relations, Nehru's mind remained preoccupied with the problem of evolving a global pattern for international economic cooperation. Articles 54 and 55 of the U.N. Charter provided a base. He was interested in the Economic and Social Commission, Food and Agriculture Organization and International Labour Organization. India played a leading role in the United Nation's decision to designate the 1960s as the First Development Decade. Nehru found time to keep himself in touch with the progress of work in the Preparatory Committee for bringing into being a new international organisation, to further "a bold new programme of international economic cooperation." Finally, the first United Nations Conference on Trade and Development met in 1964 in Geneva.

The Conference was initially divided into three groups to facilitate the organisation of its business. I was asked to preside over Group C. South Africa and Israel had by some clever device been put in that group. As was feared by some and expected by others, strong feelings were aroused. It appeared for a moment that the cause of development might be lost in a desultory debate on the demand for exclusion of South Africa and Israel. It was suggested from the chair that the order of business might be reversed so that the common problem of underdevelopment was taken up first. No one dissented. A group of seven representatives was quickly set up. The representatives did not know one another and practical experience was sadly lacking. Nevertheless, when we met we found we had common problems, and we felt instinctively that we should strive for common solutions. Within fifteen days, we were able to reach an agreement on what the developing countries would wish the conference to do. In their name, a "Charter of Demands" was presented formally. It formed the basis for negotiations with developed countries in the following months.

Eventually on June 16, the Conference adopted the "Final Act." Nehru's vision of developing countries acting in concert had been more or less realised. A little later we participated in the negotiations with the developed countries which proved to be quite difficult. There were the usual differences of approach embracing the whole spectrum between the "hawks", and the "doves". Manubhai Shah, the leader of the Indian Delegation, recalled in an impassioned speech his experiences in the fight for India's freedom. The atmosphere in the meetings of the developing countries was charged with deep emotion; I found it as uplifting when as a young student I had attended some political meetings in Delhi in the nineteen thirties. Since the final agreements that could be reached with developed countries at that stage of their understanding of our problems proved inadequate, the developing countries decided to form a pressure group of their own. This has since come to be known as "Group 77". At the end of the conference, this group issued a joint declaration. From that day, the group has continued to function, with varying degrees of effectiveness, in different international bodies to improve the efficiency of economic cooperation and to promote structural changes in international economic relationships. As happens in all movements for political change at the international level, the Group of 77 suffers from differences and dissensions. Currently, its disunity has weakened its force in international affairs. To the pessimist it might even look that it may not again capture its original elan and initial momentum. A narrow view of national interests inevitably creates rifts and engenders misgivings. However, I remain convinced that the relentless pressure of our common problems will compel us to revive our unity and to pool our strength.

Throughout, there has been a general apprehension that the unity of the economic interests of developing countries could be adversely affected by political developments in the international situation. The movement for non-alignment developed its economic content to provide sustained support to the struggle of the developing world. At Belgrade, on September 2, 1962, Nehru had asked the non-aligned nations to recognise that "we are socially and economically backward countries, and it is not an easy matter to get rid of this inheritance of backwardness and underdevelopment. It requires clear thinking; it requires action; it requires a tremendous amount of hard work....It is the positive constructive work we do that gives us strength to make our countries free." The participants in the Conference demanded that "all the gains of scientific and technological revolution be applied in all fields of economic development to hasten the achievement of international justice." It was not until the Lusaka Conference in 1970 that the non-aligned movement was able to give substance to Nehru's approach and to declare that "economic development is an obligation of the whole international community, that it is the duty of all countries to contribute to the rapid evolution of a new and just economic order under which all nations can live without fear and rise to their full stature in the family of nations."

In 1970, the General Assembly of the United Nations accepted economic and social progress to be "the common and shared responsibility of the entire international Community." While declaring the seventies to be the "Second Development Decade," the member-states of the United Nations pledged "themselves individually and collectively, to pursue policies designed to create a more just and rational world economic order in which quality of opportunity should be as much a prerogative of nations as of individuals within a nation." Thus the statement made by Nehru to the Canadian Parliament in 1949 virtually came to be accepted in 1970 as an essential ingredient of international thought and action. And his concept of combining economic growth with social justice on the national stage was beginning to be accepted as a basis for the restructuring of economic relations between the developing and the developed world.

Reference has already been made to the isolation of the socialist countries from the free market economies of the world and of Nehru's attempt to build bridges with them. The United Nations Conference on Trade and Development included in its Final Act "general principle 6" requiring all countries to cooperate in creating conditions of international trade conducive "to the promotion of expansion and diversification of trade between countries... having different economic and social systems." This is an aspect of Nehru's contribution to the evolution of international economic cooperation which has not yet received sufficient attention.

VI

India was able to have some small but basic changes introduced in the trading and monetary structure evolved by the free market economy countries at Brettonwoods and in the GATT, enabling the developing countries to overcome some of the handicaps implicit in that system. The Indian delegation led by L.K. Jha succeeded in introducing Article XVIII in the General Agreement on Trade and Tariffs, permitting developing countries to impose import restrictions to implement programmes and policies of economic development. It is well-known that the import restrictions imposed through our Red Book helped to persuade industrial organisations in the western world to think in terms of jumping over our protective walls and collaborate with Indian entrepreneurs in organising industrial production to meet domestic needs. In consequence, we were able to transform our production. We soon began to think of augmenting our foreign income by the export of our new manufactures.

Our manufactured product was itself new. Even the Indians found it difficult to overcome their preference for the imported brand. How then could an overseas consumer wish to buy our product? Moreover the industrial nations had high tariff walls to protect their industry, and it was not easy to make a dent in their complex and sophisticated system of marketing.

Another struggle ensued in Geneva. As a result, Articles XXXVI to XXXVIII were added to the GATT. The need for positive efforts on the part of "Contracting Parties" to secure for developing countries a fair share in international trade was recognised. A blanket standstill on customs charges was accepted. Appropriate measures were to be devised to attain equitable prices for primary products. Consideration was also to be given to the adoption of other measures to provide greater scope for the development of imports of new manufactures from developing countries. The "Contracting Parties" were not yet ready to accord preferential treatment to these imports. The first proposal to this effect was greeted with derisive comment. "How dare you preach such heresy in this hall of orthodoxy?" I was asked. I enquired in reply, "Have you heard of Luther? Have you forgotten the good that Reformation did to the world?"

It was only four years later that UNCTAD II in Delhi accorded its approval in principle to the Generalised Scheme of Preferences in favour of products from developing countries. While some industrial countries have given partial effect to it, others are only preparing to do so. It is nevertheless a matter for satisfaction that at last the suggestion tentatively put forward by Nehru in 1962 to the Commonwealth Prime Ministers' Conference at London was taking practical shape.

The movement for the developing countries to accord preferential treatment to one another's trade has been even slower to develop. It was usual under the colonial system for the dominating economy to grant preferences to the products of the dominated countries. As long as this system endures, it is impossible for developing countries to exchange their new manufactures with one another. When it was proposed that developed countries should voluntarily abandon their rights under the old system and agree to permit developing countries to accord preferential treatment over limited areas to one another, a delegate from a developed country accused us of trying to destroy the GATT. We argued that formal adherence to the principle of equality and non-discrimination only sustained inequality and perpetuated discrimination against developing countries. (We have the same trouble on the national stage. The more dynamic elements in our society are quick to take advantage of the measures which Government institutes for the benefit of the weaker sections with the result that the gulf between the weak and the strong, instead of narrowing, widens.) After a further struggle the "Contracting Parties" were persuaded to accept the need for "special measures" in trade relations between developing countries. Much hard work, however, lies ahead before these measures can have their impact on the course of the world economy.

If we continue to press forward steadily along the path shown to us by Nehru, it will gradually become easier to obtain from our expanding external trade a greater part of the means needed to finance our further progress. As stated earlier in the fifties, special steps had been taken by us to facilitate the import of dry fruits from Afghanistan, of dates from Iraq and Iran and of coconut oil from Sri Lanka. Is it not time for this concept to be extended to cover new manufactures from developing countries? Such a step could bring advantage to our industry and to our consumers. It could also serve to impart strength and momentum to the movement for international cooperation. Imagine the effect on Sri Lanka if we were to agree to grant national treatment to rubber manufactures, especially tyres, from that country. Would not such a step fire Sri Lanka's imagination and make it easier for developing countries to cooperate with one another in developing their respective resources for their mutual benefit?

VII

The movement for the restructuring of international financial and monetary relationships on the basis of the principles of cooperation has been even slower. It has not been easy to ensure that the financial strength of industrial nations is employed to the real advantage of developing countries and to the ultimate good of the world as a whole. Nehru tried to disentangle the beneficent aspects of financial relationship from its deleterious consequences for developing countries. Referring to the investment of foreign private capital, Nehru observed: "But India from long experience of foreign domination is most sensitive on this subject and would resist anything leading to the creation of powerful foreign vested interests." He, therefore, tried to provide that participation of foreign capital and enterprise was carefully regulated in the national interest.

State borrowing generates its own problems. Nehru was well aware of this. And yet, the needs of our long arrested development were pressing. In 1958 he permitted himself to observe: "Help from other countries is useful, and in their own time all the great countries of the world have been helped. Before hundred years even the United States of America was the place for investment of British and other capital. There is nothing disparaging about it. But the point I wish to make is that we should not develop a mentality of relying on outside help all the time."

Developing countries face a great dilemma. Financial assistance is necessary for them for the development of self reliance; at the same time it could have the effect of perpetuating dependence on sources of foreign capital. Nehru sought to deal with the dilemma by dissociating economics from politics and by turning his back on offers with visible or invisible strings. He preferred to rely on the World Bank to muster financial resources from friendly nations to meet our needs for ready cash. The World Bank succeeded in organising substantial flows of development funds to help overcome the difficulties we encountered in implementing our Second Five Year Plan and to facilitate the achievement of the target we set ourselves in our Third Plan.

The element of assistance in development loans was minimal. In consequence our debt grew apace. A large part of the loans we now receive is devoted to meeting the obligations we had contracted earlier. We wish to get out of this vicious circle. A good solution in conformity with Nehru's approach for the dilemma the developing countries face has still to be found. Nehru had himself posed this dilemma in the following words:

> We are not opposed to cooperation with the world. We are in need of new markets. We are in need of new sources of capital. But we do not want these markets, we do not want capital on old terms. The meaning I attach to our policy in this respect is we do not want aid with political strings, we do not want aid which, instead of providing new capital for our further development, further growth, further social justice, provides instead a system by which our development does not remain in our hands.

We can succeed in finding a good solution if we press on with the effort to change financial relationships to meet the emerging needs of world economy.

No nation is wholly rich or poor. We may be poor in finance. Our resources in technology and science may not be sufficient to cope with our accumulated needs. But the nations which are rich in finance and technology are comparatively less well endowed with human and material resources. These nations have been endeavouring to overcome their inadequacies by automation, by imported labour, and by substituting industrial raw materials with synthetic products. These endeavours, I am convinced, will bring them only limited solutions. They are already coming to the conclusion that it is better to import goods than to import labour. They are also beginning to discover that they cannot free themselves from their dependence on at least some of the resources which can be found only in the developing world. They are, therefore, looking beyond their confines for the solution of problems posed by the inadequacy of their resources in manpower, energy and some raw materials. To my mind, this provides a convenient conjuncture for marrying the riches of industrial nations to the resources of developing countries. The time will soon be ripe in my view for proper value to be assigned to our human and material resources, to make it easier for us to exchange what we have for what we need to have to develop our potential.

This, however, would need some basic changes in monetary management and in terms of trade. There has so far been only a small movement in the direction of alleviating the difficulties which arise for developing countries from the Brettonwoods System. It will be recalled that a new method of stand-by arrangement was introduced in 1952. In 1963, a system of compensatory financing was evolved. In 1969, the Board of Governors of the IMF approved a proposal to allocate Special Drawing Rights in order to improve international liquidity. It has, so far, not been possible to make a really deep study of the basic causes of fundamental disequilibrium in the economies of developing countries. The International Monetary Fund generally insisted on adjustment of exchange rates whenever disequilibrium appeared in the payments position of a developing country, even though such disequilibrium may have partly stemmed from the inequitably low value assigned to its products. However, when the industrial nations found themselves caught up in some difficulties, the exchange adjustment mechanism was soon found to be inadequate. Even, the United States in August 1971 found itself unable to continue to convert freely its currency into gold. In consequence, the world monetary system is now in the melting pot. The time is opportune for the needs of developing countries to be taken into account while refashioning this system.

There does seem something wrong in the system that determines the relative values of what we have in surplus and of that which we need to import from industrial nations. That may, of course, not be the whole explanation for our present difficulties. Some of them derive from historical causes, from the compulsions of the colonial system which deprived us of the opportunities provided by technological development to improve the productivity of our labour. The international community is, in my view, under an obligation to overcome this problem of the back-log.

The financial factor is a very important element in the power-structure of the world. The management of the world monetary system has so far been in the hands of those who have been financially powerful. Their inability to appreciate the problems of the developing countries or their reluctance to find appropriate solutions is understandable. Under pressure from UNCTAD, the representatives of the developing countries joined the original Group of Ten in the exercise undertaken by the International Monetary Fund. They are pressing for a link to be established between the creation of the SDRs and flows of development finance. It is too early to say whether their suggestion will be accepted or whether it will prove to be an adequate solution.

The current difficulties of world economy derive at least partly from the slow growth of developing countries. Their solution may lie in applying to the international field some of the lessons learnt by more developed nations on the national stage. There is no alternative to pressing forward the effort to transform international, financial and monetary relationships by applying—to the extent practicable—the concepts of cooperation evolved by Nehru, with redoubled vigour, with increasing knowledge and with even greater determination.

Nehru spoke and wrote in the context of his own times. It would not be proper merely to extrapolate his words into our present problems. His was an innovative mind, a humanistic mind. Several of his concepts, objectives and principles for national and international action, would seem to be relevant as the international environment unfolds inself. Growth, freedom and justice, within the nation and in its relationship with other nations—these were Nehru's watch-words. If we keep them in our mind, if we study the development in the Nehru era, if we apply his concepts and methods imaginatively to the solution of contemporary problems, we may not find our difficulties as formidable as they may appear at this turning point in our history.

P. N. KIRPAL

Jawaharlal Nehru and the Unesco

THE RELATIONSHIP BETWEEN Jawaharlal Nehru and the United Nations Educational, Scientific and Cultural Organization was somewhat complex and hard to define. He was rarely involved in any important decision making concerning India's participation in the work of the Unesco. Though he was both Prime Minister and Minister for External Affairs, he left the conduct of India's relations with Unesco to his illustrious colleague, Abul Kalam Azad, the Education Minister, and to a few other brilliant men, notably Sarvepalli Radhakrishnan and Homi Bhabha. Considering the extraordinary range of subjects on which Nehru spoke frequently, his speeches with a direct bearing on Unesco were relatively few. It might appear at first sight that Nehru was mainly concerned with the political and economic structures of the United Nations. A deeper study of Nehru's relationship with Unesco would, however, reveal that he took keen interest in its aims and ideals.

I propose to begin the story from the end; the passing away of Nehru and its aftermath revealed vividly the strange but powerful role that Nehru played in Unesco.

On the morning of May 27, 1964 when the news of Jawaharlal Nehru's death was received in Unesco House at the Place de Fontenoy I was in Paris. The Executive Board of Unesco was then in session for its long spring meeting. The Indian member of the Executive Board, Shrimati Indira Gandhi, could not participate in that meeting and I was attending it as her deputy. I remember we were in a small committee of the Executive Board finalizing a working document on programme and budget for the consideration of the Executive Board later in the day. Suddenly the Director-General, Rene Maheu, looking pale and distraught, rushed into the Committee room, and informed me of the news of Jawaharlal Nehru's death which had been announced by the B.B.C. The committee dispersed. Soon the news was confirmed through French Government sources. It was decided to adjourn the Board's morning session as a mark of respect to Nehru's memory and to meet again in the afternoon to mourn the world's loss.

The time between the sudden shock of the morning and the commencement of the Executive Board's afternoon meeting was for me an unusual experience which I find it difficult to describe. I was in a daze, a state of mind in which one is so shaken that while the normal reflexes and sensibilities become numbed, others that are hidden inside wake up to receive new perceptions and patterns. In such a daze I could feel a sudden upsurge of emotion that had taken hold of almost every one of the two thousand persons belonging to various nationalities forming the Unesco's international Secretariat and the permanent delegations. In that emotional upsurge grief was mingled with awe and inspiration, as if ordinary mortals had been reminded of the reality and immortality of the spirit of man in the passing away of a fellow-being in whose work and person they suddenly recognized the greatness of that spirit which all shared and valued. The news travelled instantly and was reflected in both sadness and elation visible in faces and glances. Work was suspended and the languages of the conference were muted that morning, but the small community of Unesco's Secretariat was more than ever made intensely aware of the great human mission of their organization. The range, depth and spontaneity of that rare and indefinable mood has remained as an unforgettable experience with me.

Outside, in the streets of Paris, the same mood prevailed. People talked in hushed voices in the open air cafes on a bright summer day. Students in the Sorbonne left their classes to congregate in small groups all over the Latin Quarter. While I paced the streets aimlessly, I received spontaneously from all passers—by an intangible message of sympathy and recognition—a kind of communication in which one realizes momentarily the reality of human solidarity that is much talked about but rarely experienced.

Paris has been called the city of light. On that late May day of 1964 the light of gaiety and abandon did go out of the hearts of many men and women, but the light of human sensitivity, which is also the light of Paris, glowed brightly in the sad remembrance of one who had evidently touched the heart of France.

To go back to the Executive Board. Before describing the afternoon meeting called especially to pay homage to Nehru, a word of explanation about the composition and significance of this body may be useful. Established as one of the three main organs of the organization, along with the General Conference of all member states and the International Secretariat, the Executive Board consisted in 1964 of thirty members representing the world's diverse cultures and elected as persons distinguished in the fields of Unesco's competence by its 113 member-states whom they represented individually and collectively while deriving, at the same time, their mandate from their respective governments. In the United Nations set-up a member of the Unesco's Board has a unique role; he functions as a person discharging the trust reposed by the general body of delegations reflecting the world community and at the same time represents his country for whose government he speaks as its official spokesman. He is expected to interpret and express the undefined and intangible area of intellectual and moral solidarity of mankind as embodied in the constitution as well as the policies and resolutions of the General Conference, and also the will of his government derived from specific instructions and directives received from his national authorities. Such a blend of responsibilities, sometimes delicate, even precarious, expresses a spirit of internationalism which is in tune with the essence of Unesco's mission that is derived from the things of the mind and the spirit and is impossible to confine within national boundaries and governmental institutions. The President of the General Conference sits as an honoured observer in the meetings of the Board that are assisted by the Director-General personally and by his spokesmen from the Secretariat.

The tributes paid to Nehru by the Executive Board have been published in full by Unesco in a publication entitled "Jawaharlal Nehru—In Memoriam." All members of the Board along with its Chairman, the President of the General Conference and the Director-General participated. Speeches were made in a mood of spontaneity and often under the stress of emotion; and for this reason they were more authentic and revealing than the calculated and official pronouncements, usually heard in the Board. The Director-General, Rene Maheu summed up the feeling of all those present:

> Jawaharlal Nehru has radiated over the world like a beacon of tolerance and understanding among the peoples. This is because, all his life long, he never ceased to believe in the supremacy of the spirit in history and because never, not even while in prison and not even while holding power—which is also a prison in many respects—did he allow the call of human brotherhood and the demands of individual and national freedom to become separate spiritual aspirations.
>
> Others will speak of the great void he has left in the affairs of the world. We will lay stress on the unique place that he occupied in the hearts of men. Others will speak of his glory and his remarkable destiny as party leader and head of government. We will recall his tireless quest for truth and love. Others will calculate the effects of his death on the balance and future of the forces in his own country, in the vast expanse of Asia, and indeed in the whole world. We, for our part, wonder how, deprived of this guide and this example, we shall be able to choose and follow our path amid the raging confusion of this world in upheaval, now that the kindliness of that smile, often so gay then suddenly so tired, the warmth of those brown eyes, the charm of that red rose, have disappeared from our view.

II

I propose now to turn briefly to India's role in Unesco during the life-time of Nehru and touch upon some concrete features of policy and action in the sphere of international cultural cooperation.

Within the United Nations system, consisting of its central political organ and a number of specialized agencies, and other bodies, Unesco occupies a rather special place both in regard to the nature of its functions and the manner of its working. As a specialized agency of the United Nations and in accordance with its agreement concluded with the United Nations in 1946, it participates in the coordinating activities of the Economic and Social Council, and functions, by virtue of its constitution, as the main organ of international cooperation in the vast fields of education, science, culture, and information; it enjoys independence and autonomy within the coordinated system of the United Nations. Its originality lies in the vastness of its fields, the basic and intangible character of the things of the mind and the spirit with which it deals, and the essentially moral and ethical role which devolves upon it from the very nature of its functions. Its constitution is distinguished from the strictly inter-governmental character of all the organs of the United Nations, by the provision of National Commissions, composed of non-governmental elements, to assist governments in advancing its objectives and in the implementation of its programmes.

Often, the effectiveness of a country's participation in Unesco's programmes of international cooperation is determined by the health, autonomy and scope of its National Commission which enlists the interest and assistance of such influential groups as teachers, students, scientists, artists, journalists and specialists operating the media of information. If a National Commission reflects adequately the creative forces in the fields of education, science, culture and communication, has the capacity to mobilise and draw upon the enthusiasm of the general public, and possesses resources and possibilities of vigorous, independent action, it can contribute to the work of Unesco in a way that is not open to the strictly other governmental organs of United Nations.

Unesco is also closely associated with International non-governmental organizations of intellectual disciplines and cultural fields and must work with them to advance knowledge and international cooperation. Both by the nature of its responsibilities and its functioning through the multiplicity of governmental and non-governmental organs, it is singularly fitted to contribute to the furtherance of peace, human rights and development, and to their convergence towards an overall concept of life's meaning and quality. It is the essence of its mission and of its overriding responsibility to help create in our world of tensions and fears, of greed and selfishness, a new climate of ethics and morality, of idealism and harmony. It is in this way that man may rediscover himself in his identity with others, express himself in love and service to his fellow-beings, and transcend his own nature by partaking of the universal and thereby directing his own evolution especially in the moral and spiritual realms.

Considering the unique character and objectives of Unesco, it is not surprising that of all organs of the United Nations, Unesco should have had a special appeal for the mind of new India, nurtured on the ideals of Gandhi and Nehru and the great struggle led by them. Ideas and urges contributing to the objectives of democracy, equality, synthesis of cultures, supremacy of moral and spiritual values, the pursuit of scientific objectivity and reason as well as the ancient, values of love and compassion, which were cherished by the leaders of modern India, were the same which lay at the heart of Unesco's mission. Their faith in diffusion and improvement of education, in the harnessing of science and technology for economic development, and the use of cultural activities and media of communication for increasing mutual understanding and trust among diverse peoples and cultures, is also the mandate of Unesco as well. It is therefore, not surprising that in the formative years of the world's cultural organization, India should have played an active and conspicuous role in its development and also derived inspiration and assistance from it.

In the things of the mind and the spirit there is no limit to what people can share with each other. India has given as abundantly to Unesco as it has received from it in the fields of education, science and culture, and both the giving and the receiving have strengthened international cooperation.

Unesco and the United Nations are what the world community of nations make of them, and it is in the action and commitment of its constituent units that the ultimate strength of the organization resides. India's record in the development of Unesco is creditable. Many things were attempted and achieved, but I shall mention only a few important aspects merely to indicate the range and nature of India's cooperation with Unesco.

From 1946 to 1964 India sent to Unesco's General Conference large and distinguished delegations which played a significant role in Unesco's evolving mission and in the formulation of its rapidly expanding programmes and policies. We supported strongly the reconstruction of the educational systems of Europe and its cultural life which had been devastated during the Second World War. Our efforts were also directed to the liquidation of colonialism and racialism and the spread of freedom in dependent and subjugated territories. Special stress was laid on education for international understanding, and India herself developed a massive programme of associated schools under Unesco's experimental programme. In 1960, after more than a decade of numerous proliferating activities, it was the joint initiative of the Indian and the United Kingdom delegations which led to a measure of concentration of Unesco's effort by according an overriding priority to education. Earlier, in 1956, at the ninth Session of the General Conference held in New Delhi (the only venue of the World Assembly so far in Asia) it was due to the leading role played by India, and especially by S. Radhakrishnan and Abul Kalam Azad, that Unesco's major project for the mutual appreciation of Eastern and Western cultural values was launched. Indian historians collaborated in the preparation of the 'Scientific and Cultural History of Mankind.' The concepts of basic and social education evolved in India exercised a considerable influence over the development of Unesco's own programmes of Fundamental Education and functional literacy. The Arid Zones Research Project was proposed by India and adopted by the General Conference. The eminent Indian scientist, the late Homi Bhabha presided over many distinguished gathering of scientists and took India near the centre of the growing network of scientific cooperation. The programme for the application of science and technology to development found powerful support from Indian delegations. Indian specialists were prominent in the development of educational planning in different parts of the world especially in Asia.

Two examples of India's faith in international cooperation which also bring out the nature of her open, democratic society in the Nehru era deserve to be mentioned. Soon after her independence, the government of India requested Unesco to provide specialists from outside to study the internal tensions of Indian society, a step which probably has no precedent in any other part of the world. A distinguished group of social scientists studied the problems with great objectivity, contributing to the development of methodology as well as the discovery of new data on social tensions. In 1964, India's Education Minister, M.C. Chagla, appointed an Education Commission composed of Indian and foreign specialists provided by Unesco, to examine all aspects of Indian education. The report of this Commission, the first international effort of massive dimensions, has inspired improvements in the quality of education in several developing countries and India's example of including foreign specialists in a National Commission has been followed by others.

The measure of India's interest in Unesco is evident from the fact that two former Presidents of the Indian Union, Dr. S. Radhakrishnan and Dr. Zakir Husain and the present Prime Minister, Shrimati Indira Gandhi, have before taking up these highest offices in the land, represented this country on Unesco's Executive Board. Unesco is the only organ of the United Nations in which India has retained a permanent place on the Governing Body and has virtually assumed the role of one of the major "cultural powers." India has always been represented at the Supreme Steering Committee of the General Conference. In little over twenty years, Unesco has honoured India by electing two Indians as presidents of the General Conference and three Indian members of the Executive Board as its Chairman. No other member state of Unesco has had such a distinction. Unesco has drawn upon the services of Indian specialists in all fields. India is the third largest supplier of experts rendering technical assistance to developing countries in the fields of Unesco.

Over the years, India received considerable technical and material assistance from Unesco through its regular and extra-budgetary sources. Numerous projects were launched, and some of them achieved outstanding results. India asked for Unesco's assistance mainly in the fields of science and technology. The Indian Institute of Technology in Bombay which was launched and developed with Unesco's assistance, is one of the best institutions of its kind in Asia. Unesco assisted centres of advanced study at the universities and in reorganising science teaching in secondary schools.

Among projects which have benefited from Unesco's assistance are Power Engineering Research Institute; Central Mechanical Engineering Research Institute, Durgapur; Central Scientific Instruments Organisation; Refining and Petrochemical Division of the Indian Institute of Petroleum at Dehra Dun; Teacher Training for Engineering Colleges, Warangal; National Institute of Foundry and Forge Technology at Ranchi; six Regional Colleges of Engineering; Post-graduate Agricultural Education and Research; Television Production and Studio Technical Operation Training Centre, Poona, and Post-graduate education of engineers. Unesco has also helped various programmes of book development. The Delhi Public Library was established as a joint Unesco-India project. Indian classics have been translated and works of art reproduced and published in the Unesco series. Recording of

Indian music have been popularized by the International Music
Council. The Asian Theatre Institute, the Asian Institute of Educational Planning and Administration and the South Asia Science
Cooperation Office in Delhi were established and operated with
assistance from Unesco. These examples show the nature and
magnitude of Unesco's cooperation; and behind each project
it is not so much the financial resources as cooperative action and
rare skills that have been of great value. Throughout the Nehru
era there was no obsession with material aid to the exclusion of
intellectual cooperation and ethical action, which always received
high priority from Indian government and delegations.

Thus India continued to be an active and prominent member
of Unesco. She gave to it her loyalty and commitment and
received valuable aid for her own development. Ultimately, in the
field of international cooperation, especially concerning things
of the mind, what we give is even more important than what we
receive. India strove to elevate the role of Unesco in the family
of the United Nations, and thereby strengthen the forces of peace,
cooperation and development.

III

The direction of Unesco's growth and the making of its policies,
which is the ultimate responsibility of member-states, is a task of
unusual complexity, and the difficulties encountered in the early
years were formidable. In this respect, the Nehru period can be
roughly divided into two almost equal parts, the nine years 1946-55
being the teething time, of searchings and gropings, of idealism
and proliferation of programme activities, followed by the years
1956-64 when Unesco had to face concrete tasks and realities,
demanding the difficult choice of programme priorities and concentration of effort. In the earlier period, culture and the programmes
for international understanding, along with the stress on freedom
and human dignity, were conspicuous; in the latter period education
and science held primacy for the promotion of equality and development. Soon after the idealistic fervour of the earlier years, the
"Great Powers" began to suspect Unesco's role in terms of
ideology and the emerging world trends towards the eradication of
colonialism and racialism. The liberation of Africa and Asia brought

new member-states to the community of nations, and the concrete forms of the Afro-Asian idea and its more alarming potentialities began to be resented by the prosperous countries of the West. The McCarthy nightmare of the United States, cast its shadow on international cooperation and Unesco was not left unscathed.

In those years of unreason and intolerance, India stood steadfastly as a champion of Unesco's principles and policies and of the newly liberated and less affluent countries. This role and its responsibility were exercised with greater restraint and wisdom here than it was in the political organ of the United Nations.

India gave unfailing support to the idea of universality; this is evident from it's support to China's membership of the United Nations and to recognition of the civilization and cultures of Asia and Africa. Successive Indian delegations pursued the objective of decentralising programmes and operational activities, stressing always the needs of the Asian region. On every occasion and in all matters relating to the strengthening of the intellectual and moral solidarity of mankind, promotion of freedom and human rights and the ethical role of Unesco, the voice of India was respectfully heard, and contributed to compromise and conciliation between conflicting points of view. In the allocation of budgetary resources and the extension of political responsibilities India gave significant support to Unesco. Contributions to both development and international understanding received constant attention from our delegations. In developing the modalities of action we emphasized the role of National Commissions and the universalization of international non-governmental Organizations.

Although Unesco is a specialized agency for performing a technical role, the nature of its responsibilities often gave rise to political and ideological problems. On such occasions India tried, often successfully, to build bridges of understanding. The responsibility of steering controversial resolutions on such delicate subjects as peaceful-coexistence, eradication of colonialism and the preservation of cultural property in the occupied territories of the Middle East was often entrusted to the Indian delegation. For example, early in Unesco's history in 1948, I was invited to conduct a survey of the educational needs of Arab refugees in the Middle East, this resulted in a massive programme which has continued and developed over the years.

Curiously enough India attained a remarkable measure of

preeminence in Unesco affairs without developing adequate and viable mechanisms for this purpose. The Ministry of Education had a very small staff to serve its Unesco unit; the Indian National Commission, after a promising start, languished for want of financial resources and ministerial interests; an effective inter-ministerial cooperation on a continuing basis failed to emerge, and to this day India has no whole-time Permanent Representative at the Unesco headquarters. These and other handicaps were offset by the high quality of leadership provided by our delegations, and especially by some brilliant individuals who enjoyed the trust and confidence of Nehru personally.

The most outstanding figure who became one of the makers of Unesco and brilliantly expounded its early idealism was Sarvepalli Radhakrishnan. Enjoying the reputation of being one of the foremost philosophers of our time, and a bridge-builder between the civilizations of the East and the West, he led several Indian delegations to the General Conference, was elected its president in Paris and served a term as Chairman of the Executive Board. In the early years he discharged his duties as a member of the Executive Board from his Professorship in Oxford, while acting at the same time as Vice-Chancellor of the Banaras Hindu University—a remarkable combination. From London, where I was posted as Educational Adviser to the Indian High Commissioner I often accompanied him to Paris to assist in the work of the Board and to represent him as an alternate member in his absence. Radhakrishnan enjoyed the confidence of Nehru, some time acted without instructions from the Government, but corresponded regularly with the Prime Minister on all important matters. He kept Nehru in touch with what was going on in Unesco and also wrote occasionally to Maulana Azad, the Education Minister. He was usually the opening speaker at the General Policy Debate in the General Conference and his eloquence never failed to cast a spell on all who listened.

His knowledge of Christianity and western philosophies was vast and western delegates were often amazed at the range of his learning. He exercised the weight of his moral and intellectual authority in favour of restraint and compromise and for the extension of a spirit of tolerance to tide over serious differences in ideology and power politics that plagued the world. Even in the growing tensions and fears of the cold war period Radhakrishnan's pleas for sanity and reason, peace and good-will were received in good spirit, without the slightest irritation or resentment. This was not so in the United Nations where India's utterances were often irksome to certain power blocs. What was received in Unesco as a simple and courageous reminder on the need for reason and good sense was often construed by some as arrogant sermonizing or "holier than thou" attitude in the political climate of the United Nations. Apart from the weight of his learning and the power of his oratory, Radhakrishnan drew the admiration and affection of most delegates for his personal qualities of humanity and kindliness.

The defence of humanism also drew another great Indian, Maulana Abul Kalam Azad, to the mission and work of Unesco. The Maulana was, however, reserved and aloof in temperament, isolated from people by his shyness and solitude, and somewhat wrapped up in a dream-world of the Asian cultures of the past in which he was really at home. His mind was luminous, his sensitivity keen and often quick to be injured, and the range of his interests was vast and varied. Nehru's choice of Azad as his Minister of Education, Science and Culture, indicated the importance he attached to the fields of Unesco's action. When the Director-General Torres Bodet of Mexico visited India in 1951, Azad was impressed by Unesco's programmes of fundamental education and decided to launch new activities in this field under the label of "Social Education." The enrichment of the humanities by due emphasis on Asian traditions, and the development of cultural relations with Asian countries, beginning with Turkey and the Arab World, were his passionate interests. Science he did not understand as well as education and culture, but in consultation with Nehru he chose eminent scientists for the making and projection of the scientific policies and horizons of free India.

The Indian scientist who made the greatest impression on the world of science at home and abroad was undoubtedly Homi Bhabha. In Unesco's General Conferences, scientists from various delegations seemed to settle down quickly to their work and functioned as a homogeneous group, motivated more by the universal concerns of science, than by the national interests and problems of their own countries. Their orderly functioning was always in glaring contrast to the confusions and bickerings that characterized the discussions in other groups of educationists, social scientists, cultural leaders and specialists in mass media. For the neater and more fruitful performance of the scientists much of the credit is due to the leadership of Homi Bhabha, who was repeatedly elected by them as their Chairman in contravention of precedent and convention which required geographical rotation in such matters. Younger in age than most of his colleagues, including some of his professors from Cambridge, Homi Bhabha always assumed quickly and effortlessly the personal authority due to one who was not only a great scientist and a science administrator, but also distinguished in a wide range of knowledge and the arts. He was quite a dazzling figure in the early years of Unesco. Few could, however, see his deep commitment to the cause of modernisation in his own country, expressed brilliantly in his relentless efforts to use all sources of knowledge and a wealth of personal contacts for building up an infrastructure needed to exploit atomic energy in the service of economic development. At the core of his vast and varied interests there was a remarkable strength of purpose and single-mindedness which was directed to the planting of atomic science and technology in India. His work and personality brought him close to Nehru. Both of them had faith and hope in the power of science to contribute to human welfare.

Another eminent personality, reflecting Nehru's broad human concerns, was that of Dr. Zakir Husain, who took Dr. Radhakrishnan's place when the latter became Vice-President of India. Dr. Zakir Husain's tenure was cut short by his appointment as Governor of Bihar, but both as a member of the Unesco's Executive Board and as an educationist of distinction, he exercised considerable influence on Unesco's activities in the fields of education and culture. Visiting Paris rarely, he yet received frequently in his home in an atmosphere of warm hospitality and culture, numerous friends of Unesco who visited India from all parts of the world.

A successor to Dr. Zakir Husain on the Executive Board, Dr. Lakshamanaswami Mudaliar, brought to Unesco his distinction in the medical sciences and the experience in the W.H.O. as well as higher education. He impressed his colleagues by his balanced judgement, and remarkable capacity for detailed and constructive work. His sights were directed to practical tasks and urgent needs, and as Chairman of the Board he contributed effectively to the choice of programme priorities and greater concentration on achieving tangible results. His preference for down-to-earth policies and solid work in the field contrasted with the philosophical flights of Radhakrishnan, but though different in their style and methods, both expressed the spirit and policies of Nehru.

Indira Gandhi's tenure at the Executive Board was short, and her important duties at home and increasing responsibilities in national politics prevented her from attending the meetings in Paris regularly. Inspite of this, the impact of her personality was great, and among influential sections of the Board's membership her name was mentioned as a possible Director-General —the first lady who might head an Agency of the United Nations. The American member, Senator William Benton, was an enthusiastic supporter of this idea, and a suggestion by him was conveyed to the Indian Government. Indira Gandhi was, however, destined to assume far greater responsibilities at home, and her commitment to national politics and national development was paramount. All the same, her short association with Unesco left a mark on the delegations and the Secretariat.

Apart from the few names of importance I have just mentioned, there were a host of others, distinguished delegates and specialists, and dedicated members of the Unesco National Commission and the International Secretariat in Paris. Tara Chand, Humayun Kabir and K.G. Saiyidain were active in the field of education, Krishnan and Kothari contributed to scientific cooperation and K.M. Panikkar and R.C. Majumdar participated prominently in the preparation of the Scientific and Cultural History of Mankind.

IV

India's fruitful cooperation with Unesco reflected in the making of programmes and policies and in the contribution of her delegates and cultural leaders was ultimately inspired by Nehru himself and bore the stamp of his personality. For his direct influence on Unesco, let me go a little further in time and quote the following resolution which was voted unanimously by 120 member-states during the 13th session of the General Conference of Unesco in November 1964. The General Conference resolved:

Having weighed the loss of India, to the world and to Unesco of this pioneer in international reconciliation and this guide for

all those who work toward greater international understanding
and co-operation;

Assembled once again to carry out the fundamental aims of
Unesco which by its Constitution is dedicated to the intellectual
and moral solidarity of mankind; and

Believing that in our world of tensions and divisions, now deprived of his physical presence, the name and spirit of Jawaharlal
Nehru should live;

Declares that it is altogether fitting that Unesco, which Jawaharlal
Nehru befriended so early in its history and helped to foster to
the end of his days, should commemorate his name and his spirit
in a living memorial which would carry forward this great task;

Requests that a round table be organized on Jawaharlal Nehru's
role in the modern world. These debates would bring together
thinkers, philosophers, scientists, educationists, writers, artists
and publicists, and all over the world, to consider some of the
great themes of human civilization which distinguish eastern and
western cultures and reveal their common bonds;

Expresses the hope that, on that occasion, consideration will be
given to means of paying a more lasting tribute to the name and
spirit of Nehru.

This resolution which was sponsored by several Western countries,
including France and the Federal Republic of Germany, was unique
in the history of Unesco and indeed, of the entire United Nations
system. It was the first time in its twenty years of existence that
Unesco had decided to honour a statesman of one of its member
states. In conformity with this resolution, an International Round
Table on Jawaharlal Nehru was held in New Delhi in 1966 and
its proceedings were summed up in a publication *Nehru and the
World* edited by B.R. Nanda, Director of the Nehru Memorial
Museum and Library.

The four themes chosen for discussion by the International
Round Table sponsored by Unesco are significant. These were:
Jawaharlal Nehru's Ideal and Action of Unesco; Jawaharlal
Nehru—Man of Two Cultures and One World; Jawaharlal Nehru—
Social Justice and National Development; and Jawaharlal Nehru—
Fight for Independence and International Peace. The discussions
in the Round Table were lively and often profound, and brought
out many aspects of the relationship between Nehru's life and work

and the ideals and action of Unesco. The Resolution of the General Conference, which I have just quoted, expressed the hope that the Round Table would consider the means of paying a lasting tribute to the name and spirit of Nehru. Several suggestions for this purpose were made by participants, but the most striking idea that emerged was the relevance and urgency of finding integrated patterns of development directed to the attainment of quality of life by each society, choosing its own path of development in complete freedom from the imposition of alien models, usually derived from the example of the affluent West. This idea of new developmental goals encouraged and assisted by international action and cooperation was called "Design of Living", and had been inspired by the following statement made by Nehru himself in the course of his Azad Memorial Lecture in 1959:

> Tomorrow's India will be what we make it by today's labours. I have no doubt that India will progress industrially and otherwise; that she will advance in science and technology; that our peoples' standards will rise, that education, will spread and that health conditions will be better, and that art and culture will enrich peoples' lives....What I am concerned with is not merely our material progress, but the quality and depth of our people. Gaining power through industrial progress, will they lose themselves in the quest of individual wealth and soft living? That would be a tragedy, for that would be a negation of what India has stood for in the past, and I think in the present time also, as exemplified by Gandhi. Power is necessary, but wisdom is essential. It is only power with wisdom that is good....Can we combine the progress of science and technology with this progress of the mind and spirit also?

The concept of a "Design of Living" was projected forcefully by the Indian Delegation at Unesco's General Conference in 1966 and received positive and eager response from the developing countries. Unfortunately, it did not take a concrete form and languished for lack of adequate action.

Jawaharlal Nehru's abiding appeal to Unesco, gratefully acknowledged by the resolution of 120 member-states, is, I believe, based on his constant quest for the quality of life needed by all humanity, but especially and urgently, by the developing countries.

The concept of quality of life is implicit in all that he said not only about Unesco, but in the context of his thinking about Unesco's vast fields of education, science, culture and communication. He was, indeed, the first significant exponent of the concept of quality of life in the modern world as applied to the practical conduct of human affairs at both the national and international levels of thought and action. The special bond between him and Unesco rests upon his creative role in defining and promoting a living concept of quality of life for his own peoples and for the world at large. All organizations of the United Nations system and, indeed of the wider spectrum of international cooperation, must contribute to the idea of the quality of life; but Unesco's role especially its ethical role is of paramount importance. Nehru's awareness of this special role is well expressed in the following words, addressed to the ninth General Conference of Unesco in November 1956, when a war of aggression was suddenly launched in the Middle East :

> Man does not live by politics alone, nor indeed, wholly by economics. And so Unesco came into being to represent something that was vital to human existence and progress. Even as the United Nations General Assembly represented the political will of the world community, Unesco tried to represent the finer and the deeper sides of human life, and, indeed, might be said to represent the conscience of the World community....
> I have called this great assembly *the conscience of the World community*. The problems we have to face, many and complicated as they are, will never be solved except on the basis of good morals and conscience. It is for this reason that I beg of you, distinguished delegates from the nations of the world, to pay heed to this *collapse of conscience and good morals* that we see around us, for unless we do so our fine ideals and the good work you have done will be shattered into nothingness.

Six years later on the occasion of his visit to Unesco Headquarters, Nehru dwelt on the quality of life and Unesco's special mission in realizing it:

> We in India, as in many other countries of Asia and Africa, are trying to develop ourselves so as to put an end to our poverty

and raise the standards of hundreds of millions of our people, ultimately aiming at the good life for all. This cannot be done we think, without the help of science and modern techniques. The problem before us is whether in adopting the methods and techniques of science we might not create a society full of internal conflict and the urge for power which brings it into conflict with other groups. Can we succeed in bringing about a synthesis of modern science with something of the spiritual background which has ennobled life throughout the ages? Without science and modern technology, we cannot better our lot or indeed even maintain our freedom, but without spiritual background also the minds of men turn into wrong directions and conflicts occur resulting in great destruction and the degradation of man.

Unesco has set the right ideal before it to try to turn the minds of men and the way it is trying to do so is not the direct method of facing our many problems and conflicts but the indirect way of creating appreciation and understanding of art and culture. Presumably this is a surer method of dealing with these problems than the direct political method, though of course both methods have to be tried. In any event, it is of the utmost importance that the purposes and objectives of Unesco should be remembered and we should always also remember that wars and conflicts begin in the minds of men and peace therefore has to be established there. In the measure that Unesco succeeds in this high endeavour, will it help in the establishment of peace and rid humanity of the danger of war, and all the fears that encompass it.

Unesco's task for the promotion of human rights and establishing a just and lasting peace by organizing international relations in the intellectual sphere is based upon the belief in the power of the mind to shape the course of history. In search of an ideology which was initially thought to lie in a scientific rationalism derived from both positivism and evolutionism, and then in mere pragmatism, Unesco came to believe in the ideology of Human Rights, a system of ideas and values that provides an explanation of history and a guide to action.

Unesco's ideology of a dynamic humanism stemming from its constitution (which proclaims that it should achieve its highest objectives in the minds of men) is identical with Nehru's passionate belief in the sanctity and supremacy of the mind and the spirit of man. Human thought, (Nehru wrote) is

> ever advancing, ever grappling with, trying to understand the problems of nature and the universe. To me there is a great fascination in this challenge of the human mind, and how it soars up to the uttermost corners of the universe and tries to fathom its mysteries, and dares to grasp and measure what appear to be the infinitely big as well as infinitely small.
>
> We may be specks of dust on a soap-bubble universe, but that speck of dust contained something that was the mind and spirit of man. Through the ages this has grown and made itself master of this earth and drawn power from its inner-most bowels as well as from the thunderbolt in the skies. It has tried to fathom the secrets of the universe and brought the vagaries of nature itself to its use. More wonderful than the earth and the heavens is this mind and spirit of man which grows ever mightier and seeks fresh worlds to conquer.

Unesco should not only be thought of in terms of the paraphernalia of an International Secretariat, manned by a relatively small number of functionaries and specialists and financed by a regular annual budget considerably smaller in size than the resources of a single medium-sized American University. To this modest organisational enterprise of government of member-states of Unesco should be added the "National Commissions" representing the relevant institutions and groups at the national level, and hundreds of international non-governmental organizations forming a vast net-work of intellectual and cultural cooperation. And beyond these institutions and persons Unesco must remain deeply involved in the world of ideas and values that mould the historical development of civilizations and cultures. It is this larger Unesco, with its deep relevance to history, as the perennial process of ceaseless change and transcendence of the human spirit, that will remember the faith and thought of Nehru in the early formative years of a world organization that remains the boldest experiment of our time.

Jawaharlal Nehru's influence on Unesco, was large though intangible. His strong and constant championship of Unesco's principles and ideals, as enshrined in its constitution, drew him closer to it. His belief in the supremacy of ideas and his vision of history coincided with the only basis on which Unesco must stand, grow and even leap up to new vistas of evolution, or falter, fail and fall into oblivion. And finally, (and this to my mind is the key to the understanding of the true meaning and significance of what happened in Unesco's headquarters and in the city of Paris on the day of Nehru's death), the remarkable relationship between Nehru and Unesco was based on an inbuilt contradiction within the world organization and in the great statesman himself who befriended it. An inter-governmental organization charged with the constitutional responsibility of operating in the minds of men was as rare and challenging a phenomenon in human affairs, as the individual who tried to guide the destinies of the second largest democracy in the world according to the light of man's conscience and human values. To Unesco it seemed, for a moment in its history, that Nehru had resolved in his own life and person the contradiction between national sovereignty and the intellectual and moral solidarity of mankind.

BHABANI SEN GUPTA

India and Disarmament

DISARMAMENT MIRRORS THE most serious dilemma that the world faces in these troubled times. Whether it is the world of the developed nations, or that of the developing ones, more and more resources of organised political societies are being devoted to arms and armaments: what we have been witnessing since 1945 is an unabated, ever-menacing, arms race. According to the Stockholm International Peace Research Institute Yearbook of World Armaments and Disarmament (SIPRI) 1972, the proportion of the world's resources devoted to military expenditure is now about six per cent. In 1971 more than 180 billion went to military expenditure; this is roughly equal to what the nations of the world spent on health and education put together. While practically all countries are engaged in the arms race, 80 per cent of world military spending is shared by just six nations: the United States, the Soviet Union, China, West Germany, France and the United Kingdom. On military research and development, which is the single greatest source of advances in weapon technology, these six countries spent about 95 per cent of all the world expenditure.[1] At the summit of the international system, the two super-powers, armed with an enormous "overkill" of nuclear weapons, have shown no restraint in the further development of their strategic forces. Both have actively continued to improve, qualitatively if not quantitatively, their strategic nuclear forces. The main nuclear arms race has continued unabated; advances in military technology have significantly increased its already formidable and frightening momentum.[2]

This appalling arms race has proceeded amidst almost uninterrup-

ted "negotiations" for disarmament or arms limitation and control.
Since 1945, Soviet and American negotiators have met officially
some six thousand times. The Conference of the Committee on
Disarmament in Geneva held its 500th meeting in 1971. The United
Nations General Assembly had adopted till the end of 1967, fifty
resolutions calling for disarmament, 14 of them demanding a complete ban on nuclear weapon testing. All that this colossal effort has
been able to produce is seven agreements—the Moscow Partial
Test Ban Treaty (1963); the treaty banning the placing of nuclear
weapons in Outer Space (1967); the Non-proliferation Treaty (1968);
the Latin American Nuclear Free Zone Treaty (1967); the Antarctic
Treaty (1959); the Seabed Treaty (1972); and SALT (1972).[3] Even
the combined impact of these agreements has not imposed any
meaningful restraint on the world-wide arms race, nuclear or conventional. If anything, they have exalted the small club of nuclear
powers to a position where they can hardly be effectively influenced
any longer by the non-nuclear nations' demand for a halt to the
nuclear arms race. In no sphere of collective international endeavour,
since 1945, has so much noise been made, resources spent, time
devoted and paper consumed with so little palpable result as in
the field of disarmament.

Those who have spent the last years of their life labouring for
disarmament have therefore been driven to the conclusion that
unless there is a major, unexpected transformation of super-power
relations, there is little or no hope that the process of the arms race
will be reversed. A decade of disarmament efforts has convinced
Mrs. Alva Myrdal, for instance, that "we have accomplished no
real disarmament and that we can see hardly any tangible results of
our work, and that the underlying major cause must be that the
superpowers have not seriously tried to achieve disarmament. The
prophecy must also be made that there will be no disarmament."
Mrs. Myrdal has correctly described the history of disarmament
as a history of "wilfully squandered opportunities."[4]

II

With this melancholy landscape as a background we look back on
India's efforts, during the Nehru period to push disarmament,
particularly nuclear disarmament, to the forefront of US-Soviet

negotiations. Indian studies of the politics of the Nehru period, domestic as well as international, have just begun to show a certain degree of sophistication. One of the areas, however, where sophistication still seems to be largely unattained is that of disarmament. There is no comprehensive account of India's contribution to the disarmament negotiations since 1946; it still remains to be written. We have a study by Arthur Lall of the complex, and often tortuous, negotiations at the Eighteen-Nation Disarmament Conference in Geneva during the first two years (1962-64). But Arthur Lall undertook the job for Cornell University, and although it includes a fair and sometimes illuminating account of the contribution made by the non-aligned group, particularly India, to the negotiations leading to the partial test ban treaty, it is a super-power-oriented study, and it contributes to the mythology that the superpowers are seriously engaged in negotiating a meaningful disarmament treaty.[5] Disarmament occupies a relatively marginal place in several books written by Indian scholars on India's foreign policy during the Nehru period. The Report of a Study Group set up by the Indian Council of World Affairs in the mid-fifties, to evaluate India's attitude to the United Nations gave less than six of its 213 pages to our contribution to the disarmament negotiations.[6]

If these superficial accounts leave us dissatisfied, it is largely because we do not find in them a grasp of the Indian perspective. What was Jawaharlal Nehru trying to do by his efforts to put forward nuclear disarmament as one of the most urgent and pressing problems facing mankind? Was he merely trying to pursue an ideal which he knew could not be realised by all the pursuasiveness that India and the rest of the non-nuclear world could command? Were his disarmament initiatives divorced from the general thrust of his foreign policy? And if, as he himself told Michael Brecher, foreign policy in the ultimate analysis related itself "chiefly with the national interest of the country concerned?" What specific national interests of India did he hope to secure by his disarmament initiatives? Did Nehru sincerely believe that the nuclear powers intended to disarm? Was he fully aware of the deceptions of the disarmament game? Did those Indian officials who took part in disarmament debates at the United Nations keep him adequately informed? Did they themselves realise the meaning of the game? We are not quite able to answer these questions with sufficient objectivity mainly because of an information gap which remains to be filled. While studying

Nehru's disarmament initiatives we have to rely mostly on declaratory material: his own statements and speeches, of which there are not many, and the proceedings of the debates at the United Nations and the 18-nation disarmament committee (ENDC) in Geneva. We do not yet have access to the communications that passed between Nehru and the Ministry of External Affairs on the one hand and our UN delegations on the other. The disarmament negotiations at the United Nations and at the numerous UN related forums reflected the prevailing power equations of the post-war world; behind the countless resolutions and counter-resolutions and the endless rhetoric, the Powers were constantly probing for the weak points in each other's armour. The disarmament negotiations, in reality, camouflagedt he great armaments game of the nuclear powers. For a really satisfying study of Nehru's foreign policy, including his disarmament initiatives, we need access to source material which is not yet open for research.

I am using the phrase "disarmament initiative" rather than the phrase "disarmament policy" with some deliberation. India could not have a disarmament policy, because it was not a nuclear power; she was not running the race either for nuclear or conventional arms; she could only take a few timely initiatives in order to press the nuclear powers to negotiate seriously, to iron out differences between the two super-powers, and to place at the disposal of negotiating agencies such specialised services as she could provide, such as drafting of documents and summing up the points of accord, apart from the psychological impact of the art of gentle pursuasion, which in any case was never very great. Yet, behind the disarmament initiatives taken by Nehru during the nineteen fifties lay certain vital issues of his foreign policy and of India's national interest, as he perceived it.

All these disarmament initiatives taken by Nehru were at the United Nations; this is true of other non-aligned countries also. It had to be so, because, being a non-nuclear power, India could not be admitted into the corridors of nuclear power politics. Over the years, a huge and tragic contradiction revealed itself at the UN. While the vast majority of its members, all non-nuclear, showed an increasing concern about the continued nuclear arms race, a concern that was reflected in the debates at each session of the General Assembly and in the resolutions adopted, especially since 1957, the United Nations itself gradually ceased to be a forum for meaningful disarmament negotiations. In other words, the greater the capacity of the International body to make noise, the less effective is that noise in inducing the super-powers to disarm. And the crowning irony is that since 1962 the super-powers have effectively shifted arms control talks from the UN to the level of bilateral negotiations, making it more or less an exclusive province of their own.

The weakness of the United Nations stems partly from its Charter, and partly from the cold realities of power politics. Anglo-American wartime planning for the structure of the post-war world relegated the pursuit of general and universal disarmament to a minor role. Both the Atlantic Charter and the UN Charter contain only passing references to disarmament and stress its economic advantages rather than its contribution to peace. Indeed, the entire UN plan for the organisation of the postwar world was based upon the continuing strength of the major allies working in cooperation. The UN Charter itself established an order of priorities in this field, which was intended to avoid the fruitless disarmament discussions of the League of Nations. The first task was, of course, the forced disarmament of the "enemy states;" secondly, the creation of an international military force under the Security Council to guarantee world security. Once this had been established, the Security Council was to consider and prepare plans "for the regulation of armaments," and finally, the General Assembly was empowered to consider "principles of disarmament."[7] A more complete break with the emphasis of the League of Nations would be difficult to imagine, and this was inspite of the fact that only days after the signing of the Charter, the first atomic weapons were exploded. The Charter specified no exact procedures for dealing with "a disarmament problem."

This is the main reason why disarmament has been almost continuously in search of an effective, stable forum for negotiations. The negotiations that have taken place have used at least twenty different forums and agencies, beginning with the Security Council, and ending with secret bilateral forums of the two super-powers. There have been endless committees, commissions, and sub-committees. Disarmament has figured prominently at great power summits and sub-summits such as meetings of the big power foreign ministers. At the UN itself, three distinct phases can be identified. In the early fifties, disarmament was almost the exclusive province of the Security Council and of the major powers. Since the mid-fifties the General Assembly tried to seize some initiative, thanks to the enlargement of membership and the emergence of the non-aligned group as a major element. The culmination of this initiative was the establishment of the Eighteen Nations Disarmament Committee (ENDC) with eight representatives of the non-aligned group and five each from the two blocs. The super-powers however, refused to yield to the floor members of the United Nations more than a marginal role in working out accords. Since 1963, they seem to have agreed to work out between themselves a series of limited arms control accords, which stabilise the mutual deterrent, permit the continuance of a qualitative vertical nuclear arms race, and put actual disarmament in cold storage.

Nehru's disarmament initiatives came mostly in the years 1953-54, 1957-58, and 1962. The initiatives aimed at securing one single objective: *nuclear disarmament*. Interestingly, India did not show much interest in the negotiations and proposals for conventional disarmament. It was not because India was building up its arms strength; in fact, it was just the opposite during the fifties, when Nehru kept the defence budget strictly under control. The situation was different after India's military conflict with China. In the fifties, however, the conventional might of the major powers posed no immediate threat to India. Besides, in the days of American monopoly of, or overwhelming superiority in nuclear weapons, Nehru probably felt that the Soviet Union's superiority in conventional arms gave the precarious bipolar world balance of power a certain amount of stability. We cannot ignore the fact that Soviet nuclear and thermonuclear explosions of 1949 and 1953 were not condemned by the Indian Government, and that Nehru's first major disarmament initiative came only *after* the USSR had become a full-fledged thermonuclear power. Nehru was realistic enough to realise that his call for a halt in the nuclear arms race had a chance of being heard only after there had come to be established a certain balance of nuclear power between the two cold-war blocs.

Why was India's initiative focussed on nuclear disarmament? The answer lies in Nehru's genuine sense of horror at the nuclear menace and his passionate belief that India, while developing nuclear energy for peaceful purposes, must not ever go in for nuclear weapons. Here, as far as Nehru was concerned, we have a combination of idealism and realism, which, as Nehru told Brecher, must inform the foreign policy of each great nation.

In 1946, India supported the Baruch Plan of the American Government. The central thought of the Baruch Plan was its provision for complete international control of the entire process of producing atomic weapons from the uranium and thorium mines to the complete weapons. In the context of the US monopoly, and American domination of the United Nations, the Soviet Union regarded the Baruch Plan as a move to establish American control over the world's nuclear weapon resources and capability. During the forties and early fifties American and Soviet disarmament proposals had two entirely contradictory thrusts. The Soviets wanted to ban nuclear weapons, destroy stockpiles and delivery systems. The Americans wanted to substantially reduce Soviet conventional military power and to instal an inspection and control system that would prevent or at least delay—Russia going nuclear. Neither set of proposals had any chance of being accepted by the other, or by the United Nations, where the Russians could kill any American move with their veto or by just ignoring it.

India's support for the Baruch Plan was not surprising. After all, the British were still in power for all practical purposes in 1946, and our representative at the UN was Girja Shankar Bajpai. Besides, India's economic and military dependence on the Western powers, especially on Britain, in the first years of independence made it very difficult for New Delhi to oppose a major American initiative at the United Nations, which had the full backing of the United Kingdom. In any case the Soviet Union killed the Baruch Plan; the United States, Government itself had lost interest in it, and so when it died, no tears were shed.

III

The first outlines of Nehru's nuclear diplomacy emerged in 1948 when he took the momentous decision to make India a *peaceful* nuclear Power, the first newly liberated country to take such a decision. Negotiations began with the Western powers to secure one or two nuclear reactors; very tough bargaining was involved. At the United Nations, the Baruch Plan had died, but the American Government was pressing with a plan during the period 1948-54 to bring the world's nuclear energy resources under international control. Having decided to build for India an autonomous peaceful nuclear capability, Nehru decided to oppose the American move. Intervening in the debate in the First Committee of the General Assembly in 1948, Mrs. Pandit pleaded that India, an underdeveloped country lacking in energy resources, might have to depend greatly on nuclear energy for peaceful development. It could not therefore separate the proposal for international control of nuclear energy resources from the control of all other power-producing materials such as coal and oil. If nuclear energy resources were to be brought under international control, so must be the case with oil, natural gas and coal.[8]

This was a policy position entirely in defence of India's national interest. In 1954, Nehru could take a much bolder and categorical stand on the question of control of nuclear energy. In the course of a statement in the Indian Parliament on May 10, he rejected the Eisenhower Administration's proposal to impose international control over the world's nuclear energy resources. The UN itself was not fully representative of the international political realities, Nehru pointed out, and what was more objectionable was the American bid to set up, through the UN, a supra-UN agency which would "have the right to maintain its own guards on the territory of any foreign State licensed to engage in any of the processes of the production of, or research in, atomic energy." "This is a very far-reaching provision" said Nehru, "It means that all our raw materials and our mines would be owned and controlled by that independent body, which is independent even of the United Nations after it is created.... An immediate consideration is, who will be in it. Either you make the body as big as the United Nations with all the countries represented, or it will be some relatively small body, inevitably the Great Powers sitting in it and lording it over. I say with all respect to them that they will have a grip over all the atomic energy areas and raw materials in every country. Now, for a country like India, is it a desirable prospect?"[9]

We have to look at India's 1953-54 initiatives in the context of the major international events of the early fifties and of the results of disarmament negotiations. Specifically, three significant changes emerged during this period in the negotiating positions of the Soviet Union and the Western powers. First, the United States no longer insisted on an improvement in the international political climate as a precondition to disarmament negotiations. Secondly, the

Western powers recognised that any measures of disarmament to be effective must be acceptable to the USSR—the mustering of majority votes at the United Nations had become meaningless. Thirdly, the USSR showed willingness to conduct negotiations on the basis of Western proposals for nuclear as well as conventional disarmament. In 1953, the Disarmament Commission held only one meeting, but for the first time it adopted a unanimous report which expressed the hope that recent international events, like the end of the Korean war and changes in the governments of the United States and the Soviet Union, would create a more propitious atmosphere for reconsideration of the disarmament question.[10]

1953 was, then, favourable for the first major initiative taken by Nehru in accelerating the pace of disarmament negotiations. As a result of amendments moved by the Indian delegation, the resolution adopted by the 1953 session of the UN Assembly incorporated an "affirmation" as well as a "provision."[11] The affirmation was of the Assembly's "earnest desire for the elimination and prohibition of atomic, hydrogen, bacterial, chemical and other weapons of war and mass destruction and for the attainment of these ends through effective means." The provision was for setting up a sub-committee consisting of the Powers principally involved to sit in private and at places of its own choosing to implement the purposes of the Disarmament Commission. On April 19, 1954, the Disarmament Commission, by a vote of nine to one, with two abstentions, created a sub-committee consisting of Canada, France, the Soviet Union, the United Kingdom and the United States. A Soviet proposal to add the People's Republic of China, Czechoslovakia and India was rejected by ten votes to one, with one abstention; that is, it was supported only by the USSR.

IV

In the spring of 1954 the incalculable destructive power of the hydrogen bomb was dramatised by the American explosion at Bikini. A number of Japanese fishermen operating peacefully, nearly a hundred miles downwind, were exposed to its radiation and suffered severe burns. According to an American account, as a result of this single explosion, "about 7,000 square miles of territory downwind from the point of burst was so contaminated that survival might have depended upon prompt evacuation of the area or upon taking shelter and other protective measures."[12] Winston Churchill, then Prime Minister of Britain, said in a statement, "with all its horrors the atomic bomb did not seem unmanageable as an instrument of war, and the fact that the Americans have such an immense preponderance over Russia has given us passage through eight anxious and troublous years. But the hydrogen bomb carries us into dimensions which have never confronted practical human thought."[13]

On April 2, a month after the Bikini explosion, Nehru came out with his famous statement on the hydrogen bomb and with four concrete proposals to control the nuclear arms race. Speaking in the Lok Sabha, he said: "A new weapon of unprecedented power both in volume and intensity, with an unascertained, and probably unascertainable, range of destructive potential in respect of time and space, that is, both as regards duration and the extent of consequences, is being tested, unleashing its massive power, for use as a weapon of war. We know that its use threatens the existence of man and civilisation as we know it. We are told that there is no effective protection against the hydrogen bomb and that millions of people may be exterminated by a single explosion and many more injured, and perhaps still many more condemned to slow death or to live under the shadow of the fear of disease and death."

The concrete measures he suggested to arrest the race of civilisation towards "the dire end," were a standstill agreement in respect of actual explosions "even if agreements about the discontinuance of production and stockpiling must await more substantial agreements amongst those principally concerned;" full publicity by the United Nations and by all governments of the destructive power and the known effects of these weapons and also of their unknown and probable effects; immediate and continuing private meetings of the sub-committee of the Disarmament Commission to consider a standstill agreement and "active steps by States and peoples of the world who, though not directly concerned with the production of these weapons, are very much concerned with the possible use of them." Nehru said, "They would, I venture to hope, express their concern and add their voices and influence in as effective a manner as possible to arrest the progress of this destructive potential which menaces all alike." And a little later he added: "It is of great concern to us that Asia and her peoples appear to be always nearer these occurrences and experiments and their fearsome consequences, actual and potential."

The Indian initiative made little impact on the major powers. The United Nations General Assembly in November 1954, referred the Indian proposals to the Disarmament Commission for appropriate consideration. The resolution adopted by the General Assembly on disarmament in 1954 carried no imprint of the Indian suggestions.[14]

Nevertheless, Nehru's initiative was not without significance. It was the first concrete move on behalf of the non-aligned countries to call for an immediate suspension of nuclear weapons tests. While India still recognised the Disarmament Commission and its sub-committee as the appropriate forum of disarmament negotiations, thus accepting, in effect, that disarmament was primarily the province of the nuclear powers, by moving a formal resolution in the General Assembly, India took the lead in registering the right of the non-aligned countries, or rather the non-nuclear nations, to intervene in the negotiations. This was the beginning of an effort, on the part of India and other non-aligned countries, that culminated in the admission of eight non-aligned nations in 1962 to the corridors of nuclear power politics.

In his statement in the Lok Sabha, Nehru had called for active steps by the governments and peoples of the world to bring about a halt to the nuclear arms race, and he seemed to visualise in this a special role for Asia which alone had actually tasted the bitter fruits of nuclear blasts. Was he thinking in terms of a world-wide campaign against nuclear weapons? There was, as we know, no such campaign. True, thousands of scientists in the United States and Europe petitioned the UN Secretary-General, urging a ban on nuclear weapon tests. But the only people's campaign against the nuclear bomb was the one organised by Bertrand Russell and others in the United Kingdom. It aroused a certain response amongst intellectuals and young people in a few West European countries, but had no impact on Britain's nuclear policy, not to speak of the nuclear policies of the super-powers. Nehru expressed his sympathy with this campaign, but took no initiative to mobilise world opinion or even Asian opinion against the nuclear bomb. His government brought out a publication narrating with vivid authenticity the destructive power and potential of nuclear weapons and other weapons of mass destruction.[15] In 1957, the Lok Sabha, adopted a resolution calling for an immediate agreement banning all nuclear weapon tests. It was, however, a private member's resolution to which the Defence Minister, V.K. Krishna Menon, moved a couple of amendments. Nehru was anxious that the resolution was framed in soft language and did not blame or condemn any particular power. "If we have attained some respect in the eyes of the other countries of the world," he told the House on May 22, 1957, "it is because we have spoken with some sense of responsibility, and because, while certainly expressing our opinion with firmness, we have always tried not to condemn but to win over the other peoples. This is our deliberate, well-thought-out policy. The whole point is that while dealing with a situation like this, the moment we enter the sphere of strong language and condemnation, we cease to have any real effect. Immediately, whether we wish it or not, we become parties to the cold war, and the appeal to reason or to the emotions of the other party is lost."

He turned down the suggestion made by several members to convene an international conference against nuclear weapon tests. "Am I to summon the leaders of the USA, the USSR, the UK and other countries and tell them what to do? Even if a conference is held, it will be of persons in conflict with each other. Therefore, how are we to proceed?" Clearly, he was not thinking in terms of mobilising public opinion in the non-nuclear world or in Asia against nuclear weapon tests. He was anxious that India did not even appear to get involved in the cold war, and he was equally anxious to work with the nuclear powers through the United Nations.

Nehru's political style was not populist, but elitist, and his approach to international politics was essentially Grotian. He believed in the existence and potential of common interests among the states of the world and he looked for patterns of accord by harmonisation of the forces and interests which he considered to be actually at play in international politics. Hence, the thrust of his non-alignment policy was to build bridges, to bring the opposing forces together, to work for a consensus, to avoid confrontation. He was convinced that, despite differences in social systems and ideologies, and with all their rivalries and competitiveness, the great powers had a common interest in protecting the world and themselves from nuclear annihilation.

In 1957, instead of trying to build a people's campaign in Asia, Africa and Latin America against continued nuclear weapon tests,

Nehru made a fervent appeal to the United States and the Soviet Union to stop all of these tests. He was overwhelmed by the thought of the crisis in civilisation that the world was facing, the like of which it had never faced before. "I believe," he said in his appeal, "that it is in the power of America and Russia to solve this crisis and save humanity from the ultimate disaster that faces it." They had in their hands the power to put an end to the horror that was enveloping the world. "Millions of people", he said, "believe in what is called Western capitalism; millions also believe in Communism. But there are many millions who are not committed to either of these ideologies and yet seek, in friendship with others, a better life and a more hopeful future. I speak for myself, but I believe that I echo the thoughts of vast numbers of people in my country as well as in other countries of the world. I venture therefore to make this appeal to the great powers, more especially the leaders of America and Russia, in whose hands fate and destiny have placed such tremendous power today to mould this world and either to raise it to undreamt of heights or to hurl it into the pit of disaster. I appeal to them to stop all nuclear test explosions and thus to show to the world that they are determined to end this menace and to proceed also to bring about effective disarmament."[16]

V

Between 1955 and 1957 some major developments had occurred in great power relationship and these had a direct bearing on disarmament negotiations. In May 1955, the Soviet Union came up with the most comprehensive and detailed programme for disarmament up to that time, accepting some of the hitherto rejected concepts and proposals put forward by the Western powers.[17] Disarmament figured prominently at the Geneva summit conference in July. The disarmament resolution adopted by the General Assembly in 1955 for the first time directed the Disarmament sub-committee to give priority to confidence-building measures such as the "Open Skies" proposal of President Eisenhower, while continuing to work for comprehensive disarmament.[18]

In 1956, both the Soviet and Western sides moved toward limited measures of disarmament prior to agreement on a coordinated and comprehensive programme. Simultaneously the Western powers proposed to create special international disarmament organs outside the United Nations, both to negotiate and to implement disarmament agreements. Also in 1956, the United States, after a prolonged policy reconsideration, decided to espouse the concept of arms control and partial disarmament *as an end in itself* rather than a prelude to comprehensive disarmament. The chief American disarmament negotiator, Harold Stassen, summed up the approach: "It is our view that if an effort is made to reduce armaments, armed forces and military expenditures to a level that is too low, to a level that reflects weakness, it would not be conducive to stability in the world and to the best interests of peace." Essentially, this was the concept of the stability of the mutual deterrent, which went against the basic philosophy of disarmament. In 1957 the Soviet Union accepted the Western proposals for inspection posts for the control and detection of nuclear weapon tests, coming nearer than ever before to the Western position. And in 1957, alarmed at the Sputnik's demonstration of Soviet rocketry, the United States suddenly went back on many of the disarmament proposals it had put forward in the preceding years.

At the United Nations, a change of milieu took place by 1957, which was reflected in the disarmament resolutions adopted by the General Assembly. Among the non-aligned members, a new posture emerged. It was a posture of asserting their own perspective with regard to disarmament, in contrast with the tendency hitherto followed of leaving the matter more or less to the major powers. As Arthur Lall reports: "By 1957 this posture had gained so many adherents that the non-aligned countries and their friends could stop any other single group in the United Nations from getting its way—from mustering the requisite two-thirds vote for adopting a resolution. From this time on, there has been at the United Nations the floating uncommitted vote on which neither side could count. The debates on disarmament have ceased to be a dialogue between the political West and East and have become world debates in which the two sides have been increasingly under pressure to justify their proposals and attitudes to the third world."[19] What this new posture meant, in reality, was that the United States could no longer count on a two-thirds majority to get Western proposals adopted. The days of American hegemony at the United Nations were fast coming to an end.

The new posture at the UN may be seen in the disarmament

resolutions adopted since 1957. From now on the first priority in the General Assembly resolutions came to be given to "immediate suspension of testing of nuclear weapons," under an effective system of inspection and control. In fact, the 1957 resolution spelled out in concrete details the steps the General Assembly expected the nuclear powers to take to bring about effective nuclear disarmament.[20] India took a lot of initiative in the General Assembly debates in backstage negotiations, in the drafting of resolutions, in sponsoring them, and in mobilising votes in favour of these resolutions.

The major powers now realised that they could no longer prevent the non-aligned nations from taking part in disarmament negotiations. This realisation led to the specific contradiction between the General Assembly and the nuclear super-powers. Organisationally, the role of the UN in disarmament negotiations began to be steadily downgraded. In the realm of ideas and concepts, while the non-nuclear small powers went on calling for disarmament, the super powers began to be sold to the limited and deceptive device of "arms control."

It seems doubtful that the full implication of the American doctrine of arms control or stability of the mutual deterrent was grasped by the Indian Government in the late fifties and early sixties. From published material, including Nehru's speeches and Arthur Lall's book, there is no evidence to suggest that the Government of India had a serious doubt about the intentions of the superpowers to disarm, or that it realised that the pressure of world public opinion for nuclear disarmament was only driving the superpowers toward a new strategy of bilateral negotiation to stabilise the nuclear military balance. In any case, Nehru himself never accepted the doctrine of arms control. During the early fifties India, like the Soviet Union, pressed for comprehensive disarmament, and played a very low profile role in the sphere of conventional disarmament negotiations. After 1955, however, Nehru opted for partial disarmament, even for collatoral confidence-building accords, but always as first steps toward meaningful disarmament. In a statement on September 2, 1957, he said: "We have always suggested that a partial agreement is better than no agreement provided *that it is a step toward* (a full) agreement."[21] He asked the nuclear powers to suspend tests if they could not immediately agree to abandon them altogether, but here again he at once added the condition: "if you can abandon them later." He was one of the most enthusiastic supporters of the emerging *detente* between the United States and Soviet Union, and his support for partial disarmament measures was in harmony with his perspective of super-power relations.

In 1961, the Soviet Union also appeared to be moving toward the doctrine of arms control and stability of the mutual deterrent. As a result of secret negotiations between Moscow and Washington during June-September 1961, the two governments issued a statement incorporating agreed principles of disarmament to form the basis for further negotiations.[22] One of these principles was "All measures of general and complete disarmament should be balanced so that at no stage of the implementation of the treaty could any State or group of States gain military advantage and the security is ensured equally for all." Perhaps without suspecting a subtle and significant shift in the super-power approach to a stable deterrent, India sought to utilise the super-power accord on the basic principles to re-start negotiations which had practically come to a standstill in 1960. The Indian delegation submitted a draft resolution at the 1961 session of the UN General Assembly, which was later co-sponsored by Ghana and the UAR, whereby the Assembly would urge the super-powers to reach agreement on the composition of a negotiating body which both they and the rest of the world could regard as satisfactory.[23] This was the genesis of the Eighteen Nation Disarmament Committee (ENDC). At long last, the "rest of the world" was accepted as partners in the process of disarmament negotiations. ENDC held its first meeting in Geneva on March 14, 1962. It had a mandate from the General Assembly to undertake negotiations "as a matter of urgency" with a view to reaching an "agreement on general and complete disarmament under effective international control."[24] France did not take part in the proceedings, partly because President de Gaulle refused to concede to the non-nuclear powers the right to participate in the negotiations, and also because in his view, the essential question was not the halting of tests but the halting of the manufacture of nuclear weapons. The eight non-aligned members of ENDC took up the work of the body more seriously than did the super-powers. One of the first important moves of the eight was to transfer the nuclear test ban issue to the agenda of ENDC from that of the Geneva Conference on the Discontinuance of Nuclear Weapons Tests. The Conference on the Discontinuance of Nuclear Weapons Tests consisting of the three nuclear powers and Canada, had worked for four years without producing any positive results.

At ENDC the initiative was quickly seized by the non-aligned group of eight. First, they pressed the three nuclear powers to form a sub-committee in order to produce a convention prohibiting nuclear weapon tests. This sub-committee quickly reached a deadlock. The Western powers would not have a test ban treaty without effective international inspection and control, and the Soviet Union would agree to a ban that would rely entirely on a national system of inspection and control. On April 3, 1962, the British delegate asked Zorin, "Does the Soviet Union really offer us hope of any form of international inspection of any unidentified events in the Soviet Union in any circumstances, short of achievement of general and complete disarmament?" Next day, Zorin replied, "I shall not beat about the bush. There is no hope."[25]

The group of eight, however, refused to be daunted by the deadlock. At the first session of ENDC, Krishna Menon and Arthur Lall stressed the need for quick progress in disarmament rather than a gradualistic approach, which placed India somewhat closer to the Soviet position than the American.[26] Within a month ENDC's work, the eight presented a memorandum offering a new scheme for a comprehensive ban on nuclear weapons testing. This scheme outlined a radically simplified, but effective system of inspection and control on a purely scientific and non-political basis. The system relied mainly on existing or improved means of observation by seismological methods, but referred also to the possibility of setting up an international scientific commission for the verification of contested cases of violation.

The memorandum was drafted by the delegates of Ethiopia, India and Sweden. The Americans did not regard the contribution of Arthur Lall to be very helpful; it resulted in a "less intelligible document," they commented.[27] However, Lall showed the document to both the American and Soviet delegates before it was formally presented, and to quote his words, "both reacted with vigorous opposition."[28] When the memorandum was formally introduced to ENDC on April 16, 1962, the Soviet delegate expressed his willingness to study the eight nation proposals as a basis for further negotiations, and similar sentiments were expressed by the American side also. ENDC worked diligently on detailed proposals relating to structures and provisions of a comprehensive nuclear test ban as well as the structure and modalities of the control scheme. Arthur

Lall claims that three significant gains emerged from the eight-nation memorandum. First, there was a major shift in the Soviet attitude towards inspection: Zorin declared that the USSR would agree to invite the proposed international control commission to visit certain scenes of doubtful events and would submit to a "degree of on site inspection." Secondly, the United States agreed that there could be a ban on tests in atmosphere and outer space without international control. And thirdly, the memorandum "very much" enhanced the standing of the non-aligned group as partners in negotiations at the Geneva conference.[29]

Meanwhile, Nehru was worried over reports that the nuclear powers would soon embark upon a new series of tests. In a statement in the Lok Sabha on April 24, 1962, he welcomed the super-powers' positive reaction to the eight-nation proposals. He said he was greatly concerned about the prospects of resumption of tests, "because there can be no doubt that if the United States resumes them, then, undoubtedly the Soviet Union will also do the same." He did not wish to blame either party: "I am not here to blame, but to beg and to appeal to the nuclear powers to refrain from having these tests, giving full chance to the Geneva conference to come to an agreement."

The appeal fell on deaf ears. President Kennedy authorised the new tests. On April 26, the United States resumed testing in the atmosphere. When ENDC met next, Arthur Lall observed, "We meet under (the) unwelcome shadow (of the tests). It is a strange irony that these tests should take place at a place which is called Christmas Island, a name which raises associations in our minds of a message of peace and goodwill."[30]

VI

The world of nuclear power moved pretty fast in the summer of 1962 with what looked like studied indifference to the labours of the non-aligned at Geneva. On May 1, France effected its first thermo-nuclear explosion in Sahara. By recording the Sahara explosion, the United States demolished its own argument that on-site inspection was essential to identify nuclear blasts.[31] The US Defence Secretary, Robert McNamara, came out in 1962 with a new strategic doctrine. Its two central points were, first, the two super-powers had already accumulated an overkill of nuclear weaponry, which made the continued nuclear arms race not only counterproductive, but also unbearably expensive. What was needed therefore was a stable mutual deterrent, in other words, nuclear arms control rather than disarmament. McNamara's second main point was that NATO should concentrate on building its conventional forces and abandon its nuclear ambitions. In reality this meant that the United States no longer regarded a multinational nuclear force for Western Europe, a viable proposition, and was no longer interested in making West Germany a nuclear power. Encouraged by the McNamara doctrine, the US Arms Control and Disarmament Agency came out with a position paper detailing four alternative policies for the government. One of these suggested a treaty banning nuclear weapon tests in the atmosphere, outer space and under water without on-site inspection or control posts on Soviet territory. On August 5, the USSR started a new series of tests, many of them in the megaton range. At ENDC, Krishna Menon expressed India's regret at the Soviet tests, but Khrushchev was in no greater mood to listen to the voice of the non-aligned group than had been John F. Kennedy.[32] On August 5, the West submitted two draft resolutions at ENDC, one for a comprehensive test ban treaty, the other for a partial ban.[33] Both were summarily rejected by the Soviet Union. A partial test ban treaty, said the Soviet delegate, would only "legalise" underground tests and would not prevent proliferation of independent nuclear capability.[34] Arthur Lall's intervention at this stage of the debate indicated that India was inclined to accept a partial test ban accord.[35]

The concept of a partial test ban treaty gained ground rapidly at the United Nations when the General Assembly met in the fall of 1962. The disarmament resolution finally adopted by the General Assembly, with both super-powers abstaining, urged Washington and Moscow to reach an interim partial test ban treaty if a comprehensive accord continued to be beyond their grasp.[36] Then came the Cuban crisis, and with it, a metamorphosis in super-power relationship.

The exercise in nuclear brinkmanship hammered upon both super-powers the inescapable compulsion to bring the nuclear demon under control. Secret bilateral negotiations began between Washington and Moscow. On December 10, Premier Khrushchev in a letter to President Kennedy offered to accept two to three-on-site inspections on Soviet territory in a year; the USSR even agreed to accept foreign personnel on the inspection teams. This significant concession was made by Khrushchev as a result of an understanding reached during the secret talks that this would lead to a treaty banning all nuclear tests. The United States, however, denied that any such understanding had been reached, but, according to one authority, the non-aligned group at Geneva was inclined to accept the Soviet version of the secret understanding.[37]

Another deadlock followed. It was broken only when Khrushchev threatened in August 1963 to withdraw his offer of two to three on-site inspections if it were not accepted by the United States soon. This threat opened up channels of communication between Washington, Moscow and London. Kennedy and Macmillan despatched Harriman and Hailsham to Moscow. Secret talks began in mid-July; by then, the Washington-Moscow "hot line" had already been set up.

Thus, while ENDC in Geneva had been labouring for well over a year for a total test ban treaty without being able to bring the nuclear powers to an agreement, the two super-powers transferred the negotiations to the bilateral level, and *within a week* came out an agreement for *partial* test ban. The accord was hailed all over the world except in France and China. At ENDC, it was hailed by the non-aligned eight; it was hailed by Nehru. Years later, Mrs. Alva Myrdal, one of the most active participants at ENDC, stated with candour: "I must confess that we did not wake up to understand the sombre reality even when the super-powers suddenly in the summer of 1963 switched the test ban negotiations from Geneva. . . . So doped in hope were we that we euphorically hailed this agreement as one of utmost importance. We took it for granted, as we were told, that it was the first step towards the discontinuance of all tests."[38]

The Preamble to the Moscow Treaty did explicitly spell out the commitment of the nuclear powers to seek to achieve "the discontinuance of all test explosions of nuclear weapons for all time." They were, said the Preamble, "determined to continue negotiations to this end." The non-aligned countries, including India, took these words at face value and believed that the partial test ban could curtail further qualitative development of nuclear weapons. The truth was entirely different. As Mrs. Myrdal noted years later: "The Moscow treaty has not had any restrictive effect whatsoever on nuclear weapons development or even on the number and yield of tests made by those nations who already possess such weapons." "Our naivete and credulity were such," Mrs. Myrdal added, "that we the smaller nations did not at that time realise that no disarmament was intended."[39]

This naivete was allowed even in the face of President Kennedy's explicit promise to the military interests that America's testing facilities would not be closed. Said President Kennedy: "The United States has more experience in underground testing than any other nation, and we intend to use this capacity to maintain the adequacy of our arsenal. Our atomic laboratories will maintain an active development programme, including underground testing, and we will be ready to resume testing in the atmosphere, if necessary."[40] Thus, by the Moscow treaty the super-powers did not curb their capacity to perfect new generations of nuclear bombs, as by the non-proliferation treaty five years later, they did not sacrifice one iota of their existing and future nuclear weapons capabilities.

The Government of India hastened to hail the partial test ban treaty. In a statement issued on July 27, 1963, that is within twenty-four hours of the signing of the draft treaty in Moscow, the Government of India hailed it as a "landmark in international cooperation." It trusted that this "first step, along with other collateral tension-reducing measures, would build up international confidence and speedily lead to a treaty on general and complete disarmament. This was a trust that was completely misplaced. Nehru hailed the treaty as what it was not; he gave the super-powers credit for what they did not achieve. But he was not the only one to be deceived. He had most of the world with him.

I am not suggesting that India should not have signed the Moscow treaty. The year was 1963, and India needed help from both super-powers to meet the situation created by the Sino-Indian conflict in 1962. But while signing it, India could have taken a more realistic position and told the super-powers that they had not really given the world anything, and that if they could not proceed towards at least a comprehensive test ban treaty within a stipulated period of time, the treaty would lose all its meaning for the world. A stand like this could have mobilised international pressure on the nuclear powers to bring about nuclear disarmament. By exalting the Moscow treaty to a level it did not attain, India and the other non-aligned countries actually helped the super-powers to elevate nuclear power politics to a superior level, beyond the reach of the non-nuclear powers. It is a grim irony that the partial test ban treaty was signed at a time when the world was expecting China's first nuclear bang any day. The Chinese Government alone called the Moscow treaty a great fraud on the world, which, in reality, it was.

We have given so much attention to the negotiations leading to the Moscow partial test ban treaty because most of India's labours in the field of disarmament during the Nehru period had been focussed on securing an agreement banning all nuclear weapon tests. To justify his policy of peaceful development of nuclear energy in India, Nehru needed at least some substantial nuclear disarmament by the major powers. He also needed another condition: *there must be no proliferation of nuclear weapons capability.* In 1959, when France announced its intention to conduct a nuclear test in the Sahara, India joined 21 other Afro-Asian nations to sponsor a resolution that would have expressed the UN Assembly's grave concern over the French intention and urged France to refrain from such tests. The General Assembly finally adopted a somewhat mellower resolution introduced by Britain, Italy and Peru "requesting" France not to conduct the test. On February 14, 1960, the day after the first French nuclear weapon test, India and 21 other nations asked for a special session of the General Assembly to consider the question of French tests in the Sahara. As the number of nations asking for the special session was less than the majority of 42 required under the Assembly's rules of procedure the request fell through and no special session was held.

In March 1962, India formally proposed that earnest negotiations begin for the conclusion of a nuclear non-proliferation treaty, but, as Arthur Lall has reported, the issue was discussed only "off and on," not systematically.[41] Definitive agreement to put it on the active agenda of items before ENDC was not arrived at till June 18, 1964, Nehru had passed away three weaks earlier.

For several years before Nehru's death, the shadow of China about to go nuclear had been looming across the World. Did the prospect of a nuclear China worry Jawaharlal Nehru? In October 1961, he confessed to Leonard Beaton that the Government of India had not given the matter much thought. He had himself occasionally given his mind to it. Beaton wrote that Nehru was quite categorical that the Chinese Bomb would not push India to go nuclear. "They will not induce us to jump into the nuclear fray. The idea of using these bombs is horrible to me and to a large number of us."[42] On

December 31, 1962, less than six weeks after the ceasefire in the Himalayas, Nehru was closely questioned at a press conference in New Delhi whether India had "for ever" committed itself against the use of nuclear energy as a deterrent. His reply was, "To be quite practical, either you have a very powerful deterrent...it is not good having something showy...some weakened people in India might have their knees wobbling and develop cold feet. It will not have the slightest effect on India if they (the Chinese) have a test tomorrow.... We are not going to make bombs, not even thinking of making bombs, (although) we are in nuclear science more advanced than China."[43]

The shadows of the coming Chinese Bomb figured prominently in the Lok Sabha when on March 25, 1963, it debated the budget grants of the department of Atomic Energy. Nehru was unyielding to suggestions that the Government's "no-Bomb" policy be reviewed and at least the issue be kept open. India, he said, had been asking the nuclear powers to give up tests. "How can we, without showing the utter insincerity of what we have always said, go in for doing the very thing which we have repeatedly asked the other powers not to do?" And, finally, nine days before his death, Nehru remained unshaken and clear-sighted in his policy. In a television interview screened in New York on May 18, 1964, he declared, "We are determined not to use (nuclear) weapons for war purposes. We do not make atom bombs. I do not think we will."[44]

If the super-powers could conclude a comprehensive test ban treaty, they would have adopted a genuine measure of nuclear disarmament and made non-proliferation a practicable and fruitful option perhaps for all non-nuclear nations except China. They would certainly have strengthened the movement for non-proliferation, of which Nehru was such an ardent and indomitable champion. They let down Jawaharlal Nehru and the entire case for non-proliferation.

Nehru's very gentleness with regard to the super-powers, his reluctance to criticise them in strong words and to blame them, proved counterproductive. He did not make a distinction, which his successors did, of India not going nuclear and India articulating strongly and unequivocally its sense of disappointment and dissatisfaction with the utter nuclear selfishness of the nuclear powers. Don Quincy Adams once said, "I know of no change of policy, but I know of changes in circumstances." Since the early sixties, the super-powers saw a change in international circumstances and steadily came together to protect their exalted nuclear power. For India neither policy nor circumstances changed.

During the fifties disarmament remained almost the exclusive concern of Nehru and Krishna Menon, as far as India was concerned. Within the broad framework of policy laid down by Nehru, it was mostly Krishna Menon who designed India's contribution to the debates and negotiations. In the Ministry of External Affairs, M.J. Desai, Foreign Secretary, and V.C. Trivedi, Joint Secretary, were probably the only two officials who were involved in disarmament. Homi J. Bhabha was probably the only other person whom Nehru occasionally consulted on the nuclear disarmament issue. In 1962, however, when India became a member of ENDC, a disarmament desk was created in the Ministry of External Affairs as part of the UN division, and the services of an officer in the Defence Ministry were obtained to man it. This is the only Indian official who has been continually involved with disarmament issues for the last ten or eleven years. During the sixties, however, several Indians took part in the complex disarmament negotiations. Apart from gathering a lot of expertise, they also learned the rules of the great game of deception. They played very different roles, in accordance with changes in circumstances; the role played by Arthur Lall during the first two years of ENDC, the period of test ban negotiations, was very different from the role played by V.C. Trivedi during the negotiations on Non-proliferation Treaty. India learned to speak up, to articulate unpleasant truths, to demand of the nuclear powers what they were most reluctant to give.

Jawaharlal Nehru was consumed by the desire to see some concrete progress toward a world rid of the nuclear menace, and he died without his dream of a world free of nuclear menace being realized. But by the time he died and soon thereafter, India saw through the disarmament game, was able to shed its innocence, and was no longer prepared to be duped by hope and doped by the deceptive rhetoric of the super-powers. India still did not speak nuclear, but its accents smelled mildly of defiance, which was symbolised by its refusal to sign the Nuclear Non-proliferation Treaty.

NOTES

INTRODUCTION

1. Nehru's letter to *Manchester Guardian*, September 8, 1938, Nehru Papers.
2. *National Herald*, July 2, 1946.
3. *Jawaharlal Nehru's Speeches*, September 1946-May 1949, Vol. I, (Delhi, 1949) pp. 2–4.
4. George Kennan, *Memoirs* (London, 1973), p. 90.
5. *New York Herald Tribune*, January 18, 1947.
6. Meany's reported remarks that he felt "stronger than ever that [Nehru] is an agent of the Soviet Union and I hope to see him and tell him so to his face" in *New Republic*, December 31, 1956, cited in A. Appodorai, *Essays in Politics and International Relations* (Delhi, 1969), p. 149.
7. Dean Acheson, *Present at the Creation* (London, 1970), p. 336.
8. K.P.S. Menon, *India and the Soviet Union*, See below p. 139.
9. Mao Tse-tung in a message dated October 19, 1949 to the Communist Party of India expressed the hope that under its leadership, India would certainly not remain long "under the yoke of imperialism and its collaborators." Text in V.B. Karnik (ed.) *Indian Communist Party Documents*, 1930–1956 (Bombay, 1957), p. 48.
10. Letter to Provincial Congress Committee Presidents, July 4, 1954. *Congress Bulletin*, June–July 1954, p. 245.
11. B.N. Rau, *India's Constitution in the Making* (Calcutta, 1960), p. 355.
12. Nicholas Mansergh, *Documents and Speeches on Commonwealth Affairs*, Vol. II, (London, 1963), p. 734.
13. Jawaharlal Nehru, *India's Foreign Policy: Selected Speeches* (Delhi, 1961), p. 133.
14. Jawaharlal Nehru, *Speeches*, Lok Sabha, May 17, 1949.
15. R.K. Karanjia, *The Philosophy of Mr. Nehru* (London, 1966), p. 68.
16. A.P. Thoronton, *For the File On Empire* (London, 1968), p. 366.
17. Nicholas Mansergh, *The Commonwealth Experience* (London, 1969), p. 396.
18. Escott Reid, "Nehru's India", *India Quarterly*, April-June, 1965, p. 185.
19. S.C. Gangal, *India and the Commonwealth* (Agra, 1970), p. 87.
20. R.K. Karanjia, *op. cit.*, p. 124.
21. K.P.S. Menon, *Many Worlds; An Autobiography* (Bombay, 1965), p. 268.
22. "The concept of limited warfare—of warfare conducted for limited objectives and ending with the achievement of those objectives by compromise with the existing enemy regime—was not only foreign to but was deeply repugnant to the American military and political mind. One had already had a clear illustration of this in Korea." (It was illustrated again fifteen to twenty years later in Vietnam). George Kennan, *op cit.*, p. 95.

23. D.R. SarDesai, "India and South East Asia", see below p. 86
24. Jawaharlal Nehru, *India's Foreign Policy: Selected Speeches, op cit.*, p. 399.
25. Pierre Mendes–France, the French Prime Minister at the time of the Geneva Agreement, was of the view that if the Western countries, especially the United States Government, had understood the uses for world peace which could be made of Nehru the evolution of contemporary history would have been different. Interview with the author in October 1971.
26. Surjit Mansingh, "India and the United States", see below p. 111.
27. Selig Harrison, "America, India and Pakistan: A Chance For A Fresh Start," *Harper's Magazine*, July 1966.
28. John Kenneth Galbraith, *Ambassador's Journal* (London, 1969), p. 77.
29. Chester Bowles, *Promises To Keep* (Delhi, 1972), p. 494.
30. Rafiq Zakaria (Ed.) *A Study of Nehru* (Bombay, 1959), p. 84.
31. *Ibid.*, p. 243.
32. R.K. Karanjia, *op. cit.* p. 111.
33. *Ibid.*, p. 109.
34. In October 1951 in a talk with the American Ambassador, Chester Bowles, Nehru expressed "concern over the long–term problem Communist China posed for India. But he was convinced that the non–aligned bridge-building role he was playing in Asia was not only in India's interest but in the interest of Asian stability, and indeed in the interest of the United States and the cause of world peace. He staked his hopes for a peaceful relationship, not only on Chinese goodwill, but on the assumption that the Chinese leaders needed a period of peace in which to solidify their revolution and to build a solid economic base." Chester Bowles, *op. cit.*, p. 490.
35. Jawaharlal Nehru, *op. cit.*, p. 355.
36. Quoted in S.S. Khera, *India's Defence Problem* (Delhi, 1968), p. 158.
37. Neville Maxwell, *India's China War* (London, 1970), pp. 158–62.
38. India's sole national interest in the Hungarian situation was to see that no war emerged from that breeding–ground of two world wars, Eastern Europe. See Surjit Mansingh, "India and the Hungarian, Revolution," in *India Quarterly*, April–June, 1965, p. 155.
39. Willy Brandt, the Chancellor of Federal Republic of Germany in October 1971 told the author in regard to the West Berlin crisis, Mr. Nehru used his influence "with the Soviet Union to calm down the crisis."
40. Chancellor Kreisky told the author in November 1971 that "Nehru had already, before 1955, begun to mediate between Austria and the Soviet Union and it was at a time when I was Under–Secretary and Mr. Gruber was Foreign Minister, and we asked Nehru to tell the Soviets that if the Soviets were to sign a treaty Austria would become a neutral country ...." Kreisky had no doubt that Nehru "made a tremendous contribution to the settlement of the Austrian question."
41. Walter Crocker, *Nehru* (London, 1966), p. 118.
42. Badr–ud–Din Tyabji, *Indian Policies and Practices* (Delhi, 1972), p. 7.
43. K.B. Lall's "Nehru and International Economic Cooperation" See below. pp. 190-6.
44. George Kennan, *op. cit.*, p. 103.
45. K. Subrahmanyam, "Nehru and the India–China Conflict of 1962," see

below. p. 113.
46. Neville Maxwell, "Jawaharlal Nehru: Of Pride and Principle," in *Foreign Affairs*, April 1974, p. 643.
47. Address by Henry A. Kissinger to the Indian Council of World Affairs, October 28, 1974 (New Delhi, 1974).

CHAPTER I

1. *Constituent Assembly Debates*, January 1947, vol. II, p. 324.
   "I will read the Resolution
      This Constituent Assembly declares its firm and solemn resolve to pro--claim India as an Independent Sovereign Republic and to draw up for her future governance a Constitution.
      (2) WHEREIN the territories that now comprise British India, the territories that now form the Indian States, and such other parts of India as are outside British India and the States as well as such other territories as are willing to be constituted into the Independent Sovereign India shall be a Union of them all; and
      (3) WHEREIN the said territories, whether with their present boundaries or with such others as may be determined by the Constituent Assembly and thereafter according to the law of the Constitution, shall possess and retain the status of autonomous units, together with residuary powers, and exercise all powers and functions of government and administration, save and except such powers and functions as are vested in or assigned to the Union, or as are inherent or implied in the Union or resulting therefrom; and
      (4) WHEREIN all power and authority of the Sovereign Independent India, its constituent parts and organs of government, are derived from the people; and
      (5) WHEREIN shall be guaranteed and secured to all the people of India justice, social, economic, and political; equality of status, of opportu--nity, and before the law; freedom of thought, expression ,belief, faith, worship vocation, association and action, subject to law and public morality; and
      (6) WHEREIN adequate safeguards shall be provided for minorities, backward and tribal areas, and depressed and other backward classes; and
      (7) WHEREBY shall be maintained the integrity of the territory of the Republic and its sovereign rights on land, sea and air according to justice and the law of civilised nations; and
      (8) this ancient land attain its rightful and honoured place in the world and make its full and willing contribution to the promotion of world peace and the welfare of mankind."
2. See S.R. Mehrotra, *India and the Commonwealth*, 1885-1929 (London, 1965), p. 138.
3. *Ibid*.
4. *Ibid.*, p. 142.
5. Jawaharlal Nehru, *An Autobiography* (Bombay, 1962), p. 612.
6. Jawaharlal Nehru, *Glimpses of World History* (Bombay, 1962), pp. 717–18.

7. Jawaharlal Nehru, *India and the World* (London, 1936), pp. 204-5.
8. S.R. Mehrotra, *op. cit.*, p. 139.
9. *Ibid.*, pp. 145-6.
10. Jawaharlal Nehru, *An Autobiography*, pp. 418-19.
11. Jawaharlal Nehru, *The Discovery of India* (Bombay, 1961), p. 495.
12. Jawaharlal Nehru's *Speeches* (Delhi, 1954-68), vol. I, p. 3.
13. *Ibid.*, pp. 13-15.
14. *Ibid.*, pp .21-2
15. N. Mansergh (ed.) *Documents and Speeches on British Commonwealth Affairs 1931-1952* (London, 1953), vol. II, p. 660.
16. Jawaharlal Nehru's *Speeches*, vol. I, pp. 13-15, 20-21, 38-39.
17. *Ibid.*, pp. 13, 19.
18. N. Mansergh, *The Commonwealth Experience* (London, 1969), p. 329.
19. See A. Campbell–Johnson, *Mission with Mountbatten* (London, 1951), pp. 72, 81, 87-88, 109, 129, 214, 219, 242, 255, 257, 269, 290–1, 310–11, 329; N. Mansergh, *The Commonwealth Experience*, pp. 329-30; and V.P. Menon, *The Transfer of Power in India* (Bombay, 1968), p. 448.
20. N. Mansergh, *The Commonwealth Experience*, p. 337.
21. Jawaharlal Nehru's *Speeches*, vol. I, pp. 268-9.
22. *Ibid.*, pp. 38-39.
23. N.V. Rajkumar (ed.) *The Background of India's Foreign Policy* (New Delhi, 1952), p. 96.
24. For the evolution of the formula, see H. Duncan Hall, *Commonwealth* (London, 1971) pp. 831-62; N. Mansergh, *The Commonwealth Experience*, pp. 333-6; P. Gordon Walker, *The Commonwealth* (London, 1965), pp. 137-9, 182-5; M. Brecher, *India and World Politics* (London, 1968), pp. 18-27; and Durga Das (ed.), *Sardar Patel's Correspondence 1945-50* (Ahmedabad, 1971-4), vol. VIII, pp. 1-25.
25. The full text is available in N. Mansergh (ed.), *Documents and Speeches on British Commonwealth Affairs*, vol. II, pp. 846-7.
26. *Constituent Assembly Debates*, May-June, 1949, vol. VIII, p. 72. "Resolved that this Assembly do hereby ratify the declaration, agreed to by the Prime Minister of India, on the continued membership of India in the Commonwealth of Nations, as set out in the official statement issued at the conclusion of the Conference of the Commonwealth Prime Ministers in London April 27, 1949."
27. N.V. Rajkumar (ed.), *op.*, *cit.*, p. 98.
28. N. Mansergh, *Survey of British Commonwealth Affairs: Problems of Wartime Co–operation and Post–War Change 1939–1952* (London, 1958), p. 252; also N. Mansergh, *The Commonwealth Experience*, p. 336.
29. S.R. Mehrotra, *op. cit*, pp. 94-98.
30. M. Brecher, *Nehru: A Political Biography* (London, 1959), p. 415.
31. S.R. Mehrotra, *op. cit.*, pp. 122-6.
32. *Ibid.*, pp. 142-3.
33. *Ibid.*, pp. 144-5. See also S.R. Mehrotra, "Gandhi and the British Commonwealth", *India Quarterly*, vol. XVII, No. 1, January–March 1961, pp. 44-57.
34. Quoted in A. Campbell–Johnson, *Mission with Mountbatten*, p. 353.
35. Jawaharlal Nehru's *Speeches*, vol. I, p. 284.

36. N. Mansergh (ed.), *Documents and Speeches on British Commonwealth Affairs*, vol. II, p. 616.

37. Jawaharlal Nehru's *Speeches*, vol. I, pp. 268; 282; vol. III, pp. 314, 316; also R.K. Karanjia, *The Mind of Mr. Nehru* (London, 1960), p. 91–92. On the role of India in transforming the Commonwealth see M.S. Rajan, *The Post-War Transformation of the Commonwealth* (Bombay, 1963), and J.D.B. Miller, *Survey of Commonwealth Affairs: Problems of Expansion and Attrition* 1953–1969 (London, 1974), pp. 11–13.

38. On May 16, 1949 Nehru said: "In the world today where there are so many disruptive forces at work, where we are often on the verge of war, I think it is not a safe thing to encourage the breaking up of any association that one has. Break up the evil part of it, break up anything that may come in the way of your growth, because nobody dare agree to anything that comes in the way of a nation's growth. Otherwise....it is better to keep going a co-operative association...Some people have thought that by joining or continuing to remain in the Commonwealth of Nations we are drifting away from our neighbours in Asia, or that it has become more difficult for us to co-operate with other countries, great countries in the world. But I think it is easier for us to develop closer relations with other countries while we are in the Commonwealth than it might have been otherwise. This is rather peculiar thing to say. Nevertheless, I say it, and I have given a great deal of thought to this matter." *Jawaharlal Nehru's Speeches*, vol. I, pp. 281, 285.

39. A. Campbell–Johnson and H.V. Hodson suggest that the fear of some of the recalcitrant Indian princely states declaring their independence and seeking separate Commonwealth membership might have been a make-weight in determining Nehru's policy of keeping India in the Commonwealth in 1947–8. See A. Campbell–Johnson, *Mission with Mountbatten*, pp. 88, 135, 329; and H.V. Hodson, *The Great Divide* (London, 1969), p. 379.

40. B.N. Rau, *India's Constitution in the Making* (Bombay, 1960), p. 344.

41. *Jawaharlal Nehru's Speeches*, vol. 1, p. 285.

42. *Ibid.*, p. 281.

43. Speaking in the Lok Sabha on February 3, 1950, Nehru remarked: "Apart from the general reason, namely, that there is absolutely no object in our breaking in association which might help and certainly cannot hinder and which helps in the larger context of world affairs, there is one major reason for our remaining in the Commonwealth and that is that a large number of Indians live abroad in what are called British colonies or dependencies.... By our remaining in the Commonwealth, these Indians are in a better position than they would be otherwise. In the latter case, they would have to make a sudden choice and break with India or with the country where they reside. Had we left the Commonwealth it would have put millions of our people in a very difficult position, quite unnecessarily." *Jawaharlal Nehru's Speeches*, vol. II, p. 130.

44. N. Mansergh, *The Commonwealth Experience*, p. 393. Selwyn Lloyd, the British Foreign Secretary, on the other hand, remarked in 1956 that Nehru was "one of the ablest expounders of what the Commonwealth really means at the present time." See *The Hindu*, July 6, 1956, quoted in M.S. Rajan, *India in World Affairs 1954-56* (Bombay, 1964), p. 350.

45. *Jawaharlal Nehru's Speeches,* vol. 1, p. 287.
46. N. Mansergh, *The Commonwealth Experience,* p. 394. Speaking in the Indian Constituent Assembly on May 17, 1949, Nehru claimed that his decision to keep India in the Commonwealth would "have met with the approval of Gandhiji." See *Jawaharlal Nehru's Speeches,* vol. 1, p. 292.
47. Jawaharlal Nehru's *Speeches,* vol. 1, p. 279.
48. See P. Gordon Walker, *The Commonwealth,* pp. 175–6.
49. Jawaharlal Nehru's *Speeches,* vol. II, p. 129.
50. *The Hindu,* July 6, 1956, quoted in M.S. Rajan, *India in World Affairs,* pp. 342-3.
51. Jawaharlal Nehru's *Speeches,* vol. II, p. 129. Speaking in the Lok Sabha on December 5, 1956, Nehru observed: "India can be influenced by other countries, but it should be remembered that India also can influence other countries, and has done so to a remarkable extent in the past few years." *Ibid.,* vol. III, p. 316.
52. See J.D.B. Miller, *The Commonwealth in the World* (London, 1958), pp. 155–8.

CHAPTER III

1. South Yemen attained statehood in 1967. Decolonization of the Arab world was accomplished in 1971 when Bahrain, Qatar and the United Arab Emirates (comprising Abu Dhabi, Dubai, Shajra, Fujaira, Uman al-Quwayn, and Ajman) became independent.
2. Jawaharlal Nehru, *A Bunch of Old Letters* (Bombay, 1958), pp. 304–5.
3. Valentine Chirol, *The Middle East Question or Some Political Problems of Indian Defence,* (London, 1903), p. 5.
4. *Jawaharlal Nehru's Speeches,* September 1946– May 1947 (Delhi, 1967), p. 235.
5. See *Journal of Industry and Trade* (New Delhi), July 1965, vol. XV, p. 1040.
6. Hamilton Gibb (ed.), *The Travels of Ibn Battuta* (London, 1962), vol. II, p. 372.
7. *Jawaharlal Nehru's Speeches, op. cit,* p. 27.
8. Quoted in Robert St. John, *The Boss: The Story of Gamal Abdel Nasser* (London, 1961), pp. 131-2.
9. D.G. Tendulkar, *Mahatma,* vol. IV (Bombay, 1961), pp. 311–12; and vol. VII (Bombay, 1962), pp. 158–59.
10. See Gamal Abdel Nasser, "My Revolutionary Life", *Sunday Times* (London), June 24, 1962, pp. 21–22.
11. *Jawaharlal Nehru's Speeches, op. cit,* p. 164.
12. Yugoslav Government, *The Conference of Heads of State or Governments of Non–Aligned Countries* (Belgrade, 1961), pp. 107–9.
13. Nehru's statement quoted in H.E.B. Catley, "India and Pakistan Relations with the Middle East", *Asian Review* (London) July 1954, vol. L p. 205.
14. *Jawaharlal Nehru's Speeches,* op cit, pp. 94–96.
15. *Ibid.,* p. 282.
16. Lok Sabha, Debates, part II, vol. VI, col. 1561 (July 31, 1956).
17. *Jawaharlal Nehru's Speeches, op. cit,* p. 527–32.
18. Lok Sabha Secretariat, *Foreign Policy of India: Texts of Documents, 1947-64* (New Delhi, 1966), pp. 252–53.

19. *The Egyptian Gazette* (Cairo), August 22, 1956.
20. *The Hindu,* November 2, 1956; and *Jawaharlal Nehru's Speeches, op. cit.* p. 535.
21. UN General Assembly, *Official Records,* 2nd session, United Nations Special Committee on Palestine, vol. II, p. 47.
22. Quoted in *The Hindu,* May 13, 1949.
23. See Government of India, External Publicity Division, *India and Palestine: The Evolution of a Policy* (New Delhi, n.d.), p. 31.
24. Arif Hussain, *Pakistan: Its Ideology and Foreign Policy* (London, 1966), p. 149.

CHAPTER IV

1. For more comprehensive studies on India's relations with the region, see Ton That Thien, *India and South East Asia, 1947-1960* (Geneva, 1963) and D.R. Sardesai, *Indian Foreign Policy in Cambodia, Laos and Vietnam, 1947-1964* (Berkeley, 1968).
2. K.M. Panikkar, *Asia and Western Dominance* (London, 1953), is sub-titled "A Survey of the Vasco-da-Gama Epoch of Asian History, 1498-1945."
3. N.V. Rajkumar, *Background of India's Foreign Policy* (New Delhi, 1952), p.91.
4. *The New York Times,* January 1, 1946.
5. Quoted in Ton That Thien, *op. cit.,* p. 163.
6. *The Times* (London), January 4, 1947.
7. Bose's support came principally from ex–servicemen of the INA. Offers of help also came from as far away as Ceylon, Burma, Singapore. *The Hindu,* January 6, 12, 14, 22 and February 13, 1947.
8. Asian Relations Organization, *Asian Relations Conference Report* (New Delhi, 1948), p. 77.
9. India, Constituent Assembly, (Legislative) *Debates,* vol. I, ii (February 18, 1947), p. 764.
10. *Asian Relations Conference Report,* pp. 77–78.
11. Quoted in Dorothy Woodman, *The Republic of Indonesia* (New York, 1955), p. 237.
12. United Nations, Security Council, *Official Records,* 171st meeting, July 31, 1947, s/447.
13. Russell Fifield, *The Diplomacy of South–East Asia, 1945-1958* (New York, 1959), p. 150.
14. Quoted in Ton That Thien, *op. cit.,* p. 123.
15. *The Statesman,* December 20, 1948.
16. Security Council, *Official Records,* 406th meeting, January 28, 1948, s/1234.
17. *India Record,* January 29, 1949.
18. Text of the speech in William L. Holland, ed., *Asian Nationalism and the West* (New York, 1953), p. 244.
19. Monetary help was provided by buying Burmese rice at prices higher than the market prices at a time when Indian did not need rice imports. In 1955, U Nu disclosed that he had received arms from India on two occasions, *Burma Weekly Bulletin,* September 13, 1955. On March 6, 1949, Nehru told a press conference in reply to a question whether India had given mili-

tary assistance to Burma that Burmese Government had probably bought arms in Indian free market, *The Statesman,* April 13, 1949. It must be noted that India was not a free market for arms. On May 13, 1953, he admitted in Parliament that ships had left India for Burma with a consignment of cartridges. India, House of the People, *Parliamentary Debates,* vol. II, i, May 13, 1953, col. 3082.

20. Great Britain, His Majesty's Stationery Office, *Agreement between the Governments of the United Kingdom ot Great Britain and Northern Ireland, Australia, India, Pakistan, Ceylon and the Government of the Union of Burma regarding a loan to Burma, June 28, 1950, Cmd. 897* (London, 1950), p. 2.

21. *The Statesman,* May 7, 1949.

22. Ruth T. McVey, *The Calcutta Conference and the South East Asia Uprisings* (Ithaca, 1958), mimeo.

23. Lok Sabha, *Foreign Policy of India, Texts of Documents, 1947-59* (New Delhi, 1959), p. 3.

24. Ministry of Home Affairs, *Communist Violence in India* (New Delhi, 1949), pp. 3–7.

25. Gene D. Overstreet and Marshall Windmiller, *Communism in India* (Berkeley, 1959), pp. 279–80.

26. *Ibid.,* pp. 135–42.

27. New China News Agency, November 23, 1949.

28. For details see Werner Levi, *Free India in Asia* (Minneapolis, 1952), pp. 115–8; Russell Fifield, "The Future of French India," *Far Eastern Survey*, vol. XIX (1950), pp. 62–64; Lok Sabha, *Debates,* vol. VII, ii, September 20, 1954, col. 2532; and India, House of the People, *Parl. Debates,* vol. III, ii, April 6, 1954, cols. 4140–4152.

29. Information Service of India, *Nehru visits U.S.A.* (Washington, D.C., 1949), pp. 11–12; *Asian Relations Conference Report,* p. 23.

30. Norman Cousins, *Talks with Nehru* (New York, 1951), p. 54.

31. Quoted in Girilal Jain, *Panchasheela and After* (London, 1960). p. 5.

32. *Ibid.,* p. 7.

33. Telegram dated October 19, 1949 from Mao Tse–tung to B.T. Ranadive, text in V.B. Karnik, ed., *Indian Communist Party Documents, 1930-1956* (Bombay, 1957), p. 48.

34. Dulles to U.N. General Assembly, text in United States, Government Printing Office, *American Foreign Policy, 1950-1955, Basic Documents* (Washington, 1957), vol. I, p. 3.

35. *The New York Times,* November 8, 1953.

36. *Le Monde,* December 16, 1953.

37. According to J.H. Brimmel, the communist policy switch had come even before Stalin's death and was evident in the later's concluding remarks to the Nineteenth Party Congress in Moscow in October 1952. The change in policy was to exploit all anti–Western elements in Asia, and was connected with events in China and based on Chinese advice. J.H. Brimmel, *Communism in Southeast Asia* (London, 1959), pp. 280-2.

38. *Hindustan Times,* July 21, 1954.

39. Nehru to Presidents of State Congress Committees, July 7, 1954, *Commonwealth Survey, 153* (August 6, 1954), p. 9.

40. India, House of the People, *Parl. Debates,* vol. IV, ii, April 24, 1954, col. 5581.

41. Nehru condemned NATO only when Portugal claimed its protection extended to her colonies in India. Ministry of Information, *Jawaharlal Nehru's Speeches, 1949-1953* (New Delhi, 1954), p. 223.

42. India, House of the People, *Parl. Debates,* vol. IV, ii, April 24, 1954, col. 5581.

43. *Le Monde,* June 24, 1954.

44. India, Lok Sabha Secretariat, *Foreign Policy of India: Texts of Documents, 1947-1959* (New Delhi, 1959), p. 113.

45. *Jawaharlal Nehru's Speeches,* 1953-57, p. 299.

46. *New China News Agency,* April 25, 1955, p. 5; *Lao Presse,* April 26, 1955.

47. SarDesai, *Indian Foreign Policy in Laos, Cambodia and Vietnam,* pp. 117-21, Modesty apart, this is the most comprehensive study of the ICC's work, particularly the Indian role in it.

48. ICC Cambodia, *Minutes,* 79th meeting, April 20, 1956.

49. *Times of India,* October 26, 1962.

50. *Pravda,* December 12, 1962; *Hindu,* December 27, 1962.

51. Great Britain, Foreign Office, International Commission for Supervision and Control in Vietnam, *Special Report to the Co-Chairmen of the Geneva Conference on Indochina, June 2, 1942,* Cmnd 1755 (London, 1962).

52. *Ibid.*

53. Nehru admitted in the Rajya Sabha that non-alignment was helped by the "new development in international situation." *Hindustan Times,* September 3, 1963.

54. See the two reports by Saville R. Davis, "The Long Shadow of China," *Christian Science Monitor,* February 25, 27, 1963.

55. *Asian Recorder,* January 9-14, 1963, p. 4979.

56. *Ibid.,* p. 4980.

57. *Nhan Dan,* October 24 and November 3, 1962, quoted in King Chen, "North Vietnam in Sino-Soviet Dispute, 1962-64," *Asian Survey,* September 4, 1964, p. 1025.

58. *Vietnam Information Bulletin,* December 1, 1962.

CHAPTER V

1. Jawaharlal Nehru, *An Autobiography,* (London, 1936), p. 84.

2. Congress Bulletin of October 24, 1940, quoted in Bimal Prasad, *The Origins of Indian Foreign Policy,* (Calcutta, 1962), p. 185.

3. Jawaharlal Nehru, *The Discovery of India,* (Calcutta, 1946), p. 566.

4. *Jawharlal Nehru's Speeches,* vol. I, (New Delhi, 1967), pp. 238-40.

5. *Jawaharlal Nehrn's Speeches,* vol. II, (New Delhi, 1967), p. 146.

6. *Ibid.,* p. 195.

7. Frank Moraes, *Witness To An Era* (London, 1973), pp. 220-21.

8. D.R. Mankekar, *The Guilty Men of 1962* (Bombay, 1968), p. 110.

9. Prime Minister on Sino-Indian Relations, *Lok Sabha Debates,* 1959, vol. xxxv, pp. 2186-2214.

10. K.M. Munshi, *Bhavan's Journal*, February 26, 1967, vol. XIII.

11. *Jawaharlal Nehru's Speeches, op. cit*, p. 3.

12. K.P. Karunakaran, *India in World Affairs*, (Delhi, 1952), vol. I, p. 101.

13. Bimal Prasad, *op. cit.*, p. 189.

14. Dorothy Norman (ed.), *Nehru, The First Sixty Years*, (Bombay, 1965), vol. II, p. 179.

15. B.N. Mullik, *My Years with Nehru*, (New Delhi, 1972), pp. 290–91.

16. Keesing's *Contemporary Archives*, (London, 1950–52), vol. VIII, p. 11564.

17. Letter dated December 7, 1950 to the Indian Ambassador to U.N., quoted in B. Shiva Rao in "Nehru and the U.N. during the Korean Crisis", *The Statesman Weekly*, December 11, 1965.

18. Chester Bowles, *Promises to Keep* (New Delhi, 1972), p. 489.

19. *Ibid.*, p. 494.

20. Harold Macmillan, *Tides of Fortune* (London, 1969), p. 619.

21. John Gittings, *Survey of the Sino-Soviet Dispute*, (London, 1968), p. 160.

22. *Ibid.*, p. 83.

23. *Jawaharlal Nehru's Speeches*, (New Delhi, 1958), vol. III, pp. 40–41.

24. Seminar, July 1962, pp. 14–15.

25. Vikas Publications, *Defence of India* (Delhi, 1969), pp. 24–25.

26. B.N. Mullik, *The Chinese Betrayal* (New Delhi, 1971).

27. Prime Minister on Indo-China Relations, Lok Sabha, *Debates*, 1959, vol. xxiv, p. 8125.

28. John Gittings, *op. cit.*, p. 114.

29. *Ibid.*, pp. 115, 124.

30. Donald S. Zagoria, *The Sino–Soviet Conflict*, 1956–61, (London, 1962), p. 344.

31. John Gittings, *op. cit.*, pp. 161-62.

32. B.M. Kaul, *The Untold Story* (New Delhi, 1967), p. 334.

33. B.N. Mullik, *The Chinese Betrayal*, pp. 551–52.

34. B.M. Kaul, *op cit*, . p. 341.

35. P.V.R. Rao, IDSA Journal, vol. I, No. I, July 1968, and General J.N. Chaudhuri, USI Centennial Lecture, January 1971.

36. Neville Maxwell, *India's China War* (Bombay, 1970), pp. 232–34.

37. P.V.R. Rao, *Defence Without Rift* (Bombay, 1970), p. 309.

38. Neville Maxwell, *op. cit.*, p. 130.

39. *Ibid.*, p. 234.

40. John Gittings, *op. cit.*, p. 186.

41. Harold C. Hinton, *China's Turbulent Quest* (London, 1970), p. 92.

42. *Motherland*, June 2, 1972.

43. These aspects have been dealt with extensively in K. Subrahmanyam, "U.S. Policy Tawards India" in *China Report*, Vol. VIII, No. 1 and 2, January-February, March–April, 1972, and "Indo-Soviet Relations" in *Quest* No. 82, May-June, 1973.

CHAPTER VII

1. Ithiel Pool and Kali Prasad, "Indian Student Images of Foreign People," *The Public Opinion Quarterly*, (Cambridge, Mass.,1958) vol. XXII, 3.

2. Jawaharlal Nehru, *Visit to America* (New York, 1950), p. 173.

3. See for a thorough discussion, M.S. Venkataramani and B.K. Shrivastava, "The United States and the Cripps Mission", *India Quarterly*, vol. XIX, 3, July-September 1963; and "The United States and the 'Quit India' Demand," *ibid.*, vol. XX, 2, April-June 1964.

4. Nehru's famous statement to the Constituent Assembly in April 1949, *Constituent Assembly Debates*, vol. IV, pt. II, p. 2385.

5. See G.L. Mehta, "As Others See Us: An Indian View," *Foreign Affairs*, vol. XXXVII, October 1, 1958.

6. Vide Dean Acheson: "He was one of the most difficult men with whom I have ever had to deal." *Present at the Creation*, (New York, 1969) p. 336, President Kennedy is reported to have described to Arthur M. Schlesinger his first meeting with Nehru as "a disaster...the worst head of state [sic] visit I have had", *A Thousand Days* (Boston, 1965), p. 526.

7. Acheson, *op. cit.*, p. 420.

8. See Harold Isaacs, "Scratches on Our Minds, "*The Public Opinion Quarterly*, *op. cit.*, vol. XX, 1, Spring 1956 and an equally perceptive book of the same title (New York, 1958).

9. Dorothy Jones, "The Portrayal of China and India on the American Screen 1896-1955", (Communications Program, E/55-12, MIT, U.S.A.) the consistent themes in movies about India were: mysterious religions, jungle life, the conquering Englishmen, and primitive tribesmen.

10. Nehru said the resolution "seemed like converting the UN into a larger edition of the Atlantic Pact and making it a war organisation more than one devoted to international peace." *Press Conferences*, 1950, quoted in Charles Heimsath and Surjit Mansingh, *Diplomatic History of Modern India,* (New Delhi, 1971), p. 69.

11. Ministry of External Affairs, *Japanese Peace Treaty U.S.—U.K. Draft—Selected Documents*, (New Delhi, 1951). Besides India's stated reasons for not attending the San Francisco conference or signing the draft treaty, Dulles' disinterest in consulting India must be taken into account.

12. John Kenneth Galbraith, *Amassador's Journal* (Boston, 1969), p. 194 Nehru issued a corrective statement to the press, p. 198.

13. *Ibid.*, pp. 280-92.

14. William J. Barnds, *India, Pakistan, and the Great Powers* (New York, 1972), pp. 91 ff.

15. Selig Harrison, "America, India, and Pakistan: A Chance for a Fresh Start", *Harper's Magazine,* July 1966, p. 59.

16. *Ibid.*, p. 57.

17. Selig Harrison, *ibid.*, also articles in *The New Republic*, Washington D.C., of August 10 & 24 and September 7, 1959 and December 11, 1961. Also see statement of Chester Bowles before the Joint Economic Committee of the US Congress on January 18, 1971, for a similar view.

18. Galbraith, *op. cit.*, p. 539.

19. See Heimsath & Mansingh, *op. cit.*, pp. 365-92 for a concise chapter and bibliography on "The American Tie and Foreign Enonomic Relatians."

CHAPTER VIII

1. Jawaharlal Nehru, *India's Foreign Policy* (Delhi, 1961), p. 80.
2. Michael Brecher, *Nehru, A Political Biography* (London, 1959), pp. 564-5.
3. Jawaharlal Nehru, *op. cit.*, p. 32.
4. *Ibid.*, p. 22.
5. *Ibid.*, p. 73.
6. *Ibid.*, p. 24.
7. *Ibid.*, p. 35.
8. *Ibid.*, p. 79.
9. *Ibid.*, pp. 32, 55, 98.
10. Rabindranath Tagore's letter to a friend, March 5, 1921, *Modern Review*, May 1921.
11. D.G. Tendulkar, *Mahatma, Life of Mohandas Karamchand Gandhi*, (Ahmedabad 1951-54), vol. VI, p. 331.
12. J. Bandyopadhyaya, "The Congress and Democratic Socialism," AICC *Economic Review*, 1968, p. 7.
13. Jawaharlal Nehru, *op. cit.*, pp. 68-69.
14. *Ibid.*, p. 83
15. *Ibid.*, p. 49.
16. *Ibid.*, p. 83.
17. *Ibid.*, p. 73.
18. *Ibid.*, p. 28.
19. *Ibid.*
20. Rafiq Zakaria (ed.), *A Study of Nehru* (Bombay, 1960), p. 84.
21. *Ibid.*, p. 243.
22. J. Bandyopadhyaya, *The Making of India's Foreign Policy* (Bombay, 1970), pp. 227-40.

CHAPTER XI

1. *World Armament and Disarmament, SIPRI Yearbook 1972*, Introduction, Stockholm International Peace Research Institute, 1972. Also, *Disarmament and Development, Report of the Group of Experts on the Economic and Social Consequences of Disarmament*, (United Nations, 1972).
2. SIPRI Yearbook, 1972, Introduction.
3. Four of these compacts—relating to outer space, Latin America, Antarctic and the seabed—are preventive measures, if scrupulously observed. SALT is an arms control measure. The partial test ban treaty and NPT are neither arms control nor disarmament measures; they, of course, provide an unenforceable preventive to nuclear proliferation.
4. Alva Myrdal, "The Game of Disarmament," *Impact of Science on Society*, vol. XXII, No. 3, 1972.
5. Arthur Lall, *Negotiating Disarmament; The Eighteen-Nation Disarmament Committee: The First Two Years—1962-64*, (Ithaca, Cornell 1964). See Chapter VI.
6. *India and the United Nations*, Report of a Study Group set up by the Indian

Council on World Affairs, (New York, 1957).

7. Articles 11 and 26 of the Charter. The inadequacy of the Charter to deal with disarmament came to be frequently mentioned during the first years of UN disarmament efforts. In 1947, the United States argued for an International Atomic Development Authority (Baruch Plan) outside the UN because "the question of control and development of atomic energy could not have been considered or dealt with in the framing of the United Nations Charter, which had been signed before the first atomic explosion." *The United Nations and Disarmament* 1945-1965, (New York, 1965), p. 16. Ernest Bevin remarked in the House of Commons on November 7, 1945 that if the drafters of the Charter, of whom he had been one, had known of the atomic bomb, they would have placed far greater emphasis on nuclear disarmament. *Hansard*, vol. 415, col. 1335, 1945.

8. *Official Records of the General Assembly*, 4th session 1948. The United States wanted to set up an International Atomic Development Authority outside the Charter primarily to circumvent the Soviet veto, while the USSR asked for an International Control Commission within the framework of the Charter. The Atomic Energy Commission failed to reconcile the two points of view and reported a complete deadlock to the General Assembly in 1949. In that year the USSR became a nuclear power. In January 1950 the Soviets walked out of the AEC protesting the presence of the Kuomintang delegation. AEC was dissolved on January 11, 1952 by the General Assembly which created the Disarmament Commission. For details of Indian moves at the Security Council See *U.N. Documents*, A/700, S/283 and *Official Records of the Security Council*, II year No. 22, 115th meeting.

9. Statement in Lok Sabha on April 2, 1954.

10. *The United Nations and Disarmament*, ch. 3.

11. Resolution 715 (VIII), adopted by 54 votes to none, with 5 abstentions.

12. Report by Lewis L. Strauss, *The Nature of Radioactive Fall-Out and its Effects on Man*. Hearings before the Joint Committee on Atomic Energy, 85 Congress, 1st session. Part II, p. 1947.

13. *The Times*, London, April 6, 1594.

14. Resolution No. 808 (IX) asked the Disarmament Commission to make further efforts to reach agreement on comprehensive and co-ordinated proposals for the regulation, limitation and major reduction of all armed forces and all conventional armaments; for total prohibition of the use and manufacture of nuclear weapons and weapons of mass destruction of every type; and for the establishment of effective international control. Thus, the American perspective of disarmament triumphed over the Soviet as well as non-aligned perspectives. The resolution also referred to the Disarmament Commission a draft resolution submitted jointly by Australia and Philippines.

15. *Nuclear Explosions*, (New Delhi, 1956), with a Foreword by Nehru himself.

16. The appeal was made on the floor of the Lok Sabha on November 27, 1957.

17. The Soviet plan surprised the West. Commented Jules Moch, of France, "I would almost say that the whole thing looks too good to be true...it is indeed a surprise today to see practically all of our proposals accepted." *UN Disarmament Commission, Sub-committee of the Disarmament Commission*

Verbatim Report, May 10, 1955, pp. 56-57.

18. Resolution No. 914 (X) of December 16, 1955.

19. *Negotiating Disarmament, op. cit.,* p. 3.

20. Resolution 1148 (XII) of November 14, 1957. The General Assembly also increased the membership of the Disarmament Commission by adding 14 members including India, Burma, Egypt, Tunisia and Yugoslavia. The USSR, however, refused to participate in the enlarged Disarmament Commission or its Sub-committee.

21. Nehru pleaded for step-by-step nuclear disarmament if the first step were sure to lead to the second. He told the Rajya Sabha on May 24, 1957; "We suggest that nuclear tests be suspended and ultimately banned. Even if the countries concerned agree to the proposal, I do not mean that it will put an end to all dangers...The mere fact of suspension with a view to future abandonment will itself create a new atmosphere in the world . . . . it will set people thinking in a different direction. I would welcome any step, however small, which creates the atmosphere for the next step."

22. For text of the joint declaration, see *The United Nations and Disarmament,* pp. 87-88.

A series of meetings dealing with the problem of cessation of nuclear testing began in 1958; in two years more than 400 meetings took place, and their official records ran into many thousands of pages. These negotiations proceeded independently of the outside temperature of Soviet-US relations. They did not result in an agreement but brought about an understanding of mutual points of view. By 1960, the two superpowers apparently agreed on two major points: the creation of a more stable military environment which would curtail the risk of war and permit reduction on national armed forces and armaments; and secondly, to halt what the then US Secretary of State, Christian Herter, called "the promiscuous spread of production of nuclear weapons." Mr. Herter in an address to the National Press Club in Washington on February 18, 1960, said that the nuclear proliferation issue was a danger that "we, our major allies and the Soviet Union should all view with real concern."

23. The three-nation draft resolution was approved unaimously as resolution 1660 (XVI).

23. Resolution 1722 (XVI).

24. India deplored the French decision to stay away from the negotiations. For Arthur Lall's comment on the French decision see *Negotiating Disarmament, op. cit.,* p. 7.

25. ENDC/PV 14, April 3, 1962.

26. Krishna Menon told the Committee on March 20, 1962, "...We consider that we disarm pretty quickly or the process of the rearming will go on because in any very gradual procedure anything that would be accomplished would be subject to suspicions and difficulties of various kinds...". ENDC/PV 5, March 20, 1962.

27. Harold K. Jacobson and Eric Stein, *Diplomats, Scientists and Politicians,* (Michigan, 1966), p. 373. The authors write, "Sweden and India played a leading role in formulating the concerted action for the eight. India mainly contributed the idea of constitutional and legal character. The Swedish

delegation brought to the task considerable technical knowledge as well as definite ideas about the political and legal arrangements that could be implemented in arms control agreements."

28. *Negotiating Disarmament*, p. 21. Arthur Lall says that he was "largely responsible for the contents and the language of the eight-power proposals." In his book the importance of Swedish contribution to the negotiations is somewhat minimised.

29. *Ibid.*, pp. 22-23.

30. ENDC/PV 28, April 26, 1962.

31. The UN General Assembly at its 1959 session adopted a draft resolution sponsored by 22 nations, including India, expressing its grave concern over the French intention to conduct nuclear weapon tests and requesting France to refrain from such tests. The USSR voted for the resolution, while the US and Britain voted against it. *United Nations and Disarmament*, pp. 155-6.

32. ENDC/PV 60, July 24, 1962.

33. Krishna Menon did not suggest a partial test ban treaty. Curiously, however, his passionate appeal to the superpowers to come to an agreement produced the concept of a partial test ban accord among the non-aligned eight. The day after Menon's speech, the Brazilian delegate said that since the superpowers differed on banning underground tests, the Committee should concentrate its efforts on a treaty banning tests in the atmosphere and outerspace. He was supported by several delegates. India at this stage gave no explicit support to the partial test ban treaty move, but did not oppose it either. ENDC/PV 61, July 25, 1962.

34. ENDC/PV 66, 67, August 6, 8, 1962.

35. ENDC/PV 78, September 3, 1962.

36. Arthur Lall explained the Indian position thus: "We are all well aware of the difficulties which exist at the moment in reaching a comprehensive treaty, although in our view the Eight Nation Memorandum remains a firm and solid basis for reaching an agreement on the cessation of all tests....We would like to observe that in presenting the second draft, the United States and the United Kingdom have moved forward from the position which the leaders of those countries took up in their offer of September 1961 when they proposed the cessation of nuclear weapon tests in the atmophere. Today the draft proposes the cessation of tests not only in the atmosphere but in outer space and under water, and we observe that there are no requirements of international verification. We hope that this will be acceptable with the aim of going forward and arriving at a treaty which will put an end to all nuclear tests." ENDC/PV 75, August 27, 1962.

37. The phrasing of Resolution 1762 A(XVII) was unusually strong. It condemned all nuclear weapon tests, asked that such tests should cease forthwith, urged the two superpowers to settle the remaining differences between them and reach agreement on the cessation of nuclear testing by January 1, 1963, and endorsed the 8-nation memorandum of April 16, 1962, as a basis, for negotiation. Part B of the resolution urged the 18-nation disarmament committee to seek the conclusion of a treaty with effective and prompt international verification which prohibits nuclear weapon tests in all environ-

ments for all time.

38. "Non-aligned negotiations in Geneva tended, by and large, to believe the Soviet version and to sympathise with the (Soviet) predicament. However, they did not accuse the Western negotiators of bad faith. The prevalent explanation that they favoured was that those Western negotiators who had led the USSR representatives to believe that two to four inspections might be acceptable did so in the sincere belief that this should be the case. Apparently something went wrong. They either were misinformed or underestimated the United States' internal forces opposed to a treaty." Samir Ahmed, *The Neutrals and the Test Ban Negotiations*, (New York, 1968), p. 59.

39. Alva Myrdal, "The Game of Disarmament.", *op. cit.*

40. *Negotiating Disarmament*, pp. 24-26.

41. *Documents on Disarmament*, (Washington DC, 1963), p. 300.

42. *Negotiating Disarmament*, p. 66.

43. Quoted in G.G. Mirchandani, *India's Nuclear Dilemma*, (New Delhi, 1966) p. 22.

44. *The Statesman*, January 1, 1963.

45. *The Times of India*, March 26, 1963.

46. Quoted in Mirchandani, *op. cit.*, p. 23.

INDEX